Praise for *The Lion Has Conquered*

"Aquinas scholar Daniel Waldow offers a theology of Christ and salvation that readers will treasure for its insight and clarity. The first part is a biblical tour-de-force, while the second part systematizes these insights with the aid of magisterial documents. A marvelous final chapter leads us through Catholic soteriology as inscribed in Western and Eastern Eucharistic rites, calling us to live liturgically the salvific path revealed by God in Scripture and Tradition."

— **Matthew Levering**
James N. Jr. and Mary D. Perry Chair of Theology,
Mundelein Seminary

"This book expertly weaves together a rich panoply of theological sources, unfolding the mystery of Christ's saving work both objectively in the sacrificial gift offered by Christ on the Cross and subjectively in the application of the fruits of that sacrifice to individual souls through the sacraments, and especially through the holy sacrifice of the Mass. The exposition of the nature of sacrifice against the backdrop of the ritual (external) and moral (internal) sacrifices of the Old Testament is especially valuable. The essence of sacrifice, both on the Cross and in the Mass, is the pure and perfect gift of Himself offered by Jesus Christ in the pouring out of His most precious blood to God the Father out of love and obedience on behalf of sinners. This is the one and only perfect sacrifice, in which we are called to participate and to which we must be conformed."

— **John P. Joy**
Author of *The Atoning Death of Christ:*
St. Thomas's Doctrine of Vicarious Satisfaction

"Among the most basic teachings of Christian faith is the fact that 'Jesus saves.' But what is salvation? What is sin? And how do the actions of Jesus two thousand years ago save us from sin today? In this approachable guide, Daniel Waldow introduces Catholic soteriology with remarkable brevity and breadth. Building on his masterful presentation of the Old Testament background, Waldow shows the significance of the life, death, resurrection, and ascension of Christ. Then, he explains official Catholic teaching, drawing both on the Council of Trent and on the current *Catechism of the Catholic Church*. The scriptural and magisterial sections are excellent, but what makes this book unique in my opinion is Waldow's explanation of the sacrificial dimension of the Eucharist and how this is faithfully expressed in the Church's liturgical rites. I have no doubt that *The Lion Has Conquered* will help readers of all backgrounds to contemplate Jesus Christ the Savior and His mysteries."

— **Rev. Dylan Schrader**
Veterum Sapientia Institute

"A delightful new compendium of the Savior and our salvation. Come for Waldow's learned treatments of sacrifice in the scriptures, the magisterium, and the liturgy (both East and West). Stay for his updated C.S. Lewis-style allegories of the afterlife, such as the TSA parable with the punchline: 'Hell is choosing to miss the flight and remain locked outside of the airport with the nasty dog.'"

— **Urban Hannon, FSSP**
Author of *Thomistic Mystagogy:*
St Thomas Aquinas's Commentaries on the Mass

"Newcomers to soteriology can find themselves flummoxed by contradictory theories of salvation. If you ask ten Christians how Christ saves us, you could expect a dozen different answers. In *The Lion Has Conquered*, Daniel Waldow has given us a handbook on soteriology that will serve students and popular audiences alike as a confident entry into the broader discussion about the manner in which Christ saves our souls. Readers will find the comprehension questions that accompany each chapter especially helpful for study or discussion."

— **Kevin Clarke**
Associate Professor of Theology, Sacred Heart Major Seminary

THE LION HAS CONQUERED

THE LION HAS CONQUERED

An Introduction to Catholic Soteriology

Daniel Robert Waldow

Os Justi
Press

Os Justi Press
P.O. Box 21814
Lincoln, NE 68542
www.osjustipress.com

Send inquiries to
info@osjustipress.com

ISBN 978-1-965303-74-0 (paperback)
ISBN 978-1-965303-75-7 (hardcover)
ISBN 978-1-965303-76-4 (ebook)

Book design by Kenneth Lieblich
Cover by Julian Kwasniewski
Cover image: "The Sealed Book and the Lamb"
Apocalypse Flamande (15th cent.), BNF Néerl3, folio 6r.

I dedicate this book to my immediate and extended family and to my Godchildren. I pray that this book may help us all to know, receive, and be conformed to the saving love of Christ.

CONTENTS

ACKNOWLEDGMENTS

I thank my wife Mary Kate and our children—Peter, Emma, Leo, Magdalena, and Justin—for their support and encouragement throughout the process of writing this book. I am also grateful to colleagues who provided feedback on an initial draft of this text. Finally, I am thankful for the many priests who pray the liturgy of the Eucharist in a theocentric manner and who, consequently, have helped me to better contemplate and more fruitfully participate in the sacrifice of Christ.

PREFACE

IN THE Book of Revelation we are told, "weep not; lo, the lion of the tribe of Judah, the root of David, has conquered." We then see "a lamb, standing as though it had been slain, with seven horns and with seven eyes."[1] The lion who has conquered is Jesus. But *what* has he conquered, and *how* has he done so? The depiction of Jesus as a lamb who "stands as though slain" suggests that his conquest involves his sacrificial death and resurrection. And his numerous horns and eyes imply his divine power. But what exactly is a sacrifice? What does Jesus conquer by his death and resurrection? And what role does his divinity and humanity play in his conquest? Perhaps most importantly, what does Jesus' conquest have to do with any of us? "Soteriology" is the branch of Christian theology which engages these types of questions. The word is derived from two Greek words, *soter* (σωτὴρ) and *logos* (λόγος), meaning "savior" and "word/reason," respectively. Hence, "soteriology" literally means reasoning and speaking about the savior and the salvation that he brings. Christian soteriology focuses upon the person and work of Jesus, whom the New Testament repeatedly refers to as the "savior" of the world.[2] What does Jesus save us *from*? *How* does he do so? And how is his saving work related to God's work in the Old Testament and in the life of the Church? Soteriology seeks to provide clear, thorough, and persuasive answers to such questions.

THE PURPOSE AND STRUCTURE OF THIS BOOK

This book is a scholarly introduction to Catholic soteriology. Its primary purpose is exegetical and dogmatic insofar as it seeks to provide readers with a thorough yet concise exposition of the essential content of Catholic soteriology as contained in Sacred Scripture and

---

1 Rev. 5:5–6. All citations from Scripture use the Revised Standard Version Catholic Edition (RSVCE).
2 Lk. 2:11, 1 Jn. 4:14, etc.

Sacred Tradition. This exposition is also analytic in that it identifies, and proposes basic answers and solutions for, many of the central soteriological questions and issues which are raised by Scripture and Tradition. But this is not an exhaustive work of historical or analytic soteriology. Instead, this book is intended primarily for use in upper level undergraduate or beginning graduate and seminary courses in theology. Given its focus on Scripture and Tradition, it would be well complemented by engagement with soteriological texts from the saints, the fathers and the doctors of the Church. This book only requires that readers have a very basic knowledge of Christianity and Catholicism but it aims to lead them promptly from fundamental topics into an exploration of more advanced concepts within the Bible and Magisterial teaching. Each chapter concludes with an extensive list of comprehension questions which students can use to guide their reading and which instructors can employ for the purposes of assessment.

This book consists of an introduction, seven chapters, and a conclusion. The introduction considers the nature of soteriology as a species within the genus of Catholic theology and identifies the major questions and issues which occupy Catholic soteriological reflection. These questions and issues are exegetical and dogmatic (what do the texts of Scripture and Tradition say about Christ's saving work?) and analytic or philosophical (are these claims about the saving work of Christ intelligible, defensible, and persuasive to reason?). We continually return to these questions and issues throughout the ensuing chapters and invite the reader to ponder them from various positions.

Chapters 1–4 offer a succinct portrait of biblical soteriology. These chapters analyze major soteriological texts and themes within the Old and New Testaments. Chapter 1 examines the fundamental teaching of the book of Genesis on sin and sacrifice. It shows how Genesis sets the stage for the entirety of the biblical history of salvation: sin is the fundamental problem from which God seeks to save us, and sacrifice is the primary means which he employs to do so. Chapter 2 explores the origin, nature and effects of the various kinds of sacrifice which are depicted throughout the remainder of the Old Testament. It identifies the salvific value and limits of these forms of sacrifice and shows how they prepare for, and shed light upon, our understanding of the sacrifice of Christ. Chapters 3–4 engage the teaching of the New Testament, with a focus upon the four Gospels. Chapter 4 considers the salvific significance of Jesus' being and public ministry. Who is Jesus and how does his Incarnate life, prior to his Passion, contribute to our salvation? We focus especially upon the soteriological meaning of Jesus' name, titles, teaching and miracles. Chapter 4 is in a sense the zenith of the entire book, for it analyzes the New Testament's depiction of the saving value of Christ's Passion, Resurrection, and Ascension. We show how Christ's Paschal Mystery completes his saving work and fulfills and transcends the salvific sacrifices of the Old Testament.

Chapters 5–7 explore the official soteriological teaching of the Catholic Magisterium. This Tradition is contained principally in the dogmatic and doctrinal statements of ecumenical councils and Popes and is given prayerful expression above all in the liturgy of the Eucharist. Chapter 5 focuses upon the fundamental principles of Magisterial soteriology. It details the teaching of the Council of Trent and the contemporary *Catechism of the Catholic Church* on the work of Christ, the Sacraments, and the roles of grace and free will. Chapter 6 builds upon these foundational elements of Catholic soteriology by considering the place of the Eucharist within the process of salvation. It examines the teaching of Trent, Vatican II, the *Catechism*, and contemporary popes concerning the sacrificial and life-giving nature of the Eucharist. And it considers the relationship between the sacrifice of the cross and the sacrifice of the Mass. Chapter 7 brings the biblical and magisterial insights of Chapters 1–6 to bear upon the major prayers and rituals of Catholic Eucharistic liturgies. How do the Roman and Byzantine Eucharistic rites depict the salvific being, public ministry, and Paschal Mystery of Christ? How do they depict the relationship between the cross and the Eucharist and between grace and free will in the process of salvation? I then provide a conclusion which synthesizes the various biblical, magisterial and analytic fruits of the previous chapters. This synthesis aims to offer a philosophically coherent exposition of the essential and primary features of Catholic soteriology.

INTRODUCTION

PRINCIPLES AND THEMES OF CATHOLIC SOTERIOLOGY

T HIS introduction consists of two divisions with two related purposes. The first section describes the nature and principles of
soteriology as a species within the genus of Catholic theology. The
second section identifies the central questions and issues which preoccupy scholars and students of soteriology. These questions and issues can be synthesized into seven major soteriological themes. Here
we will establish the methodological principles that will be employed
throughout this book and highlight the themes to which we will repeatedly return throughout our examination of Sacred Scripture and
Sacred Tradition. Following this introduction and all ensuing chapters, a list of Comprehension Questions is provided in order to help
the reader to retain and synthesize what they have learned.

SOTERIOLOGY AS CATHOLIC THEOLOGY

Soteriology is a species within the genus of Catholic theology. Consequently, in order to do soteriology well we first need to clearly identify the object, end and methods of Catholic theology in general. The
word "theology" comes from two Greek words, "theos" (θεός) and
"logos" (λόγος), which mean "God" and "reason/word," respectively.
So "theology" is reasoning and speaking about God so as to know,
and share our knowledge of, the truth about God. The medieval
monk Anselm of Canterbury, whose book *Cur Deus homo* is one of
the most influential soteriological works of all time, described theology with the Latin phrase *fides quaerens intellectum*, faith seeking
understanding. For Anselm, the Christian life begins with an act of
faith in response to God's miraculous revelation of himself to humanity in salvation history. Through faith we trust in the truth of God's
revealed word to us, but this faith is not blind; the believer trusts in

1

the wisdom and goodness of God, and as a result they yearn to further understand the depths of divine wisdom and goodness. This is what theology does—it seeks the intelligible and persuasive reasons which explain *why* and *how* God exists, is who he says he is, and does what he does. In *Cur Deus homo*, for instance, Anselm seeks to provide a rationally satisfying explanation of why God became human and how his death on the cross was ordered towards our salvation.

The object of theology, meaning, that which the theologian studies, is God. Theology seeks to advance in understanding of the being, will and work of God. It seeks to share in the "mind of Christ" who is the "wisdom" (*sapientia*) of God.[1] In this sense, theology is "sapiential," a participation in God's own wisdom or knowledge of himself and of the relation of creatures to him.[2] Christian theology does not focus upon what can be known about God through merely natural reason and experience, but rather on the truth about God which is given in divine revelation. Revelation is God's supernatural self-communication to human beings through words and deeds in history. God's appearance and speech to Moses at the burning bush is an exemplary instance of divine revelation. The zenith and completion of revelation occurs through the incarnate life and teaching of Christ, the eternal Word made flesh (Jn. 1:14). All contemporary Christians agree that the revelation of God is recorded and handed on through Sacred Scripture. Consequently, the study of Scripture is foundational to Christian theology and debate regarding the proper interpretation of Scripture is central to dialogue within and across Christian churches and denominations.

In addition to Scripture, Catholic theology also accepts Sacred Tradition and the living Magisterium as normative witnesses of divine revelation. God's supernatural word comes to us through Scripture but also through the authoritative teachings of the Pope and the bishops in union with him. These successors of Peter and the other Apostles, respectively, were appointed by Christ not to receive new

1 1 Cor. 2:16 and 1 Cor. 1:24, respectively.
2 For a concise treatment of theology as "sapiential," see Daniel Lendman, "A Note on the Sapiential Unity of Sacred Doctrine: Editorial Essay," *Lux Veritatis: A Journal of Speculative Theology* 1.2 (2024): 126–32.

revelations, but rather to hand on, clarify, and apply the perennial teachings which they received from Christ himself prior to his Ascension into heaven. They do so through the dogmas and doctrines which they promulgate in ecumenical councils and papal writings. Scripture and Christian experience generates the questions and issues which are answered and addressed by dogmas and doctrines. And these teachings of the Church in turn help us to better understand the content of Scripture. Together, Sacred Scripture and Sacred Tradition provide the Catholic theologian with the divinely revealed material which they study in their quest to advance in understanding of God.

Given the foundational and normative function of Scripture and Tradition to all Catholic theology, Catholic soteriology must include theological exegesis and dogmatic theology. "Exegesis" refers to the task of clarifying and explaining the meaning of a text. "Theological exegesis" seeks the meaning(s) of the texts of Scripture precisely because those texts are viewed as sources of divine revelation. We want to clarify and explain the meaning of the text because the text conveys the revelation of God. Dogmatic theology is like theological exegesis applied to the texts of Sacred Tradition. It seeks to accurately identify and explain the meaning of the dogmatic and doctrinal statements of ecumenical councils and Popes. Theological exegesis and dogmatic theology are the essential first steps within all Catholic theology, including soteriology, for these disciplines are the means through which we clearly identify *what* God has revealed.

Sound theological exegesis and dogmatic theology are particularly important to ecumenical debates within soteriology. Scripture is the witness to divine revelation that all Christians share. Only Catholics acknowledge the infallible teaching authority of the Pope, but Catholics, Protestants, and Orthodox Christians all acknowledge the authority of Scripture. And beginning with Martin Luther, Protestant theology has embraced the principle that scripture alone (*sola scriptura*) is the authoritative witness of divine revelation. Given the universally recognized authority of Scripture within Christianity, inter-Christian soteriological arguments can and should revolve around the meaning of Scripture. All Christians should be ready to submit with faith to the most persuasive interpretations of Scripture that they encounter. And the assessment of all soteriological claims, including claims which are essential to particular Christian churches or denominations, must include a consideration of the degree to which those claims are consistent with Scripture. Christians who encounter an otherwise logically coherent and attractive theological claim must reject it if it is plainly contrary to the teaching of Scripture. In order to have persuasive power both within and beyond the confines of Catholicism, Catholic soteriology needs to be able to clearly identify the teachings of Sacred Tradition and show how those teachings are, at minimum, compatible with Scripture. But if Catholic soteriology is to be really persuasive, then it needs to show how the content of Sacred Tradition provides the *best* interpretation and explanation of the content of Scripture.

In addition to focusing on the proper interpretation of texts, Catholic theology is also inherently "analytic" or "philosophical." This simply means that the theologian strives to show how the content of divine revelation is in accord with reason and to draw out the logical implications of revealed claims. Are the revealed claims of Scripture and Tradition logically, metaphysically and morally possible? Can we demonstrate their necessity or show their fittingness? Are these claims consistent with the certain and persuasive discoveries of the natural sciences? Can we reason from a revealed claim to a further theological truth? Can we provide persuasive explanations of the issues which the revealed claim generates? These are the types of questions that Catholic soteriology strives to answer insofar as it is "analytic" or "philosophical."

The content and ends of Catholic theology can be "speculative" and "practical." The *content* (that which is known) of theology is more speculative when it focuses upon the nature or essence of a thing and the manner of action to which that thing is naturally ordered. The content of theology is more practical when the truth that is known pertains directly to how we ought to act and to interact with other things. For instance, knowledge of the material structure and aerodynamic capacity of a football is a more speculative truth. Knowledge of how to effectively grasp and throw a football is a more practical truth. Knowledge of a practical truth (how do I throw a football?)

presupposes knowledge of a speculative truth (what is a football?). The content of theology is speculative because it involves study of the being and activity of God. What and who is God and what has he done? The content of theology is also practical insofar as it regards what God has revealed about how we ought to act in relation to God, one another, and the rest of creation. Who God is (speculative truth) specifies how we ought to relate to God (practical truth). Regardless of whether the theological content which we study is more speculative or more practical, we can *intend* to study that content for more speculative or more practical *ends*. We study truth for a speculative end when we seek knowledge for its own sake, as a good in itself, as something which gives our will delight and rest. We study truth for a practical end when we seek knowledge as a means to some further, practical end. In such a case we may still find the knowledge delightful, but nonetheless our primary goal is to use that knowledge in a practical manner. We study theology for a practical end when we want to know the truth about God so that we can live and act properly in relation to God and in accord with his will. We study theology for a speculative end when we simply delight and rest in the knowledge of God as an end in itself.[3]

Catholic Theology gives us real, yet analogous and limited, knowledge of the truth about God. We can know the truth about God because God has endowed us with reason and supernaturally revealed himself to us through the mediation of human figures and words. Insofar as we can understand the words of Scripture and Tradition and analyze their logical content, then we can know the truth about God with great insight. But Catholic theology also maintains that God himself is incomprehensible, which means that we can never know *everything* that there is to know about God. The infinite truth and intelligibility of God is inexhaustible to our finite minds in this world and even in heaven. And the insight of our statements about God is always limited by the fact that our theological language can only ever be analogous at best. When we say things like "God is

---

3 For a concise treatment of the relation between the speculative and the practical in theology, see Taylor Patrick O'Neill, "The Primacy of the Speculative in the Science of Theology," *Lux Veritatis: A Journal of Speculative Theology* 1.1 (2024): 2–14.

love," this is a literally true statement and not a mere metaphor. But "love" is a finite word which refers primarily to finite realities, and only secondarily can it be used to describe the infinite reality that is God. All created perfections are real but partial participations in the infinite perfection and being of God. Hence, while a real similarity exists between created "love" and divine "love," there is an even greater dissimilarity. As a result, theology requires both confidence in our capacity to state the truth about God and also humble recognition that God's being is like an infinite ocean which we will never be able to fully explore.

Having established these primary features of Catholic theology, we can now relate them to the practice of soteriology. Catholic soteriology studies the supernatural self-communication of God that is conveyed in Scripture and Tradition. It attends to the salvific being and work of God which is described in the Old Testament, the New Testament, and in the authoritative teachings of the Popes and ecumenical councils. Hence, Catholic soteriology begins with sound theological exegesis and dogmatic theology. Catholic soteriology is analytic and philosophical insofar as it seeks to show how the revealed claims about the salvific being and activity of God are in accord with reason. It strives to provide a rationally clear, consistent, and persuasive explanation of the revealed claims regarding how and why God saves us. It does so for the practical end of knowing how to relate to God, receive the salvation which he offers us, and help others to know the truth of his saving work. Soteriology is done for a speculative end when we simply delight in contemplating the wisdom and love of the savior who died for us, as a lover delights in the knowledge of her beloved. And just as a bride and groom can know one another on an intimate level, and yet continue to advance in intimacy as the years go by, so too can we know God through the study of soteriology and yet never exhaust the infinite intelligibility of his wisdom and love.

QUESTIONS AND ISSUES IN SOTERIOLOGY

Now that we have identified the essential features of soteriology as a species within the genus of Catholic theology, we can proceed in this section to identify the major theological questions and issues which preoccupy soteriology and which will concern us throughout this book. The two fundamental questions of soteriology are: what does God save us from, and how does God do so? Answering these questions involves the consideration of numerous additional questions and issues, all of which can be synthesized into seven major soteriological themes: (1) sin and evil, (2) the objective work of Christ and our subjective participation in it, (3) the role of Christ's divinity and humanity in his saving work, (4) the saving value and relation between Christ's life and Paschal Mystery, (5) ends and means, (6) the relationship between grace and good works in the process of salvation, and (7) the relationship between personal, communal, temporal and eternal salvation. All of these themes are related and bear upon one another. We will encounter these themes repeatedly throughout the biblical and Magisterial texts which we examine in this book. But before we do, we will first take a closer look at the issues themselves and the questions which they raise.

Sin and Evil

This theme is focused primarily upon understanding what it is that God saves us from. The angel Gabriel instructed Joseph to name Mary's child "Jesus" because the child would "save his people from their sins."[4] But what exactly is "sin?" Providing a thorough answer to this question belongs to the theological subdiscipline known as "hamartiology," a word which is based on the New Testament's Greek word for "sin," hamartia (ἁμαρτία). "Hamartia" was originally and literally used to describe "missing the mark," as when an arrow misses its target. What is the target which humans have missed by their sins? How does missing that target consist in, and/or result from, the reality of sin? And where does sin come from? Is there a relation between sin, or, moral evil, and what we might call "physical evil," such as disease, injury, suffering and death? And what role, if any, does God's will play in relation to both moral and physical evil?

4 Mt. 1:21.

7

Christ's Objective Work and Our Subjective Participation

The *objective work* of Christ refers to the various things that Jesus said, did, and experienced for our salvation during his earthly life 2,000 years ago. It refers to the direct effects of Jesus' historical life, as well as to the continual, glorified life and works which Jesus accomplishes from heaven. *Subjective participation* refers to the way in which an individual person, through their particular choices and experiences, is affected by the life, words, and deeds of Jesus, past and present. "Subjective" and "objective" are not here meant as synonyms for "not real" and "real," respectively. Rather, I am using these terms in their phenomenological and relational senses: a subject is an individual person who acts, an object is what they know, act upon and are acted upon by. I am an individual subject, and Jesus's historical life is an object that I may or may not necessarily know about or be impacted by. But Jesus' life is an objective fact; it did happen, and it brought about various effects, and that does not change even if I choose to have nothing to do with Jesus.

We can use an analogy to illustrate this distinction between the objective work of Christ and a person's subjective participation in it. Imagine that a medieval princess has been kidnapped and locked in a dungeon which is guarded by armed men. Christ's *objective work* is like when a heroic prince arrives at the dungeon, defeats the armed men, unlocks the doors to the dungeon, and invites the princess to return with him to their native land. But *subjective participation* only occurs if the princess takes the prince's hand and allows him to lead her out of the dungeon and back home. By doing so, she experiences the full impact of what the prince did for her. But she does not need to take his hand; she can reject or ignore the prince and choose to remain in the dungeon. Yet even if she stays behind in the dungeon, this would not change the objective reality of what the prince did for her. Nor would it change the fact that the situation in which she finds herself is objectively different, and better, as a result of the prince's actions. She is still in a dungeon; but the armed guards are now gone, and the doors are unlocked. She is free, but as an acting subject she has chosen not to receive her freedom. Similarly, in soteriology we can distinguish between what Christ has done for us and the direct effects of what he has done, on the one hand, and, on the other, what we must do in response to what Christ has done in order to receive the full benefits of his work. And there is an order between these two issues: we must first be clear about what Christ has done, objectively, before we can discern how we are meant to respond, as acting subjects, to what he has done.

Christ's Divinity and Humanity

Christians who adhere to the first seven ecumenical councils profess the doctrines of the Incarnation and the hypostatic union. The former is the belief that the eternal, consubstantial Son of God assumed a fully human nature, consisting of a rational soul and physical body, in the womb of his mother Mary. The latter is the belief that Jesus is one person who possesses two complete natures, namely, a divine nature *and* a human nature. As the Ecumenical Council of Chalcedon taught, the two natures of Christ are united "without confusion or change, without division or separation" in the one person of the Son. Soteriology asks about the salvific purpose and effects of the Incarnation and Hypostatic Union. For instance, why did God become human? What role did his humanity play in his saving work? What role did his divinity play? What did Jesus do for us, as true God and true man, that could not have been done by a mere man, or by God through his divine nature alone?

Christ's Life and Paschal Mystery

Soteriological questions about Jesus' divinity and humanity are wrapped up with questions about his life on earth and his *Paschal Mystery*. The latter phrase comes from the word "Passover," and it refers to Jesus' passing-over from this life into eternity through his Passion (suffering and death), descent to the dead, resurrection from the dead, and Ascension into heaven. Most Christians and even non-Christians are familiar with the claim that Jesus died for us, and that his Passion was central to his saving activity. Yet, even as prominent a Christian apologist as C.S. Lewis once struggled to explain *how* and *why* Christ's Passion was salvific for us:

9

My puzzle was the whole doctrine of redemption: in what sense the life and death of Christ 'saved' or 'opened salvation to' the world. I could see how miraculous salvation might be necessary: one could see from ordinary experience how sin (e.g., the case of a drunkard) could get a man to such a point that he was bound to reach Hell (i.e., complete degradation and misery) in this life unless something quite beyond mere natural help or effort stepped in. And I could well imagine a whole world being in the same state and similarly in need of a miracle. What I couldn't see was how the life and death of Someone Else (whoever he was) 2000 years ago could help us here and now—except insofar as his *example* helped us. And the example business, tho' true and important, is not Christianity: right in the center of Christianity, in the Gospels and St Paul, you keep on getting something quite different and very mysterious expressed in those phrases I have so often ridiculed ('propitiation'—'sacrifice'—'the blood of the lamb')—expressions which I could only interpret in a sense that seemed to me either silly or shocking.[5]

Lewis is putting his finger on two soteriological issues: first, how were the past, *objective* experiences of Christ salvific for Lewis, a *subject* who lived 2,000 years later? And second, how are the suffering and death of Christ, in particular, supposed to save people from the state of moral wretchedness in which they find themselves? How is the state of the world, and the condition of those living within it, different before and after Christ's coming? These are perennial questions of Catholic soteriology.

But Catholic soteriology must make sure that it does not act as if the Passion is the only aspect of Christ's saving work. Good soteriology considers the Passion in light of all of the experiences of Christ that led up to and followed it. This means first looking at the Passion alongside Christ's conception in the womb of Mary, his infancy and childhood, his public ministry, and then also in relation to

5 C.S. Lewis, *The Letters of C. S. Lewis to Arthur Greeves*, Letter from Oct. 18, 1931, in *The Essential C.S. Lewis*, ed. Lyle W. Dorsett (Touchstone, 1996), 55–56.

his resurrection, Ascension, sending of the Spirit, and second coming at the end of time. In short, Catholic soteriology considers each and every aspect of Christ's life, from the moment of his conception until his last breath on the cross, from his descent to the dead to his glorious return to judge the living and the dead. As true God and true man, nothing that Christ said, did, felt or experienced was insignificant; and so we should strive to consider the salvific quality of every one of his experiences. This can be done without prejudicing the saving value of particular events, such as the Passion. In fact, the saving quality of the Passion is better understood in light of Christ's other actions and experiences.

Ends and Means

When we are thinking about the saving work of Christ, it is helpful to distinguish between an end and a means. An *end* is something that we enjoy and delight in. It is something that we do or pursue for its own sake. When we acquire an end our will attains rest; it has the thing that it sought. Examples of ends which humans pursue for their own sake are spending time with friends, reading a good book, and looking upon something beautiful such as the ocean, the stars, or a campfire. Conversely, a *means* is something that we choose for the sake of the end. While we may enjoy aspects of a means, we nonetheless choose it primarily because it leads to a desired end. People who make the seven-hour drive from Pittsburgh to the Jersey shore do so for the sake of the end, namely, being at the ocean, and not because they delight in driving seven hours. And, depending upon their life circumstances, driving may not even be a *necessary* means. If they own a plane, they could simply fly from Pittsburgh to Atlantic City. Insofar as flying is far quicker, it would be a far more *fitting* means of attaining the end.

We can see this distinction between ends and means on soteriological display if we return to our fictional situation with the medieval princess. Her problem is that she has been kidnapped and locked in a dungeon far from her home. By her own power she cannot unlock the doors or defeat the armed guards who keep watch over her. Fortunately, the prince wants to save her from her predicament. The prince's end is clear and singular: free the princess from the dungeon and give her the opportunity to return home (if she so desires). But there are a variety of *means* by which the prince may pursue that end: he could attempt to fight the guards by himself; he could try to recruit a band of noble souls to help him fight the guards; he could offer to pay a ransom to free the princess; he could employ stealth, such as by digging a tunnel into the princess's dungeon, etc. Some of these means may be more fitting than others, and in the end one may prove to be necessary: if tunneling and persuasion fail, then armed conflict is the only option left. If the Prince manages to defeat the guards, find the key, and unlock the doors, then he has attained his end: the princess is no longer bound, and is free to return home.

Soteriological reflection upon the life and Paschal Mystery of Christ has to keep this distinction between ends and means in mind. What is the end for which Christ came? What is the means which he employs to acquire that end? Which means are necessary, and which are fitting? And what makes certain means more fitting than others? The importance of these questions is felt in a particularly forceful way when we apply them to Christ's Passion. Was Jesus' suffering and death an end in itself which God willed for its own sake? Did God somehow delight in Christ's Passion? Or was the Passion merely a means to some further end? And if it was a means, how was it a necessary or fitting means? And in what way can we say that God willed this means? These types of questions are at the heart of Christian soteriology.

Grace and Good Works

How do Christians, as rational subjects, benefit from and participate in the objective, saving work of Christ? All Christians answer this question through some sort of appeal to grace, good works, or both. *Grace* refers to God's free initiative to do good to us. Through grace, God showers us with gifts, whether natural or supernatural, internal or external. For instance, God's active presence in our souls and in our lives, through the sending and work of the Holy Spirit, is typically described as supernatural and invisible grace. *Good works* refers to our free human decisions which we make in relation to the gift of God's grace. Such free human acts may be before, after, or in cooperation with the presence and work of the Holy Spirit within and upon us. Soteriology considers a variety of questions regarding grace and good works, such as: how is the life and Paschal Mystery of Christ a grace? How does Christ's life result in the sending of the Holy Spirit upon the world? And how is this sending different from the way that the Spirit was present to the world prior to the life of Christ? And must the grace of the Spirit be freely received and co-operated with, or is it given to us and enjoyed apart from our knowledge and consent?

The soteriological distinction between grace and good works is particularly relevant when considering the notion of justification and divinization. *Justification* refers to the event in which people, formerly alienated from God by sin and unbelief, are restored to a proper relationship with God. A person who is justified has been reconciled to God; the distance between God and the person has been removed. Justification is analogous to the reunion between parents and their estranged son. After many years of avoiding his parents out of pride and anger, the son finally returns home, apologizes, and receives the loving embrace of his parents. He now has a new relationship with them.[6] Reflection upon justification is bound up with reflection upon *divinization* (or, deification/theosis), which refers to persons being made like God. A divinized person shares in the divine nature and so participates, in a real and dynamic way, in the very life of God. Divinization is like when the son, having been welcomed home by his parents, starts to actively share in their everyday life: he shares in their house, meals, family business, income, recreation, vacations, etc. He starts to develop the same intellectual and moral habits that they have. He becomes like them in a real way.

Soteriology reflects upon the relationship between justification and divinization and the role of grace and good works within them. What exactly is the distinction, if any, between justification and divinization? Is our reconciliation with God purely a result of his gift of grace, or does it involve our human effort as well? Can we become

6 See the parable of the Prodigal Son in Lk. 15:11–32.

like God apart from grace, by our own power? Conversely, can we be divinized merely by grace, apart from our free choices? If both grace and good works are involved in justification and/or divinization, then what is the relationship between them? And, even more fundamentally, how is the life and Paschal Mystery of Christ related to our justification and divinization? How does the suffering and death of a man, 2,000 years ago, reconcile us to God and make us like him today? In addition to their inherent value, the answers to these questions are also of great ecumenical interest, for these issues have divided Catholic and Protestant Christians for five hundred years.

Individual and Communal, Temporal and Eternal

Soteriology asks about the relationship between the salvation of an individual person and the salvation of the human family. It also considers the ways in which this salvation is realized both on earth and in eternity. For instance, how does Christ's life and Paschal Mystery impact me as an individual as well as the human family and universe as a whole? Is there any relationship between the justification and divinization of an individual and the salvation of their family, friends, community, and society? Is salvation a merely personal and private reality, or does it bear upon social and political life as well? Is it spiritual, physical, or both? And is salvation something merely in the future, in eternity, or does it begin in a concrete way in this life? Did Christ's objective work change my situation temporally, or merely eternally? What is the connection, if any, between our experiences and choices in this life and our eternal fate?

CONCLUSION

This introduction described the nature of soteriology as a species within the genus of Catholic theology. Catholic soteriology is exegetical, dogmatic, and analytic. Its content is speculative and practical, and it may be done for speculative and/or practical ends. Soteriology employs analogous language and can never comprehend God, but nonetheless can make true statements about the salvific being and work of God. The fundamental questions which soteriology

considers are "what does God save us from?" and "how does God do
so?" Answering these questions involves the consideration of seven
major soteriological themes: sin and evil; objective and subjective
salvation; the humanity and divinity of Christ; the life and Paschal
Mystery of Christ; ends and means; grace and good works; and individual, corporate, temporal and eternal salvation.

∽

COMPREHENSION QUESTIONS

1. What does "theology" mean?
2. How does Anselm define "theology?"
3. What is the object of Catholic theology?
4. What is divine revelation and how is it transmitted?
5. What are theological exegesis and dogmatic theology?
6. What does it mean to say that theology is "analytic" or
   "philosophical?"
7. How is the content and end of theology both speculative and
   practical?
8. What does it mean to say that God is incomprehensible?
9. What is analogous theological language and what is its meta-
   physical basis?
10. What are the two fundamental questions of soteriology?
11. What are the seven major themes of speculative soteriology?
12. What are the Incarnation, Hypostatic Union, and Paschal
    Mystery?
13. What is "objective" and "subjective" salvation?
14. What is the difference between an end and a means?
15. What are grace and good works?
16. What are justification and divinization?

PART I

SOTERIOLOGY IN SACRED SCRIPTURE

SIN AND SACRIFICE IN GENESIS

W̶HAT DOES God save us from and *how* does he do so? The Bible begins to answer these questions in the Old Testament. Catholicism maintains that the Old Testament is an enduring source of revelation which is valuable in itself and which also enables us to better understand the New Testament. This is true on a basic literary level, insofar as the New Testament makes innumerable references and allusions to Old Testament persons, events and concepts. It is also true on a theological level, for Catholicism claims that the "principal purpose" of the events and ideas of the Old Testament was to "prepare for the coming of Christ."[1] It does so above all through prophecies which "announce this coming" and types which "indicate its meaning."[2] Due to these prophecies and types, the Old Testament contains "the mystery of our salvation" in "a hidden way." The New Testament is "hidden in the Old" and the Old Testament is "made manifest in the New." As a result, the Old Testament books "acquire and show forth their full meaning in the New Testament" and yet at the same time they "shed light on" and "explain" the New Testament. Thus, Catholic soteriology must approach the Old Testament as an essential source of revelation and as a key to understanding the saving work of Christ that is described in the New Testament. This chapter explores fundamental soteriological texts in the first book of the Old Testament, Genesis. The first section examines Genesis's depiction of the origins and nature of sin and its consequences. The

---

1 For what follows, see Second Vatican Council, *Dei Verbum* (1965), §§15–16.
2 A *prophecy* is a statement or deed in the Old Testament which provides detail regarding the future being, works, and teachings of Christ. For instance, Isa. 53:1–12 is typically interpreted as a prophecy of Christ's Passion. A *type* is a person or event which prefigures some aspect of Christ's work, e.g., God's revelation of the Ten Commandments on Mt Sinai prefigures the moral teaching of Christ delivered in the Sermon on the Mount in Mt. 5–7.

second section shows how in Genesis God begins to save his people from sin and its consequences through sacrifices.

Before we begin to examine Genesis and subsequent Old Testament texts, we first need to briefly identify the basic principles of Catholic biblical exegesis. The primary goal of biblical study is to discover the *literal sense* of Scripture, meaning, the realities (*res*) that God wills us to know through the words (*verba*) on the page.[3] The *verba* are means by which we come to know the *res*, and the *res* are primarily truths about God, morality, eternity, and the interactions between God and man in history. Any individual word or series of words in Scripture can point to multiple realities. There is no need to restrict the meaning of any given passage to one truth, so long as those multiple truths are logically compatible.[4] In order to better understand the words of Scripture, and thus the realities to which they point, readers must be attentive to (1) the literary genre, rhetorical form, and original language of the words in question, (2) the historical context in which the words were written, (3) the content and unity of the entire biblical canon, and (4) the content of Sacred Tradition and the living teaching authority of the Magisterium.[5] Thomas Aquinas nicely summarizes these principles: while some interpretations of Scripture may be more persuasive than others, all interpretations are legitimate as long as they are consistent with (a) the circumstances of the letter, (b) truths known with confidence by natural reason, and (c) the truths contained in Sacred Tradition.[6] Having established these basic principles of biblical interpretation,

---

3 Thomas Aquinas, *Summa theologiae*, I, Q. 1, art. 10. Henceforth all references to the *Summa* will be abbreviated as follows: ST I, Q. 1, art. 10. All citations from the works of Aquinas are taken from the Latin texts and English translations published by the Aquinas Institute and available online at www.aquinas.cc.

4 This notion is called the "pluriform literal sense." It was given prominence by Augustine of Hippo in Book XII of his *Confessions* and also endorsed by Thomas Aquinas in ST I, Q. 1, art. 10.

5 See Vatican II, *Dei Verbum*, §12.

6 Aquinas, *De Potentia*, Q. 4, art. 1. By "circumstances of the letter" Thomas simply means the definitions and meanings of the words in themselves and in light of the literary genre at work in the passage. For instance, interpreting the statement "the dog is red" to mean "the cat is black" would not be consistent with the "circumstances" of the former letters.

we can now proceed to examine the major soteriological themes in the book of Genesis.

THE PROBLEM: SIN AND ITS CONSEQUENCES

The history of temptation and human sin begins in Genesis 3. God commands Adam and Eve to abstain from eating of the tree of knowledge of good and evil, and he warns them that if they eat of the tree they will die. Conversely, a serpent encourages Eve to partake of the forbidden fruit, saying: "You will not die. For God knows that when you eat of it your eyes will be opened, and you will be like God, knowing good and evil."[7] The serpent tempts Eve to disobey God's command, and the foundation of his temptation is the assertion that God is not trustworthy: the fruit will not kill Eve and Adam, rather it will make them like God, and that is exactly what God does not want. God does not want Eve and Adam to know the truth about good and evil; he wants to keep them in the dark. He does not want what is best for them; rather than share his glory with them, he wants to keep his power and his knowledge to himself. Hence, God is a liar; Eve and Adam must not trust him. The initial temptation sows *doubt* regarding the goodness and honesty of God.

Genesis 3 suggests two other aspects of the temptation placed before Eve. First, after hearing the serpent's words, Eve saw that the tree of knowledge of good and evil "was good for food" and "was a delight to the eyes." The visible form of the tree and its fruit was beautiful; it appealed to the senses of Eve and elicited her positive *desire* for physical pleasure. She allowed this desire to overpower her, and so chose sensual pleasure over the will of God. Eve is thus the primordial hedonist. Second, some have suggested that Eve and Adam may have felt physically threatened by the presence of the serpent and the pressure which he placed upon them.[8] On this line of thinking, the serpent threatens Eve and Adam with physical death if they do *not* eat the forbidden fruit. Hence, the first humans are faced with

---

7 Gen. 3:4–5. For what follows, see the entirety of Gen. 3.
8 See the case made by Scott Hahn, *A Father Who Keeps his Promises: God's Covenant Love in Scripture* (Servant Publications, 1998), 64–76.

a terrible dilemma: disobey God and suffer spiritual death as well as future physical death; or, disobey the serpent and suffer immediate physical death. Eve and Adam's sin was the failure to trust God in the face of violent aggression. They succumbed to cowardice and clung to their physical lives at the cost of their spiritual lives. They were unwilling to endure martyrdom.

Tempted by the serpent, Adam and Eve eat of the forbidden fruit and bring disorder into God's creation. There are several notable results of their decision to disobey God. First, they become aware of one another's nakedness in a new way, and consequently each covers themselves by making aprons out of fig leaves. Second, their nakedness makes them "afraid" of God, and so they hide from him as he walks through the garden.[9] Third, after God calls them and asks if they have eaten the forbidden fruit, both admit the truth but fail to take responsibility for their actions. Adam blames Eve for giving him the fruit and also seemingly blames God for giving him Eve in the first place! For her part, Eve blames her disobedience on the serpent, who she claims "beguiled" her.[10] In these ways, Genesis 3 shows that Adam and Eve's sins result in immediate *estrangement* from God and from one another: their relations to God and each other are marked by fear, distrust, and obstinacy. They now hide from God and even, through clothes, from one another.

In addition to these immediate results of Adam and Eve's sin, there were also long term consequences.[11] God himself describes these consequences, saying to Eve, "I will greatly multiply your pain in childbearing; in pain you shall bring forth children, yet your desire shall be for your husband, and he shall rule over you." He then tells Adam:

> Cursed is the ground because of you; in toil you shall eat of it all the days of your life; thorns and thistles it shall bring forth to you; and you shall eat the plants of the field. In the sweat of your face you shall eat bread till you return to the ground, for out of it you were taken; you are dust, and to dust you shall return.

These curses upon Adam and Eve can be summarized as follows:

9 Gn. 3:10.   10 Gn. 3:12–13.
11 For what follows, see Gn. 3:16–24.

(1) vulnerability to physical and psychological pain; (2) moral disorder between man and woman; and (3) physical mortality. The last curse is further emphasized by the fact that Adam and Eve are now prevented from partaking of the fruit of the tree of life: to ensure that Adam and Eve do not eat of the tree and "live for ever," God banishes them from Eden and places an angel before the tree to guard it. Their physical mortality is thus accompanied by the loss of the intimate presence of God in Eden: they will no longer walk and talk with God in paradise.

Sin looms prominently in the remaining primordial history which unfolds in Genesis 4–11. Following the story of Adam and Eve, the first people we are given any moral details about are Cain, Abel, and La'mech. Cain, the oldest son of Adam and Eve, murders his younger brother Abel.[12] La'mech is a polygamist who slays a man in excessive retaliation and warns his wives that he will be avenged sevenfold if they commit any injustices against him.[13] The first human stories following Adam and Eve's story are thus stories of unjust violence and lust: moral disorder reigns between brothers and between man and woman. Genesis 5 provides a list of Adam's descendants, but the story of sin immediately picks up again in Genesis 6:1–4:

> When men began to multiply on the face of the ground, and daughters were born to them, the sons of God saw that the daughters of men were fair; and they took to wife such of them as they chose. Then the LORD said, "My spirit shall not abide in man for ever, for he is flesh, but his days shall be a hundred and twenty years." The Nephilim were on the earth in those days, and also afterward, when the sons of God came in to the daughters of men, and they bore children to them. These were the mighty men that were of old, the men of renown.

The precise identity and sins of the figures in Genesis 6:1–4 are enigmatic, but it is nonetheless clear that they represent a sinful low point in human history. For immediately after the references to these figures, Genesis states, "The Lord saw that the wickedness of man

---

12 Gn. 4:1–16.   13 Gn. 4:19–24.

was great in the earth, and that every imagination of the thoughts of his heart was only evil continually."[14] Similarly, a few verses later Genesis states, "Now the earth was corrupt in God's sight, and the earth was filled with violence. And God saw the earth, and behold, it was corrupt; for all flesh had corrupted their way upon the earth."[15]

Consequently, God decides to flood the earth, punishing sinful humanity with death and starting human history over again with the righteous Noah and his family.[16] Yet this is not the end of sin: following the flood, Noah gets drunk on wine, and while drunk becomes the victim of a heinous sexual sin committed by his son Ham. The exact nature of Ham's sin is debated, but it is so grave that it leads Noah to curse Ham and all of his descendants.[17] As soon as Noah's story is completed at the end of Genesis 10, Genesis 11 proceeds to tell the infamous "Tower of Babel" story, in which people band together to build a city featuring a tower which reaches to heaven. They do so in order to "make a name" for themselves and ensure that they are not "scattered abroad upon the face of the whole earth."[18] Their efforts were motivated by pride and idolatry, and so in response God divides human languages and scatters people into distinct places throughout the earth. The story of Babel shows that, even after the flood, humanity's proclivity to sin endures and has reached societal scales.

The story of human sin that begins in Genesis 1–11 is further fleshed out through the remainder of the Old Testament. Scripture describes too many instances of sin for us to list them all here, but we can identify a few of the more prominent examples: Abram, despite being promised by God that his wife Sarah would conceive a son, grows impatient and conceives a child with his slave, Hagar; Jacob's sons sell their brother Joseph into slavery in Egypt; the Pharaoh refuses to let the Hebrew people worship God or leave Egypt, despite the numerous miraculous signs (and warnings) which God gives him; the recently liberated Hebrews complain that God led them out of Egypt only to

---

14 Gn. 6:5.   15 Gn. 6:11–12.

16 Gn. 6:6–10:32.

17 Gn. 9:20–27. Ham's sin is typically thought to have been either rape of his drunk father or incest with his mother, i.e., Noah's wife.

18 Gn. 11:4. For what follows, see vv. 5–9.

starve them to death in the wilderness; they engage in immorality and worship a golden calf statue while Moses converses with the Lord atop Mt Sinai; the book of Judges depicts the frequent sins which the Chosen People commit, and the ensuing hardships which they must endure, throughout their initial decades in the Promised Land; they anoint Saul as their first king so that they will be like other nations, and Saul consistently puts his own will before the will of the Lord; King David commits polygamy, adultery, and murder; his son Solomon, also a polygamist, commits and supports idolatry and enslaves his people; Solomon's son Rehoboam oppresses the people even further, leading ten of the twelve tribes to secede and start the non-Davidic northern kingdom of Israel; the Kings of Israel, and the Davidic kings of Judah in the south, frequently commit and support idolatry, including the practice of child sacrifice; the result is that God allows pagan kingdoms to conquer and exile Israel in 722 BC and Judah in 587 BC; and while the exiled Judeans eventually return to Jerusalem, they are subsequently conquered by Greece (333 AD) and Rome (63 AD), and the Old Testament repeatedly identifies the Chosen People's sins as the cause of their recurring political oppression.

We can now summarize the Old Testament's answer to the question, *what does God save us from?* The main features of that answer are given in Genesis 1–11, and those features are then reiterated and further explored throughout the remainder of the Old Testament. The problems which God desires to save us from are: (1) deliberate *acts* of disobedience in response to God's commands; (2) the disordered *attitudes* and *inclinations*, intellectual and emotional, which lead to and result from acts of disobedience, such as: distrust of God; desire for illicit pleasures; fear of pain and death; shame; lust; violence; jealousy; and pride; (3) the *vulnerability* of our fallen nature to physical and psychological harm; (4) the physical *mortality* which all humans possess as a result of sin; (5) estrangement from the presence and glory of God which was enjoyed in Eden prior to sin. In sum, the problems which plague humanity are spiritual and physical. Physically, we suffer and die; spiritually, we are alienated from God and one another.

To what degree, if any, does God will these physical and moral problems which plague fallen humanity? And what can God do about these problems? On one hand, Genesis 3 indicates that human suffering and death is a natural consequence of Adam and Eve's free act of rebellion against God. God commanded them not to eat the fruit of the tree of knowledge of good and evil, and he explicitly warned them that if they did eat of it then they would die. The fact that humans now suffer and die, in both physical and spiritual ways, is due to the first couple's free choice and to the free, sinful choices which followed in history. God cannot be said to desire these sinful choices or their consequences, for he took active steps to prevent both. On the other hand, God does not immediately repair certain damages of Adam and Eve's sins despite his seeming capacity to do so. Theoretically, at least, God could have responded to the first couple's sin by immediately restoring at least their physical invulnerability and immortality: through a mere word, he could have protected them from physical harm and pain and preserved their bodily lives forever. Or, at least, he could have done so for their children. But he does not. Instead, he banishes the first couple, and consequently all of their descendants, from Eden and prevents them from accessing the tree of life.

This, of course, raises important soteriological questions. Why is there a connection between sin, pain and death? Why does God design creation in such a way that physical vulnerability and mortality are the immediate consequence of sin? Why does he allow the innocent descendants of Adam and Eve, such as preborn children, to bear the burdens of pain and mortality? We can ask similar questions regarding the spiritual condition of fallen humanity. Why didn't God immediately restore the innocence of Adam and Eve? Could he have made them forget that they were naked, remove their fig leaves, and thus eliminate their shame, fear, and selfishness? If so, why didn't he? And if not, then why? How and why does God repair and cleanse the disordered minds, wills and hearts of sinners? These are perennial questions in soteriology. In the remainder of this chapter, I will show how Genesis begins to sketch answers to these questions while also laying a foundation for understanding the fuller answers that will be provided in the remainder of the Old and New Testaments.

THE SOLUTION: SACRIFICE

After describing Adam and Eve's sin and its consequences, Genesis 3 quickly proceeds to indicate *two ways* in which God comes to the aid of his fallen children. The first way is indicated by the curse which God imposes on the serpent: "I will put enmity between you and the woman, and between your seed and her seed; he shall bruise your head, and you shall bruise his heel."[19] Eve's offspring will strike the head of the serpent's offspring, while the serpent's offspring merely strikes the heel of Eve's offspring. The implication is that Eve's offspring will be victorious, but this victory will come at a cost: humanity's heel will be wounded in battle. God promises victory to Eve's offspring, but that victory will require *sacrifice*. Genesis 3:15's divine assurance of victory through sacrifice has led many Christians to label this text as the "first Gospel" (*protoevangelium*). On this interpretation, Genesis 3:15 announces the good news of a savior, descended from Eve, who will conquer the powers of evil precisely through his self-sacrifice.

The second way in which God's mercy is manifested towards Adam and Eve is through the clothing that he provides for them. Immediately after God lists the consequences for Adam and Eve's sins, and right before he banishes them from Eden, he makes "garments of skins" for them and "clothed them."[20] God knows that the fallen man and woman now experience their nakedness as a vulnerability. And so he provides them with clothes which contribute to their protection and peace. These clothes do not fully eliminate the fear, shame, and disordered desire which sin has produced in their hearts. But the clothes do serve to mitigate those damages and partially restore a sense of order and peace between the first couple. Crucially, the clothes that God gives to the fallen man and woman are made from animal skins. This suggests that God killed animals in order to cloth sinners. *Animal sacrifice* is thus a means through which God mitigates and partially repairs the damages caused by the first man and woman's sin.

Hence, Genesis 3:15 and 21 both link God's mercy with sacrifice,

19 Gn. 3:15.   20 Gn. 3:21.

and together these passages suggest that sacrifice of some kind is an essential means by which God repairs the damages caused by sin and grants people victory over the powers of evil. But *how* does sacrifice do so? How does the death of an animal, or of a human, serve to rescue people from sin and its consequences? We can begin to answer these questions by examining the exemplary instances of sacrifice in Genesis.

Cain and Abel

The connection between sin, sacrifice, and God's mercy continues in the story of Adam and Eve's sons, Cain and Abel.[21] Cain, a farmer, "brought to the Lord an offering of the fruit of the ground" which he tilled. Abel, a shepherd, brought "some of the firstlings of his flock and of their fat portions" to God. We see here the first explicit biblical references to an "offering." An *offering* refers to the ritual presentation of a gift to God, typically upon an altar. A *sacrifice* is a ritual offering which involves the destruction of the thing that is given to God. There are three basic types of sacrifice. An animal sacrifice, such as Abel offered, involves first killing the animal and then burning at least a portion of it upon the altar; the remaining portion is eaten by the priest and perhaps the offerer. A libation is a sacrifice in which a vessel of wine is completely poured out upon the altar. And in a grain sacrifice, such as Cain offered, the grain is partially or entirely burnt upon an altar, and the remainder is consumed. All sacrifices are offerings, but not all offerings are sacrifices.

There are several significant features of the story of Cain and Abel. First, it depicts the primordial presence of ritual offerings and sacrifices in human religious activity. Second, it shows that not all ritual offerings are equal or acceptable to God, for God "had regard" for Abel's sacrifice, but not for Cain's. But Genesis 4 does not clearly identify the criteria which distinguish acceptable from non-acceptable ritual offerings. *Why was Abel's sacrifice accepted by God, while Cain's sacrifice was not?* This is an important question which we will revisit throughout this book. Third, Abel the shepherd is a clear type

---

21 See Gn. 4:1–16.

of Jesus, the good shepherd. Both Abel and Jesus are righteous men who offer pleasing worship to God, and consequently both are unjustly killed by their religious peers. Fourth, the primordial story of Abel, and the story of Jesus which it prefigures, suggests a link between ritual sacrifices and the death of those who offer such ritual sacrifices. From the beginning of human history, those who have offered pleasing ritual sacrifices to God have elicited the ire of their peers and, consequently, have become sacrificial victims themselves. The story of Cain and Abel suggests that the proper worship of God will often be met with resistance and even violence by those who do not offer right worship to God.

Noah

The next notable instances of sacrifice in Genesis are depicted in the story of Noah. Why were Noah and his family chosen by God to build the Ark, and how did they successfully survive the deluge? The answer to both of these questions is what I will call Noah's *moral sacrifice*: Noah did the will of God. As Genesis 6 indicates, when all of the world was covered in evil, Noah alone "found favor in the eyes of God," and the reason for this favor was that he "was a righteous man, blameless in his generation; Noah walked with God." The righteousness of Noah is the reason why he and his family are warned of the flood and given the instructions to build the Ark. Then, Noah and his family survive the flood because of their response to God's warnings and instructions: "Noah did this; he did all that God commanded him." The clear lesson of the story of Noah is that sin results in destruction, but obedience to God results in life. The way to survive the deluge of the fallen world is to offer the moral sacrifice of obedience to God.

Noah's story also involves an important ritual sacrifice. Once the flood has concluded and Noah has left the Ark, the first thing that he does while on dry land is build an altar and sacrifice animals upon it. Noah "took of every clean animal and of every clean bird, and offered burnt offerings on the altar."[22] These select animals were taken from

---

22 Gn. 8:20.

the larger group of animals which God commanded Noah to harbor in the Ark during the flood. God wanted Noah to protect these animals so as "to keep their kind alive upon the face of all the earth."[23] And there is no indication that God commanded Noah to sacrifice any of these animals after the flood. Yet, after Noah has killed the animals and burnt their flesh on the altar, we hear that God "smelled the pleasing odor" from the burnt offering. Consequently, God enters into a covenant with Noah and his family by blessing them and promising to never again curse the ground or destroy every living creature.[24] We thus see here the first instance in Scripture of a ritual sacrifice which results in a change to the relation of creatures to God.[25] By destroying some of the very animals which God had commanded him to save from the flood, Noah evidently anticipated that these sacrifices would be pleasing to God, and that they would bring about a better relation of creation to God. But *why* was this sacrifice pleasing to God? What is it about the death and burning of these animals that pleased God so much that he responded by showering great blessings upon Noah, his family, and the entire world?

Abraham and Melchiz'edek

Before answering these questions, we first need to examine other instances of ritual offerings and sacrifices in the Old Testament. Two of these instances involve Abram, or, as he is later called, Abraham. God establishes a covenant with Abram in Genesis 12, and in Genesis 14 Abram encounters Melchiz'edek, the king of Salem.[26] Melchiz'edek "brought out bread and wine; he was priest of God Most High." Melchiz'edek then blesses Abram and prays to God on

---

23 Gn. 7:3.   24 Gn. 8:21–2 and 9:1–17.

25 To be clear, this does not mean that a sacrificial offering changes God's being, for God's eternal substance does not change. He is always perfect, and therefore cannot improve or suffer loss. Nor does a sacrifice make God begin to love us, or love us more, for everything that God wills for us is out of love. Rather, at most, a sacrifice can lead to a change in the material (i.e., concrete) manner in which God exercises his love for us, and it can lead to a change in the human who offers the sacrifice.

26 For what follows, see Gn. 14:18–20. "Salem" was the ancient name of the city which was later to be called "Jerusalem."

his behalf: "Blessed be Abram by God Most High, maker of heaven and earth; and blessed be God Most High, who has delivered your enemies into your hand!" Melchiz'edek is a king and priest who presents a ritual offering of bread and wine to God, and who appears to do so in thanksgiving for the military victory which God had previously given to Abram. This story helps us to identify six major elements of all ritual offerings and sacrifices: 1) the person *who offers* (Melchiz'edek), (2) *what* they offer (bread and wine), (3) the *manner* in which they offer (what is done to the bread and wine), (4) *to whom* they offer (God), (5) the *ends* for which they offer (thanksgiving), and (6) the person *for whom* they offer (Abram).[27] What this story does not explicitly identify, though, is the intelligibility of the ritual act: *why would God want bread and wine ritually presented to him, and how does such a ritual express thanksgiving?*

We will examine answers to this question soon, but for now we proceed to the next notable ritual sacrifice involving Abraham as described in Genesis 22.[28] At the outset of this story, the narrator claims that God "tested" Abraham by giving him the following command: "Take your son, your only-begotten son Isaac, whom you love, and go to the land of Moriah, and offer him there as a burnt offering upon one of the mountains of which I shall tell you." Abraham attempts to carry out God's command, but before he is able to slay Isaac, an angel is sent by God and says, "Do not lay your hand on the lad or do anything to him; for now I know that you fear God, seeing you have not withheld your son, your only-begotten son, from me." Abraham then sees a ram nearby that is "caught in a thicket by his horns" and he sacrifices this ram "as a burnt offering instead of his son." He then gives the name "The Lord will provide" to the place where this occurred. God then tells Abraham that he will reward him because he has "obeyed" God and has "not withheld your son, your only-begotten son." Because of Abraham's obedience, God promises to give Abraham numerous descendants and to bless the entire world through Abraham's line.

27 See Augustine, *The Trinity*, trans. Edmund Hill, second ed. (New City Press, 1991), 171 (Bk. IV, ch. 3, no. 19).
28 For what follows, see Gn. 22:1–19.

There are several features of this story which shed light on the meaning of ritual sacrifice. First, God asks Abraham to sacrifice something *valuable*. Isaac was Abraham and Sarah's only son and was thus their only hope for any further descendants. In a sense, God is asking Abraham to give up that which he loves and cherishes the most. Second, God asks Abraham to sacrifice something which he had previously *received from God*, for Isaac had been miraculously conceived. Third, the sacrifice requires Abraham's *unconditional obedience* to God. One can hardly imagine a worse case scenario for Abraham to be in: he is asked to kill his only, beloved, miraculous son, and (consequently) to eliminate the prospect of future descendants. Despite these dire circumstances, Abraham does what God commands. Fourth, Abraham obeys God not out of fear, but because he *trusts in God's goodness*. God had promised to give Abraham descendants through Isaac. Abraham trusts that God can and will be faithful to that promise: "He considered that God was able to raise men even from the dead."[29] Fifth, Abraham *receives again* that which he offered to God in sacrifice: "hence he did receive him back."[30] Isaac was spared and given back to his father, just as Abraham had hoped for.[31]

We can now conclude this section on sacrifice with a brief synthesis. In the *protoevangelium* of Genesis 3:15, God promises that the offspring of Eve will defeat the offspring of the serpent, but the former will be wounded in the process. God clothes Adam and Eve, reducing their shame and restoring some harmony between them, through the sacrifice of an animal. Abel and Cain both offer ritual sacrifices to God, but only Abel's offering is accepted, and this leads to the death of Abel. Noah is pleasing to God and survives the flood because he offers the moral sacrifice of obedience to God's will. Noah's ritual sacrifices following the flood are pleasing to God and result in God's covenant blessing upon Noah and humanity. Melchiz'edek, the first priest mentioned in Scripture, offers bread and wine to God

---

29 Heb. 11:19. 30 Heb. 11:19.

31 Abraham may have anticipated that this test would not result in Isaac's death at all. For when Isaac asks where the animal is which they are to sacrifice, Abraham responds "God will provide himself the lamb for a burnt offering, my son" (Gn. 22:8).

in thanksgiving on behalf of Abraham. Abraham himself is willing to sacrifice his son Isaac in obedience to God, and as a result God saves Isaac and promises to bless humanity through Abraham and Isaac's descendants.

CONCLUSION

This chapter examined foundational soteriological texts and themes in the Book of Genesis. We began with an examination of the nature, origin, and consequences of sin. We then explored how God responds to the problem of sin through sacrifice, both the ritual sacrifice of animals and the moral sacrifices of human beings. In the next chapter, we will continue to explore how the Old Testament depicts different types of sacrificial offerings, different reasons for which those sacrifices are offered, and the various salvific effects which occur as a result of those offerings.

COMPREHENSION QUESTIONS

1. What is the principal purpose of the Old Testament and how is that purpose accomplished?
2. What is the literal sense of Scripture and how is it discovered?
3. What are Aquinas's three criteria for a legitimate interpretation of Scripture?
4. What are the three possible aspects of the serpent's temptation in Genesis 3?
5. What are the immediate consequences of Adam and Eve's sin?
6. What are the curses and long term consequences of their sin?
7. What sins were committed by Cain, Lamech, the sons of God and daughters of men, and Noah and Ham?
8. What sins did the Davidic kings and kings of Israel/Judah commit which led to the division, conquests and exiles of their kingdoms?
9. What are the five things which God desires to save us from, per Genesis 1–11?

10. To what degree, if any, does God will the physical and moral problems which plague humanity?
11. In Genesis 3, what are the two ways that God helps Adam and Eve following their sin?
12. What is the difference between an "offering" and a "sacrifice?"
13. What are the four major features of the story of Cain and Abel in Genesis 4?
14. What is "moral sacrifice" and how is it exemplified in the story of Noah?
15. Why are Noah's ritual sacrifices "pleasing" to God and what does God do as a result?
16. Who was Melchiz'edek and what are the six major elements of all ritual offerings and sacrifices?
17. What does Abraham do in Genesis 22 and what does God bless him with as a result?
18. What five features of ritual sacrifice are shown by the story of Genesis 22?

2

RITUAL AND MORAL SACRIFICES
IN THE OLD TESTAMENT

I N T H E previous chapter we began to examine the nature and effects of ritual and moral sacrifices in the Book of Genesis. We
saw how the first animal sacrifice occurred in Eden, after Adam and
Eve's fall, as a means of mitigating the consequences of sin. Genesis displayed additional features and effects of sacrifice in the stories of Abel, Noah, Melchiz'edek, and Abraham. In this chapter we
will continue our exploration of sacrifice in the Old Testament. In
the first section we examine the meaning and results of the various
ritual sacrifices which were conducted by Moses and the Levitical
priests. We will focus on the Passover sacrifice in Egypt, the covenant ratification sacrifices at Mt Sinai, and the numerous forms of
sacrifice which took place within the liturgy of the tabernacle and
temple. Section two explores the moral sacrifices, or lack thereof, in
the lives of prominent figures such as kings Saul and David, Job, Isaiah's Suffering Servant, and the confessors and martyrs in the books
of Daniel and Maccabees, respectively. Ultimately, our aim in this
chapter is to examine prominent Old Testament prophecies, types
and antitypes which will serve to illuminate our later examination
of the soteriological teaching of the New Testament.

THE RITUAL SACRIFICES OF MOSES AND THE LEVITES

The book of Exodus depicts God's liberation of the Hebrew people
from slavery in Egypt, and this story contains three significant mo-
ments of ritual sacrifice. The first moment occurs when God reveals
himself to Moses through the burning bush. God sends Moses and
the elders of the Hebrews to Pharaoh with a message: "The LORD,
the God of the Hebrews, has met with us; and now, we pray you, let
us go a three days' journey into the wilderness, that we may sacrifice

to the LORD our God."[1] Why did the Hebrews need to offer sacrifices to God in the wilderness rather than in Egypt? Moses tells Pharaoh that Hebrew sacrifices will be "abominable to the Egyptians," so much so that the Egyptians would stone the Hebrews if they saw their sacrifices.[2] This is because the animals which the Hebrews would sacrifice are the same animals which the Egyptians worship as deities! This highlights a symbolic element in the meaning of ritual sacrifice: the destruction of an animal can represent the rejection of the idol which that animal is equated with.[3] By destroying idols, the Hebrews concretely turn away from sin and express their dedication to the one true God.

The second moment of sacrifice in the story of God's liberation of the Hebrews involves the Passover ritual. This ritual involved five steps: (1) each household must slaughter an unblemished lamb, (2) use a branch of hyssop to spread some of the lamb's blood on the doorposts and lintels of the house, (3) eat the flesh of the lamb, along with unleavened bread and bitter herbs, (4) eat while fully dressed and ready to depart from Egypt, and (5) burn any leftover flesh that is not consumed.[4] What is the meaning of this ritual? The lamb was an idol which the pagans of Egypt worshiped. By slaughtering and eating the lamb, and then spreading its blood on the externals of their house for all to see, the Hebrews were taking a public stand against idolatry and in favor of the living God. They were effectively saying: "we don't worship lambs or any other Egyptian deity. We worship the one true God, and we are so confident that lambs are not gods that we will kill them and make a public mockery of them."

There were two important consequences of the Passover sacrifice. First, the performance of this ritual protected the Hebrews from the punishment which God was inflicting upon Egypt. God had commanded the Hebrews to perform the Passover ritual on the very night that he was passing through Egypt in order to destroy every firstborn

---

1 Ex. 3:18–19.   2 Ex. 8:26.

3 For a concise but persuasive defense of the interpretation of Jewish animal sacrifices as symbolic of idol destruction (among other things), see "Sacrifice" in *The Catholic Bible Dictionary*, ed. Scott Hahn (Doubleday, 2009), 795–99.

4 Ex. 12: 3–11.

human and beast. This was the final plague against the hard hearted Pharaoh who had refused to free the Hebrew slaves. On that night God enacted judgment "on all the gods of Egypt," for he destroyed the very animals and humans (royalty) whom the Egyptians worshiped.[5] But, seeing the blood of the lambs on the outside of Hebrew houses was a sign to God of that household's loyalty to him. So, he "passed over" those houses and spared their firstborn. Second, the Hebrew people and their surviving firstborn were able to depart from Egypt. As a result of the plague against the firstborn, the Pharaoh finally agreed to set the Hebrew slaves free. The power of the enemy of God and his people was finally broken. Those who had carried out the Passover sacrifice, in obedience to God and public recognition of his reign, were made victorious over their enemy. The Hebrews, while still physically enslaved, offered sacrifice in Egypt to the true God; and through this act of spiritual freedom, done in obedience to God, they merited their physical freedom as well.

The third moment of ritual sacrifice in Exodus's liberation story occurs when the newly freed Chosen People reach Mt Sinai in the wilderness. From Sinai God reveals his laws, such as the Ten Commandments, to Moses.[6] Moses then conveys these laws to the people, who with "one voice" promise to obey "all the words which the Lord has spoken."[7] Moses then builds an altar at the foot of Sinai along with twelve pillars which represent the twelve tribes of the people. At Moses' command, men then "offered burnt offerings and sacrificed peace offerings of oxen to the Lord." Then:

> Moses took half of the blood and put it in basins, and half of the blood he threw against the altar. Then he took the book of the covenant, and read it in the hearing of the people; and they said, "All that the LORD has spoken we will do, and we will be obedient." And Moses took the blood and threw it upon the people, and said, "Behold the blood of the covenant which the LORD has made with you in accordance with all these words." Then Moses and Aaron, Nadab, and Abi'hu, and seventy of

5 Ex. 12:12–13.   6 Ex. 20–23.
7 Ex. 24:3. For what follows, see vv. 4–11.

37

the elders of Israel went up, and they saw the God of Israel; and there was under his feet as it were a pavement of sapphire stone, like the very heaven for clearness. And he did not lay his hand on the chief men of the people of Israel; they beheld God, and ate and drank.

Why would Moses take the blood of sacrificial animals and pour half of it against the altar and sprinkle the other half upon the people? And why does this strange ritual result in Moses and 73 leaders of the people being able to ascend God's mountain, see God, and dine with him?

There are at least three layers of meaning to this Sinai sacrifice.[8] First, the sprinkling of blood upon God (the altar) and the people represents the new relationship of blood kinship that exists between them. God has revealed his will and promises to the people, and the people have agreed to abide by God's will; God and the people are now family, with new duties and responsibilities. They are one blood. Second, the sprinkling of the animal's blood upon the people represents what will happen to them if they fail to fulfill their new family obligations: they deserve death, the shedding of their own blood. Third, God and the people feast together upon some of the meat from the sacrificial animals, a shared meal which further manifests their new, familial bond: families eat together and enjoy one another's presence. In sum, the sacrificial ritual at Sinai represents the new covenant relationship between God and the people, and this new relationship involves new blessings (enjoying God's presence, eating with him, knowing his will), new duties (obedience to God's revealed commands), and consequences (death) for the failure to fulfill those familial duties.

In Exodus 24 the Hebrew people enter into a new covenant relationship with God, and this relationship includes the duty to observe the laws that God revealed through Moses on Mt Sinai. What exactly are these laws? They are listed immediately before and after Exodus 24. Laws which govern social behavior, such as the Ten

8 For what follows, see John Bergsma and Brant Pitre, *A Catholic Introduction to the Bible*, volume I: *The Old Testament* (Ignatius Press, 2018), 181–82.

Commandments, are given in Exodus 20–23. Laws about objects and acts of ritual worship, such as the tabernacle, priesthood, and sacrifices, are given in Exodus 25–31.[9] The fact that *both* social and ritual behaviors are divinely commanded show that both are necessary and that neither exhausts the requirements of divine worship on its own. Mere ritual is not enough, nor is mere justice towards one's neighbor. Those who offer the right ritual sacrifices, but fail to keep the Ten Commandments, fail in their duties towards God. And those who keep the Ten Commandments, but fail to perform the prescribed ritual acts, also fail in their duties towards God. Having established this foundational point, we can now look closer at the content and meaning of these ritual laws.

The tabernacle was the foundation of the ritual laws given at Sinai. God revealed the design for this structure and the various objects within it. The tabernacle was an elaborate, portable tent which the people set up, took down, and carried during their journey through the wilderness to the Promised Land.[10] It was understood as the "sanctuary" and "house" of God on earth, the place where he would "dwell among" his Chosen People.[11] Inside the tabernacle was the Ark of the Covenant, which was a wooden box overlaid in gold and containing the stone tablets of the Ten Commandments. The Ark had long poles on each side which enabled it to be carried around, and on top of the Ark was a gold "mercy seat" with a gold angel statue on each end.[12] The Ark was considered the "throne" and "footstool" of God on earth.[13] It resided behind a veil in the innermost room of the tabernacle, the "most holy" place.[14] The outer room in the tabernacle, the "holy place," contained a golden lampstand shaped like a tree (a menorah), a golden table upon which bread was placed, and a golden altar where incense was burned.[15] Immediately outside of the

---

9 Ex. 24 appears to be a literary interlude which depicts the people's public commitment to observe the laws listed in Ex. 20–23 and 25–31.

10 Once David conquered Jerusalem and made it his capital, he began plans to build a permanent structure which would replace the tabernacle. That structure, known as the Jerusalem temple, was built by David's son, King Solomon.

11 Ex. 25:8 and 2 Samuel 7:1–17.   12 Ex. 25:10–20.

13 Ps. 99:1–5; 1 Chr. 28:2.   14 Ex. 26:31–34.

15 Ex. 25:31–40 (lampstand), Ex. 25:23–29 (golden table), Ex. 30:1–6 (altar of

tabernacle was the "court," which contained a bronze altar for animal sacrifice and a bronze laver with water for washing.[16]

Levitical priests were responsible for the daily and annual rituals which were performed in the tabernacle/temple and its court. The high priest went into the holy place of the tabernacle twice per day in order to burn incense on the golden altar (morning and evening) and in order to light and extinguish the menorah (evening and morning, respectively). Every sabbath day he placed fresh bread and wine as an offering upon the golden table.[17] In the court outside of the temple, every day the priests had to sacrifice one lamb in the morning and one lamb in the evening upon the bronze altar. Along with these animal sacrifices, they also had to present and burn offerings of flour, oil, and wine upon the altar. All of these were "a pleasing odor, an offering by fire to the Lord."[18] While these rituals were their sole responsibility, the priests were also responsible each day for sacrificing the many animals (etc.) which other people brought to them to offer on behalf of themselves or their families. Further, there were four annual celebrations (Passover, Weeks, Booths, and the Day of Atonement) which had their own ritual and sacrificial requirements for the priests themselves and for the priests on behalf of the people.[19]

The sacrifices which priests offered at the temple can be distinguished by their physical nature, on the one hand, and the spiritual end for which they were offered, on the other.[20] In terms of the *physical ritual* performed, there were four basic types. A *holocaust* burnt an animal in its entirety upon the altar; nothing was left for the consumption of the priest or person who presented the object. A *cereal* offering consisted of flour, oil, and frankincense, part of which was burned and part of which was consumed by the priest. A *peace offering* burnt only part of an animal, while the remainder was given to the

incense).

16 Ex. 27:1–8 (bronze altar), Ex. 30:17–21 (bronze laver).
17 See Ex. 25:23–30 and 1 Sam. 21:6 (Bread of the presence), 27:20–21 (menorah), and Ex. 30:7–8 (incense).
18 Ex. 29:38–41.
19 See Ex. 23:14–17, Dt. 16:1–17, and Lev. 16.
20 For what follows in this paragraph, see Lev. 1–6 and E.P. Sanders, *Judaism: Practice and Belief, 63 BCE–66 CE* (Fortress Press, 2016), 175–86.

priest and the person who brought the offering. A *sin* or *guilt offering* burnt a portion of the animal (or flour) and gave the remainder to the priest. Depending upon the type of animal sacrifice, the blood would be sprinkled and/or poured out against the outdoor bronze altar, the altar of incense in the sanctuary, or "in front of the veil of the sanctuary."[21] And there was an absolute prohibition against the consumption of any of the animal's blood.[22] The physical act of sacrifice, therefore, includes distinct objects (what is offered) as well as distinct manners of acting (what is done to the object) upon those objects. There were four general, spiritual *ends* for which these physical sacrifices were typically performed: thanksgiving/praise, communion, petition, and atonement. Holocausts could be offered for any of the ends in question. Cereal offerings expressed communion between God and the offerer. Peace offerings were for thanksgiving, praise, communion and petition. Sin and Guilt offerings were in atonement; they purified the offerer from ritual impurity and reconciled them to God following sins against God or neighbor. And if a person had sinned against their neighbor, then before they brought an offering to God they first had to pay recompense to their neighbor.[23] Only then would their sacrifice be acceptable to God.

What was the meaning of these elaborate sacrifices and rituals which took place at the tabernacle and temple? What was the connection between the physical rituals and the spiritual ends to which they were ordered? In order to answer these questions, we first need to further identify the significance of the tabernacle, temple, and the Ark which they housed. Recall that the Ark was considered the throne or footstool of God on earth. The "pattern" for the design of the Ark and its lodging place had been revealed by God on the top of Mt Sinai, that place of privileged encounter between God and the people.[24] As the people departed from Sinai and journeyed towards the Promised Land, the Ark and Tabernacle became like a portable Sinai: God left Sinai and traveled with them.[25] Later, the Ark was

21 Lev. 4:6.   22 Lev 17:10.
23 Lev. 6:1–7.   24 Ex. 25:9 and 40.
25 For this point, and what follows in this paragraph, see Jon D. Levenson, *Sinai & Zion: An Entry Into the Jewish Bible* (Harper Collins, 1985), 89–145.

permanently housed in the new Jerusalem temple, on a new mountain, Mt Zion. The Chosen People associated and even equated Mt Zion with other biblical places in which God had been present to humanity in a radical way: Eden, where he walked and talked with Adam and Eve; and Mt Moriah, where he revealed himself to Abraham and prevented the sacrifice of Isaac.[26] As in the days of Adam and Abraham, so now, Mt Zion was the place where heaven and earth met, the place from which God spoke to his people and received their prayers. Hence, those who dared to enter the temple sanctuary, the holy of holies, were in fact entering into the eternal and heavenly sanctuary of God.[27]

This understanding of the Ark, tabernacle and temple enables us to make two basic observations regarding the meaning of the priestly ministry and sacrifices. First, priests were fundamentally *mediators* between God and his Chosen People. Priests attended to and served the divine presence in the temple, and in doing so they exercised a *"descending"* and *"ascending"* function: they brought the revelations and commandments of God down to the people, and they brought the prayers and offerings of the people up to God.[28] Second, the various rituals which the priests regularly performed—burning incense, lighting the Menorah, offering bread, wine libations, and animal sacrifices—were understood as *gifts* which they presented to God on behalf of the people.[29] Incense, for instance, was the gift of a pleasing aroma whose smell rose up to God. Sacrifices and other dietary offerings were specifically gifts of *food* for God. Grain, flour, wine and meat were placed on altars, which were simply the tables of the Lord. The people brought their gift of food to the priest, and the priest placed the food upon God's tables in his house. Then, depending upon the type of sacrifice, the priest and even the people

---

26 See Gn. 22:14 and 2 Chr. 3:1.

27 See Isa. 6:1–9, where Isaiah's vision of God in his heavenly sanctuary is a vision of God in the temple.

28 See Franck Quoëx, *Liturgical Theology in Thomas Aquinas: Sacrifice and Salvation History*, trans. and ed. Zachary J. Thomas (The Catholic University of America Press, 2023), 72; Levenson, *Sinai & Zion*, 126.

29 For what follows in this paragraph, see Patrick D. Miller, *The Religion of Ancient Israel* (Westminster John Knox Press, 2000), 126–30.

may share in a portion of the food that was presented to the Lord. In those circumstances, the sacrifice became a meal between God and his people, just as Moses and the elders ate and drank with God atop Mt Sinai.

We can thus see that ritual sacrifices had a fundamentally *symbolic* value. How do you express your praise of God? How do you thank him for the many blessings which you have received? The answer is that you bring God a gift of bread, wine, and meat, and then you sit down and share a meal with him. How do you apologize to God and be reconciled with him following your sins? You present him and his minister with a gift of food as an expression of your sorrow and as a partial reparation for the damage which your sins have caused. Gift giving, both as an expression of love and as an expression of remorse, is foundational to human relationships. A husband who wishes to express his love for his wife will take her to an expensive restaurant on their wedding anniversary. And he may do the same at any other point in the year if he has offended her and needs to atone! In the liturgy of the tabernacle and temple these elements of human relationality are enacted in our relation to God. God and his Chosen people are in a covenant, a familial relationship. God dwells with his Chosen People in his palace on Mt Zion, and from there he protects, provides for, and directs them. In return, the people bring gifts of food and sweet aromas to God.

In addition to symbolizing gifts of food for God, we can draw out several other symbolic elements of Levitical ritual sacrifice. First, the theory that Mt Zion was the very location of Eden connects animal sacrifices to the events of Eden. The sacrificial animal's death is a reminder of the death that Adam and Eve's sin brought into the world and of the clothing that God provided to them following their sins. Ritual sacrifice is thus a regular reminder of the penal consequences of sin (death) and of God's mercy in response to our sins (animal clothes). Second, the equation of Mt Zion with Mt Moriah connects Levitical sacrifices with the testing of Abraham. Every gift given to God in the temple is a reminder of the great gift of obedience and trust which Abraham gave to God, and of the obedience and trust which God asks of each one of us. Third, sacrifices and food oblations were a concrete expression of dependence upon and trust in God. Food was far more scarce and hard earned in ancient Israel than it is for many people today. And yet people would hand over significant portions of their own food to God. By doing so, they acknowledged that everything they had was in fact a gift from God, and they displayed trust that God would continue to provide them with the gifts of nourishment which they needed. In this sense, the person who offered sacrifice was merely making a partial return to God from the abundant gifts which God had first given to them.

Fourth, sin and guilt offerings had their own specific symbolism. Immediately before the animal was killed and handed over to the priest, the person who brought the animal would lay their hand upon its head and verbally confess to the priest the impurity or sin for which the animal was being offered.[30] A similar ritual took place in the "scapegoat" offering on the annual Day of Atonement. In this ritual, the high priest placed his hands upon a goat and confessed the sins of the nation, and then the goat was sent away into the wilderness.[31] It has been suggested that the laying on of hands and confession of sin represented the "identification of the offerer with the animal."[32] For instance, Leviticus 16 says that on the Day of Atonement the high priest places the nation's sins "upon the head of the [scape] goat," and then "the goat shall bear all their iniquities upon him to a solitary land" as the people chant "Bear [our sins] and be gone!"[33] The sending away of the scapegoat symbolizes and ritually enacts the nation's turning away from sin. For daily sin and guilt of-

---

30 See Num. 5: 5–10, Lev. 5:1–6, and the commentary in Sanders, *Judaism: Practice and Belief*, 178–182. Recall also that, if the sacrifice was being offered in atonement for a sin against one's neighbor, then one first had to pay recompense to one's neighbor. Hence, reparation had to be made to one's neighbor and to God.

31 Lev. 16:10 and 20–22.

32 William Lane Craig, *Atonement and the Death of Christ: An Exegetical, Historical, and Philosophical Exploration* (Baylor University Press, 2020), 25.

33 Lev. 16: 21–22 and Sanders, *Judaism: Practice and Belief*, 235. See also the analysis by Simon Gathercole, *Defending Substitution: An Essay on Atonement in Paul* (Baker Academic, 2015), 36–37, in response to the view articulated in 30–36. Notably, on the Day of Atonement the high priest did sacrifice a different goat as a sin offering to the Lord on behalf of the people, but he does not perform the laying on of hands and verbal confession on that goat.

ferings, the death of the animal may have been "a symbolic representation of what the offerer deserves" due to their sins.[34] And, or, the symbolic transference of one's sins to the animal and consequent destruction of the animal could represent the destruction of one's sinfulness through repentance.

Fifth, every animal sacrifice involved a symbolic blood ritual.[35] In holocausts and peace offerings, the priest poured out the sacrificial animal's blood against the sides of the bronze altar in the courtyard. Similarly, in all sin and guilt offerings, a portion of the blood was poured out against the base of the altar. But depending upon whom the sin or guilt offering was made for, the priest would also (1) put blood on the horns which surrounded the outdoor altar; (2) enter the holy place of the temple and sprinkle blood seven times before the veil which covered the holy of holies; (3) put blood on the horns of the altar of incense.[36] What was the meaning of these rituals and of the prohibition against consuming the sacrificial animal's blood? Leviticus 17:11–12 and 14 explain:

> For the life of the flesh is in the blood; and I have given it for you upon the altar to make atonement for your souls; for it is the blood that makes atonement, by reason of the life. Therefore I have said to the people of Israel, No person among you shall eat blood, neither shall any stranger who sojourns among you eat blood... For the life of every creature is the blood of it; therefore I have said to the people of Israel, You shall not eat the blood of any creature, for the life of every creature is its blood.[37]

The blood was the life of the animal and of every creature. It could not be consumed by any human, but rather was poured out to God on his altars and before his veil. One implication, at least, is that life belongs to God. Hence, the killing of the animal and pouring forth of

---

34 Craig, *Atonement and the Death of Christ*, 25.
35 For what follows, see Lev. 1–5.
36 For the sins of individual rulers or common people, only the first was done; for the sins of the priest or the entire people together, 2–3 were also done.
37 Lev. 17:11–12 and 14.

its blood to God represents the offerer's gift of their own life to God.[38] Additionally, the pouring out and sprinkling of blood was considered to have a purifying and atoning effect.[39] We see this meaning displayed in particular in the various rituals that were required on the annual Day of Atonement.

The Day of Atonement is the sixth and final element of Levitical sacrifice that we will examine.[40] The purpose of this day was to offer sacrifices which would "cleanse" the people and the temple itself from the various sins and impurities which had accrued throughout the year. This cleansing ensured that the temple remained a pure dwelling place for God and that the people remained fit to dwell in his presence.[41] The need to cleanse the sanctuary where God dwelt made this the only day of the year in which anyone could enter the holy of holies. To do so at any other time would be to incur death before the presence of God "in the cloud upon the mercy seat." The duty to enter the holy of holies and perform the major rituals on the Day of Atonement fell to the high priest alone. His tasks were: (1) wash and put on special vestments; (2) sacrifice a bull as a sin offering for himself; (3) enter the holy of holies with burning coals and incense, thus hiding the Mercy Seat from sight via smoke; (4) use his finger to sprinkle the bull's blood "on the front" of the Mercy Seat and Seven times "before" it; (5) return to the altar outside, place blood on the horns which surround it and sprinkle more blood seven times upon it; (6) repeat steps 2–5, but this time with a goat as a sin offering for the people; (7) perform the scapegoat ritual in the courtyard.[42] The sprinkling of blood upon the Mercy Seat and the bronze altar purified these objects from ritual impurity and ensured God's continued

---

38 On sacrifice as representative of the offerer's gift of self to God, see "Sacrifice," in *The Catholic Bible Dictionary*, ed. Scott Hahn (Doubleday, 2009), 794.

39 Miller, *The Religion of Ancient Israel*, 126.

40 Unless otherwise specified, for what follows, see Lev. 16:1–34. Lev. 1:1 implies that the Day of Atonement rituals were instituted in response to the liturgical sins of Aaron's two sons, as narrated in Lev. 10.

41 Miller, *The Religion of Ancient Israel*, 114.

42 Following the scapegoat ritual, the high priest removed his vestments and washed, and then the bull and goat sacrifices were carried outside of the temple area and burnt.

presence in the temple. And the people's life, symbolized by the animal's blood, was given to God upon his altar and his throne.[43] God accepts their gift of self, forgives the people, and allows them to continue to serve him on his holy mountain.

MORAL SACRIFICES: KINGS, PROPHETS, AND MARTYRS

The previous section showed that the Old Testament places great emphasis on the significance of ritual sacrifices within the saving plan of God. But ritual is not all that God desires from sinners. Even more fundamentally, the Old Testament shows that God desires obedience and moral righteousness from sinners. We saw this last chapter in our study of Noah and Abraham. In this section we examine additional passages in the Old Testament which further illustrate the nature and effects of moral sacrifice.

The fundamental and essential value of human obedience to God is illustrated in 1 Samuel through two stories in which King Saul performs illegitimate sacrifices. In 1 Samuel 13, Saul offers an animal sacrifice to God in order to pray for victory in an impending battle against the Philistines. The prophet Samuel then arrives and rebukes Saul: "You have done foolishly; *you have not kept the commandment of the* LORD *your God*, which he commanded you." Saul's kingdom would have endured forever, but now Samuel warns him that his throne will be taken away and given to another.[44] It is noteworthy that this significant punishment occurs as a result of a ritual action which is good in itself (animal sacrifice) and which is offered with a good intention (petition to God before battle). The problem, though, is that Saul performed this action in *direct disobedience* to the command of God conveyed through the prophet Samuel. The indication, therefore, is that God desires obedience over all else.

A similar event and lesson is depicted in 1 Samuel 15. Through Samuel, God commands Saul to do battle against the Amalekites and to

---

43 Pope Benedict XVI, *Jesus of Nazareth: Holy Week: From the Entrance into Jerusalem to the Resurrection* (Ignatius Press, 2011), 39–40.

44 1 Sam. 13:13–14, emphasis added.

place the ban upon them.[45] Saul proceeds to defeat the Amalekites, but he spares their king (Agog) and takes him captive. Saul also preserves some of the best of the Amalekites' animals in order to offer them as sacrifices to God. Samuel rebukes Saul for his disobedience, but Saul attempts to justify himself by explaining that he spared the best of the spoils in order to offer them as ritual sacrifices to God. In response, Samuel conveys God's word to Saul:

> Has the LORD as great delight in burnt offerings and sacrifices, as in obeying the voice of the LORD? Behold, to obey is better than sacrifice, and to hearken than the fat of rams. For rebellion is as the sin of divination, and stubbornness is as iniquity and idolatry. Because you have rejected the word of the LORD, he has also rejected you from being king.[46]

Obedience is better than ritual sacrifice, even ritual sacrifices which offer our greatest spoils to God and which are done with the best of intentions. Further, the identification of the ban as the object of obedience serves to hyperbolically emphasize the point: no matter what God commands, sinners must obey, and when we do we give God the gift which he desires the most.

The Psalms of King David, who replaced king Saul, provide further witness to the priority of obedience and moral righteousness over ritual sacrifice. In Psalm 50 God first acknowledges the good of ritual sacrifices offered on Mt Zion.[47] But then he seemingly rejects them and emphasizes their merely symbolic value:

> I will accept no bull from your house, nor he-goat from your folds. For every beast of the forest is mine, the cattle on a thousand hills. I know all the birds of the air, and all that moves in the field is mine. If I were hungry, I would not tell you; for the

---

45 The "ban" refers to the complete destruction of the enemy, both combatants and non-combatants. The Old Testament depicts God giving such a command on numerous occasions. While I prefer non-literal interpretations of these commands, the question of how they are to be interpreted does not impact my point here.

46 1 Sam. 15:22–23, emphasis added.

47 Ps. 50:8: "I do not reprove you for your sacrifices; your burnt offerings are continually before me."

world and all that is in it is mine. Do I eat the flesh of bulls, or drink the blood of goats?[48]

The point is that all animals already belong to God and are within his power, and so he does not need humans to feed him. Instead, God desires people to offer him thanksgiving, to fulfill their vows to him, and to call upon him when they are in trouble.[49] After establishing these points, the Psalmist proceeds to critique those who sin against their neighbor through adultery, theft, deceit, and slander. Psalm 50 then concludes by reminding the wicked that "he who brings thanksgiving as his sacrifice honors me; to him who orders his way aright I will show the salvation of God."[50] The clear emphasis of the Psalm is that gratitude to God and justice towards one's neighbors is a form of "sacrifice" which is superior to mere ritual sacrifice.

Psalm 51 expands upon these themes. This Psalm is a prayer for mercy which David makes following his sins against Bathsheba and Uriah. David acknowledges his sinfulness and asks God to "wash" and "cleanse" him.[51] And this washing must occur *within* David: "you desire truth in my inward being; therefore teach me wisdom in my secret heart," and "create in me a clean heart, O God, and put a new and right spirit within me. Cast me not away from your presence, and take not your holy Spirit from me."[52] After acknowledging his need for interior healing and strength, David states "for you take no delight in sacrifice; were I to give a burnt offering, you would not be pleased. The sacrifice acceptable to God is a broken spirit; a broken and contrite heart, O God, you will not despise."[53] Yet, when sincere repentance of heart and conversion of life is present, "then will you delight in right sacrifices, in burnt offerings and whole burnt offerings; then bulls will be offered on your altar."[54] Hence, both Psalms 50 and 51 indicate the priority and necessity of moral sacrifice (repentance, conversion, justice towards neighbor, prayer) over ritual sacrifice. But Psalm 51 adds that ritual sac-

---

48 Ps. 50:9–13.
50 Ps. 50:22–23.
52 Ps. 51:6 and 10–11, respectively.
54 Ps. 51:19.

49 Ps. 50:14–15.
51 Ps. 51:2.
53 Ps. 51:16–17.

rifices remain valuable so long as they proceed from and accompany moral sacrifice.

The necessity of moral sacrifice and the secondary value of ritual sacrifice is emphasized once again in the opening chapter of Isaiah. After lamenting the sinfulness of the Chosen People, Isaiah delivers a scathing critique of their ritual practices:

> What to me is the multitude of your sacrifices? says the LORD;
> I have had enough of burnt offerings of rams and the fat of fed
> beasts; I do not delight in the blood of bulls, or of lambs, or of
> he-goats. When you come to appear before me, who requires
> of you this trampling of my courts? Bring no more vain offer-
> ings; incense is an abomination to me. New moon and sab-
> bath and the calling of assemblies—I cannot endure iniquity
> and solemn assembly. Your new moons and your appointed
> feasts my soul hates; they have become a burden to me, and I
> am weary of bearing them.[55]

After expressing his disregard for the ritual sacrifices and feast days which the people practice amidst their sinful lives, God proceeds to describe what he actually desires from them:

> Wash yourselves; make yourselves clean; remove the evil of
> your doings from before my eyes; cease to do evil, learn to do
> good; seek justice, correct oppression; defend the fatherless,
> plead for the widow. Come now, let us reason together, says
> the LORD: though your sins are like scarlet, they shall be as
> white as snow; though they are red like crimson, they shall be-
> come like wool. If you are willing and obedient, you shall eat
> the good of the land; but if you refuse and rebel, you shall be
> devoured by the sword.[56]

The sinful people must begin to offer God moral sacrifice. They must be washed and made clean not by offering ritual sacrifices, but rather by turning away from evil, practicing justice, fighting oppression, and caring for the fatherless and widowed. In sum, the sacrifice

---

55 Isa. 1:11–15.   56 Isa. 1:16–20.

which God desires from sinners is obedience to God's commands, and especially to God's command to love one's neighbor.

The value of moral sacrifice is given a concrete example in the Book of Job, which depicts the life of a non-Jewish man named Job.[57] Job possessed numerous cattle, had many servants, was married and had ten children. But more importantly, Job was "blameless and upright, one who feared God, and turned away from evil." He would even regularly sacrifice burnt offerings in atonement for his children's sins.[58] God boasted to the devil that "there is none like him [Job] on the earth," so great is Job's righteousness. But the devil objects that Job is blameless only because he has been materially spoiled and preserved from pain. God then permits the devil to destroy all of Job's livestock, servants, and children. Yet Job continues to worship God, saying "the Lord gave, and the Lord has taken away; blessed be the name of the Lord."[59] The devil then objects that Job would not remain blameless if his own body was harmed, so God then permits the devil to afflict Job "with loathsome sores from the sole of his foot to the crown of his head." At this point Job's own wife tempts him, saying "do you still hold fast to your integrity? Curse God and die."[60] But Job refuses to do so, and he continues to preserve his moral and religious integrity throughout all of his suffering.

The remainder of the Book of Job consists primarily of a dialogue between Job and three of his friends. These friends initially come to console Job, but they then proceed to argue that he must be suffering as a punishment for his sins. In response, Job repeatedly insists that he has not committed any sins which would merit such severe punishments. At one point Job utters a lament which shows that these friends were not the only ones who condemned him: "I am repulsive to my wife, loathsome to the sons of my own mother. Even young children despise me; when I rise they talk against me. All my intimate friends abhor me, and those whom I loved have turned against

---

57 As Thomas Aquinas argues in the prologue to his *Commentary on Job*, the question of whether or not the book is about an actual historical figure or merely a fictional parable does not alter the clear meaning of the book.

58 Job 1:1–5.   59 Job 1:8–21.

60 Job 2:3–9.

me."[61] Job has been rejected by everyone; he is alone against the world. Yet, he remains faithful to the Lord and expresses a prophetic hope:

> Oh, that my words were written! Oh, that they were inscribed in a book! Oh, that with an iron pen and lead they were graven in the rock for ever! For I know that my Redeemer lives, and at last he will stand upon the earth; and after my skin has been thus destroyed, then from my flesh I shall see God, whom I shall see on my side, and my eyes shall behold, and not another. My heart faints within me![62]

Despite his horrific material, social, and physical suffering, Job continues to believe and hope that one day he will rise from the dead and, with his own eyes, see his Creator present on earth in the flesh.[63] And Job's hope is partially rewarded by the end of the book: God appears, vindicates Job, and rebukes the three friends. God commands them to sacrifice burnt offerings in atonement for their foolish words, and then he "restored the fortunes of Job, when he had prayed for his friends." Job not only preserved his innocence throughout his horrific suffering, he also prayed for those who contributed to his suffering. Job's steadfast righteousness and mercy amidst suffering was a pleasing moral sacrifice to God, so much so that God gave him "twice as much as he had before."[64]

The necessity and value of fidelity to God amidst suffering is given additional expression in the Book of Daniel. In Daniel 3, King Nebuchadnez'zar of Babylon threatens to cast Shad'rach, Me'shach, and Abed'nego into a raging furnace of fire for their refusal to worship his golden idol. They respond, "our God whom we serve is able to deliver us from the burning fiery furnace; and he will deliver us out of your hand, O king. But if not, be it known to you, O king, that we will not serve your gods or worship the golden image which you have set up." Consequently, they are cast into the flames, but are preserved

---

61 Job 19:17–19.   62 Job 19:25–27.
63 Many great Catholic theologians, such as Thomas Aquinas, have interpreted Job
    19:25–27 as evidence that Job had explicit prophetic knowledge not only of the
    resurrection of the body, but of the Incarnation as well.
64 Job 42:10.

from all harm and ultimately set free. For God "sent his angel and delivered his servants, *who trusted in him*, and set at nothing the king's command, and *yielded up their bodies* rather than serve and worship any god except their own God."[65] Similarly, in Daniel 6 the prophet Daniel is cast into a den of lions for continuing to pray and give thanks to God despite a law which required exclusive worship of the Babylonian king. But because Daniel was "blameless," God sends an angel to shut the lions' mouths and preserve Daniel from harm. The king then frees Daniel and punishes those who turned him in. These stories show that God is pleased by those who offer him the moral sacrifice of obedience in the face of death. And they depict God miraculously intervening to preserve his faithful from the death with which they were threatened.

Yet, elsewhere the Old Testament makes it clear that God does not always rescue his faithful from death: martyrdom does happen, and these holy deaths are the supreme form of moral sacrifice which humans can offer to God. One particularly dramatic account of Jewish martyrdoms occurs in 2 Maccabees 7. A Jewish mother and her seven sons are arrested for refusing to consume unclean food, "swine's flesh." They are subsequently tortured "with whips and cords," but nonetheless one of the brother's states, "we are ready to die rather than transgress the laws of our fathers." This family is ready to unconditionally obey God's commands, even commands as seemingly trivial as dietary laws. In response, the pagan king proceeds to torture and kill each of them, one at a time. He cuts off the first brother's tongue, hands, feet and scalp, then fries him alive in a pan. He does the same to the second brother, but right before this one dies he says "you dismiss us from this present life, but the King of the universe will raise us up to an everlasting renewal of life, because we have died for his laws." The third through sixth brothers endure the same violence, and together they too express their confidence that God will one day raise them from the dead and will punish their persecutors.

All the while, the mother encourages her sons. She says that the God who formed them in her womb "will in his mercy give life and

---

65 Emphasis added.

breath back to you again, since you now forget yourselves for the sake of his laws." Before torturing the seventh son, the king offers him power and wealth if he will eat the unclean food, but the son refuses. The king then pressures the mother to persuade her son, but instead the mother tells her youngest child: "Do not fear this butcher, but prove worthy of your brothers. Accept death, so that in God's mercy I may get you back again with your brothers." The son perseveres, as does his mother, and both are subsequently martyred. In his final words, the seventh son states that he has "give[n] up body and life for the laws of our fathers, appealing to God to show mercy soon to our nation … and through me and my brothers to bring to an end the wrath of the Almighty which has justly fallen on our whole nation." The seven sons believed that the persecution which they and their nation were enduring at the hands of the Greeks was a punishment for their sins.[66] But they also believed that the obedience which they gave to God amidst these persecutions, obedience even to the point of torture and death, was a sacrifice which could be offered in atonement for their sins and in petition for the deliverance of the nation. The story of the mother and her seven sons thus conveys the necessity of unconditional obedience to God, hope in the resurrection of the body, and hope that obedience unto death is a pleasing sacrifice which can be offered to God in atonement and petition.

We bring this chapter to a close by considering one final passage in which these themes converge and reach their zenith, namely, Isaiah 52:13–53:12's description of the mysterious "Suffering Servant."[67] This passage describes the condemnation, torture, death and vindication of an unnamed Servant of God. The Servant's peers view him as a miserable sinner who was being punished by God: "He was despised and rejected by men" and "we esteemed him stricken, struck down by God, and afflicted." But the truth is that the Servant was perfectly innocent, and his suffering was a consequence of humanity's sins, not his own: "he had done no violence, and there was no deceit in his mouth," and "he was wounded for our transgressions, he

---

66 See 2 Macc. 7:18, 32–33 and also 6:12–16.
67 Contemporary biblical scholars generally identify four "songs" in which this Servant is depicted: Isa. 42:1–4; 49:1–6; 50:4–9; and 52:13–53:1–12.

was bruised for our iniquities." Despite his great pains, the Servant remained innocent and passive throughout his suffering, "like a lamb that is led to the slaughter." In fact, he freely chose to endure his pains as a sacrifice which he offered to God in atonement for the sins of humanity: he "poured out his soul to death" and "makes himself an offering for sin" to give "intercession for the transgressors." Consequently, his pains "made us whole" and "with his stripes we are healed." The Servant's sacrificial death not only cleanses the people from sin, it also leads to his own reward and exaltation by God: "I will divide him a portion with the great, and he shall divide the spoil with the strong," and "he shall see his offspring, he shall prolong his days."

The text of Isaiah 53 describes the suffering Servant using the language of both ritual and moral sacrifice. The Servant is like a *lamb* who is offered as a sacrifice in atonement *for sin*. As the lamb's blood is *poured out* upon the altar, so the Servant's life is poured out. And as the high priest offered sacrifices of *intercession* to God for the sinful nation, so the Servant's suffering and death is intercession for sinful humanity. But, an animal does not offer itself; it does not practice virtue in the face of death; and it is not vindicated following its death. Conversely, the Servant is the offerer, the priest, and the sacrificial victim. His perfectly innocent and righteous life, preserved all throughout his persecution and execution, is the gift which he freely presents to God. In this sense he is like the blameless Job and the heroic figures in Daniel and Maccabees who remained obedient to God even amidst tragedy, torture and the threat of death. And as Job prayed for his enemies and was heard, and the mother and her seven sons offered their lives for the sins of the nation, so the Servant offered his life in atonement for the sins of the world. But Job and Daniel's confessors were saved merely from *temporal* suffering and death, and the martyrs of Maccabees died with mere *hope* for their resurrection and for the temporal deliverance of their nation. But the Servant is actually rewarded with new life *after* death, and his sacrifice gives sinners new life by delivering them from their *sins*, rather than from temporal pain. In fact, the story of the Servant shows that suffering and death in this world, freely endured out of love for God and neighbor, is the ultimate source of salvation from sin and eternal death. Isaiah 53 shows the ultimate fulfillment of God's initial promise of salvation given in Genesis 3:15: the Servant is the offspring of Eve who is struck by the offspring of the serpent, but the Servant also crushes the head of the serpent's offspring. Through the sacrifice of the Servant, the children of Eve conquer and are victorious over the spawn of the serpent: sin and eternal death.

CONCLUSION

In this chapter we have examined the nature and purpose of various forms of ritual and moral sacrifice in the Old Testament. We identified the numerous symbolic meanings of ritual sacrifice while also noting that these rituals do not exhaust the proper worship of God. God also requires the moral sacrifices of obedience to his commands, including his command to practice justice and service towards one's neighbors. Total and unconditional obedience to the commands of God, whether those commands be ritual or moral, is the ultimate sacrifice which pleases God, delivers humanity from sin, and establishes them in intimate communion with the Lord. These truths about sacrifice converge in the mysterious figure of the suffering Servant, a man who freely chose to offer his life in atonement for sin and who preserved his innocence throughout his persecution and death. Isaiah 53's description of the Servant serves as a helpful transition to our next chapter, in which we will begin to consider the New Testament's account of the saving work of Christ. For Christians have long insisted that Isaiah 53 is a prophecy of the Incarnation and Passion of Christ.[68] As we explore the soteriological teaching of the New Testament, we will see how Isaiah 53 and the various other sacrificial texts and themes which we have examined are brought to fulfilment in the person and work of Christ.

~

68 Thomas Aquinas, for instance, interpreted the literal sense of Isa. 53 as exclusively about Christ. See the analysis of Aquinas's view in Daniel Waldow, *The Suffering Servant in Aquinas: Isaiah 53 and Thomas's Theology of Christ's Passion* (The Catholic University of America Press, 2024).

COMPREHENSION QUESTIONS

1. Why did the Hebrews need to offer sacrifices in the wilderness rather than in Egypt?
2. What are the five steps, the meaning, and the two consequences of the Passover sacrifice?
3. What sacrifices did Moses offer at the foot of Mt Sinai and what did he and the elders do afterward?
4. What are the three meanings of the sacrificial rituals which Moses performed in Exodus 24?
5. What are the two basic types of laws which are revealed by God in Exodus 20–23 and 25–31?
6. What is the tabernacle/temple and what did it contain?
7. What were the required daily rituals which the high priest and the other priests performed in the temple and its court?
8. What were the four physical types of sacrifice?
9. What were the four spiritual ends for which sacrifices were offered?
10. What three places was the temple associated with?
11. What are the two basic meanings of priesthood and sacrifice?
12. What are three symbolic meanings of ritual sacrifice?
13. What was the symbolic meaning of the rituals connected with sin and guilt sacrifices and the scapegoat?
14. What was and was not done with the sacrificial animal's blood, and what was the symbolic meaning of these rituals?
15. What rituals did the high priest perform on the Day of Atonement and what was their purpose?
16. What sins does Saul commit in 1 Samuel 13 and 15, and what does Samuel say in response?
17. What do Psalms 50–51 and Isaiah 1:11–20 indicate about the relationship between morality and ritual sacrifice?
18. According to Psalm 51, what is the sacrifice acceptable to God?
19. Who was Job, what happened to him, how did he respond, and how does his story end?
20. What is the meaning of Job's words in Job 19:25–7?

21. How is moral sacrifice exemplified in Daniel 3, 6, and 2 Maccabees 7?
22. In 2 Maccabees 7, what do the mother and her sons hope will happen to them and to their nation as a result of their moral sacrifice?
23. How is the suffering and death of the Servant in Isaiah 53 similar to and distinct from ritual sacrifices and other moral sacrifices in the Old Testament?
24. How do Christians such as Thomas Aquinas interpret the text of Isaiah 53?

THE BEING AND PUBLIC MINISTRY
OF CHRIST

W HAT *does God save us from,* and *how does he do so?* In the previous two chapters we examined how the Old Testament began to answer those questions. We saw that ritual and moral sacrifices were central expressions of the proper worship of God and means by which God brings his sinful people back into a proper relationship with him. In this chapter we will begin to examine key soteriological texts and themes of the New Testament. Our focus in this chapter is upon the New Testament's depiction of the salvific significance of the being and life of Christ *prior to* his Passion, Resurrection and Ascension. This chapter consists of two major sections. The first section examines the soteriological meaning of the name "Jesus" and the titles "Christ" and "Son of God." These titles and name shed light on the saving mission of Jesus and on the ontological power which he possesses in order to carryout that mission. Section two treats the Gospel's presentation of the public ministry of Christ, with a focus on the saving nature of his teachings and miracles.

THE SOTERIOLOGICAL MEANING OF JESUS'
NAME AND TITLES

What does Jesus save us from and how does he do so? One way to begin to answer this question is to consider the soteriological meanings of the name and titles of Jesus that are provided in the Gospels. For instance, the opening line of the Gospel of Mark specifies that its story is about "Jesus Christ, the Son of God."[1] What does this name and those titles mean, and how do they shed light on the saving work of Jesus? In this section we will answer those questions by examining

---

1 Mk. 1:1.

the use of "Jesus," "Christ" and "Son of God" in the opening chapters of the Gospels and in light of relevant Old Testament texts.

Jesus

We can begin with the name "Jesus." In Matthew and Luke's infancy narratives, an angel tells Joseph and Mary that they are to give this name to Mary's miraculously conceived child. The angel specifies that the child is to be given this name because"he will save his people from their sins." The evangelist specifies that "all this took place to fulfill what the Lord had spoken by the prophet: 'Behold, a virgin shall conceive and bear a son, and his name shall be called Emma'nuel', which means, 'God with us.'"[2] "Jesus" is a translation of the Hebrew *Yeshua*, which literally means "YHWH saves" or "YHWH is salvation."[3] YHWH is name that God revealed to Moses at the burning bush: "God said to Moses, 'I AM WHO I AM (YHWH).'"[4] Hence, the name "Jesus" is explicitly tied to the name of God, to the name "Emmanuel," and to the power to save from sin. But this name and the meaning which the angel assigns to it raises soteriological questions: *what exactly is the relationship between Jesus and God? And how does Jesus save us from sin?* The answers to these questions will become clearer as we proceed to consider the titles "Christ" and "Son of God."

Christ, Messiah

The title "Christ" sheds some further light on the saving mission of Jesus. The wise men followed a star to Jerusalem in order to find the newborn "king of the Jews," and the wicked king Herod realized that they were seeking "the Christ." The angel of the Lord announced the birth of Jesus to shepherds, saying "to you is born this day in the city of David a Savior, who is Christ the Lord."[5] The "Christ" is thus a king

---

2 Mt. 1:22–23, quoting Isa. 7:14. Isaiah appears to refer to this same child in Isa. 9:6–7.

3 *Yeshua* was a common name in ancient Judaism. For instance, it was the name of the titular hero of the Old Testament book of "Joshua." Joshua was the successor of Moses who led the Chosen People amidst their entrance into and conquest of the Promised Land.

4 Ex. 3:14. In the Greek rendering of the Old Testament, "YHWH" was translated as *ego eimi ho on* (ἐγώ εἰμι ὁ ὤν).

5 Lk. 2:11.

and savior. His birth in Bethlehem links him with king David, whose hometown was Bethlehem. This Davidic link is emphasized in the angel Gabriel's annunciation to Mary concerning Jesus: "the Lord God will give to him *the throne of his father David.*"[6] Mary's son is a descendant of David who will take up David's royal throne and rule as a king. Hence, the title "Christ" refers to the fact that Jesus is a Davidic king and savior. But what sort of salvation does this king bring?

In order to answer this question, we first need to consider the Old Testament background to the title "Christ." The literal meaning of "Christ" is "anointed one," and it referred primarily to kings who were anointed for their royal office.[7] For instance, God sent the prophet Samuel to anoint Saul and then David as kings. And King David was a savior in his own way: he liberated and protected the Chosen People from their pagan enemies in the Promised Land, such as the giant Goliath. David also united the twelve tribes of the Chosen People under his reign, established Jerusalem as the capital of the kingdom, and brought the Ark of the Covenant to the city. God promised David a son to succeed him as king following his death, and regarding this son of David he said: "He shall build a house for my name, and I will establish the throne of his kingdom for ever. I will be his father, and he shall be my son."[8] David's son king Solomon would build a temple to God in Jerusalem, he and his successors would be known as "sons of God," and the reign of Davidic kings in the Promised Land would last forever.

Yet, due to their idolatry and sinfulness, the reign of Davidic kings did not last forever. During the reign of Solomon's tyrannical son, Rehoboam, ten of the tribes seceded and started the northern kingdom of Israel. They were subsequently conquered and scattered abroad by Assyria in 722 B C. At the same time, an influx of Assyrian pagans settled in the northern regions of Samaria and Galilee. Meanwhile, two Jewish tribes had remained under the rule of Davidic kings in what came to be known as the southern kingdom of Judah. But Judah was conquered by Babylon in 587 B C. At that point the temple of

---

6 Lk. 1:32.
7 "Christ" is the Greek form of the Hebrew "Messiah."
8 2 Sam. 7:13–14.

Solomon in Jerusalem was destroyed, the Ark was lost forever, and the Judeans who survived were exiled to Babylon. Those who survived captivity in Babylon eventually returned to Jerusalem around 539 BC and built a new temple, but they no longer had a Davidic king. In time they were conquered by the pagan Greeks (333–167 BC) and then Romans (63 BC). Hence, at the time of Jesus the Jewish people in the holy land had not had a Davidic king in nearly six hundred years; the Jews who lived in Galilee and Samaria had lived alongside pagan neighbors for 722 years; and all were now subject to Roman rule.

But throughout the centuries the prophets taught the Chosen People to hope for a time when God would come to save them and establish a new Davidic kingdom. For instance, while Daniel was exiled in Babylon he warned the Babylonian king that "the God of heaven will set up a kingdom which shall never be destroyed, nor shall its sovereignty be left to another people. It shall break in pieces all these [pagan] kingdoms and bring them to an end, and it shall stand firm forever." Like a stone "cut from a mountain by no human hand," the kingdom of God will shatter the pagan kingdoms of the world and become "a great mountain" which will fill "the whole earth."[9] Similarly, Daniel described pagan kings and their kingdoms as violent "beasts" who terrorize the world, but he promised that "their dominion" would be "taken away."[10] For God, the "ancient of days," will pronounce judgment against these beasts from his heavenly throne.[11] And God will then replace these pagan kingdoms with a kingdom of his own:

> Behold, with the clouds of heaven there came one like a son of man, and he came to the Ancient of Days and was presented before him. And to him was given dominion and glory and kingdom, that all peoples, nations, and languages should serve him; his dominion is an everlasting dominion, which shall not pass away, and his kingdom one that shall not be destroyed.[12]

This mysterious "son of man" certainly represents the holy people of God, the "saints of the most high" who "shall receive the kingdom,

9 See Dn. 2.
10 Dn. 7:17 and 12, respectively.
11 Dn. 7:9–12, 21–22 and 26.
12 Dn. 7:13–14.

and possess the kingdom forever, for ever and ever."[13] But there were ancient Jews who also identified the Son of Man as an individual, and specifically as the king of this future kingdom of God. The Son of Man was the last and greatest king whom God would anoint to take the throne of David. He is the stone which shatters the reign of the pagan kingdoms; he is *the* Christ, *the* Messiah.[14]

The book of the prophet Ezekiel provides additional background which helps us to understand the saving mission of the Christ. Ezekiel was writing to the Jewish people who were exiled in Babylon following the destruction of Jerusalem. He spoke of God as a shepherd who would come to save his sheep from wild beasts and false shepherds.[15] God will "break the bars of their yoke and deliver them from the hand of those who enslaved them." He will find the lost sheep and "rescue them from all the places where they have been scattered." He "will bring them into their own land" and "will feed them on the mountains of Israel." He will "banish wild beasts from the land" so the sheep "shall be secure in their land." And yet God will not work alone: "I will set up over them one shepherd, my servant David, and he shall feed them." Ezekiel emphasizes that God will not merely bring home the lost Judeans; he will also bring home the lost tribes of Israel and reunite everyone under the Davidic shepherd.[16] Nor will God merely bring home the lost who are still alive; he will also raise the dead back to life: "Behold," he says, "I will open your graves, and raise you from your graves, O my people, and I will bring you home into the land of Israel."[17] Following this resurrection and return from exile, the people will live in the Promised Land "for ever, and David my servant shall be their prince for ever."[18] Consequently, Ezekiel associates the Davidic shepherd or "Christ" with God's final salvific intervention in history: God and his Christ will save the people from oppression, exile, division, and even death itself.

---

13 Dn. 7:18 and 27.
14 On the ancient Jewish identification of the Son of Man with the Messiah, see Brant Pitre, *The Case for Jesus: The Biblical and Historical Evidence for Christ* (Image, 2016), 111–13.
15 For what follows, see Ez. 34.   16 Ez. 37:1–21.
17 Ez. 37:1–14.   18 Ez. 37:25.

Having established the Old Testament background to the title "Christ," we can now better understand the salvific significance of the application of this title to Jesus in the infancy narratives. The angel Gabriel announces to Mary that Jesus "will be great, and will be called the *Son of the Most high*; and the Lord God will give to him *the throne of his father David*, and he will reign over the house of Jacob *for ever*; and of his kingdom there will be *no end*."[19] While Jesus is a son of God like previous Davidic kings, he is not merely the beginning of a new succession of kings. Rather, he is the last and greatest king: he will reign forever, and his kingdom will never end. Similarly, the angelic announcement of Jesus' birth to the shepherds in Bethlehem emphasizes Jesus' royal, saving power: the angel is accompanied by "a multitude of the heavenly host" and he proclaims "good news of a great joy which will come to all the people; for to you is born this day in the city of David a Savior, who is Christ the Lord."[20] The army ("host") of angels in heaven praise Jesus, for he is the Davidic shepherd and Son of Man foretold by Ezekiel and Daniel: Jesus is the king through whom God will conquer the pagan kingdoms and free his Chosen People. The arrival of Jesus the Christ signifies the coming resurrection of the dead and the establishment of the permanent kingdom of David in the land of Israel.

Son of God

Having established the meaning of "Jesus" and "Christ," we can now say more about the soteriological significance of the title "Son of God." When Mary asks Gabriel how the conception of Jesus will occur, Gabriel responds: "the Holy Spirit will come upon you, and the power of the Most High will overshadow you; therefore the child to be born will be called holy, the Son of God." This indicates that Mary's child is the "Son of God" not *merely* in the sense of being a Davidic king, but also in a more literalistic sense: Jesus has no biological father and his conception is caused by the Holy Spirit. God "overshadows" Mary and causes Jesus to live in her womb, just as a cloud "overshadowed" the original tabernacle in the wilderness when it was filled with the

---

19 Lk. 1: 32–33, emphasis added. 20 Lk. 2: 10–14.

64

glory, or, presence, of God.[21] Does this mean that Jesus is the glory of God present within the tabernacle of Mary's body? The ensuing story of Mary visiting her cousin Elizabeth suggests as much, for it contains clear allusions to the story of David bringing the Ark of the Covenant to Jerusalem.[22] These allusions suggest that Mary is the new temple, her womb is the new Ark, and that Jesus is the God who resides in that temple and sits enthroned upon that Ark.

In order to better appreciate the soteriological significance of Luke's depiction of Mary and Jesus in cultic terms we can return once again to the prophecies of Ezekiel. We have already seen how Ezekiel foretold the resurrection of the dead and the establishment of a new and perpetual Davidic kingdom in the Promised Land. Additionally, God promised Ezekiel that with the establishment of this new kingdom God himself would come to the people and "set my sanctuary in the midst of them for evermore."[23] This sanctuary is a new temple in Jerusalem which will be filled with God's glory.[24] Alluding to the Ark, God calls this temple "the place of my throne and the place of the soles of my feet," and there God "will dwell in the midst of the sons of Israel for ever."[25] And God's presence amidst his people will be life-giving: a river will flow eastward from the temple, and "everything will live where the river goes."[26] The river will enter the sea, making its waters fresh and teeming with life for fishermen.[27] Similarly, trees will live and bear fruit perpetually along the river's banks: "their fruit will be for food, and their leaves for healing."[28] All of this takes place "because the water for them flows from the sanctuary."[29] And the life which God gives to his people in this eschatological Promised Land is not merely physical, but also spiritual:

---

21 Ex. 40:35.
22 See Lk. 1:39–56 and the essay "Mary, Ark of the Covenant" in *The Ignatius Catholic Study Bible: New Testament, Second Catholic Edition RSV*, ed. Scott Hahn and Curtis Mitch (Ignatius Press, 2010), 107.
23 Ez. 37:26–27.   24 Ez. 43:2–5.
25 Ez. 43:7.   26 Ez. 47:9.
27 Ez. 47:8–10.   28 Ez. 47:12.
29 Ez. 47:7–12.

For I will take you from the nations, and gather you from all the countries, and bring you into your own land. I will sprinkle clean water upon you, and you shall be clean from all your uncleannesses, and from all your idols I will cleanse you. A new heart I will give you, and a new spirit I will put within you; and I will take out of your flesh the heart of stone and give you a heart of flesh. And I will put my spirit within you, and cause you to walk in my statutes and be careful to observe my ordinances. You shall dwell in the land which I gave to your fathers; and you shall be my people, and I will be your God. And I will deliver you from all your uncleannesses.[30]

Through sprinkling with water, God transforms the hearts of his people, puts his Spirit within them, and consequently empowers them to avoid sin and idolatry and observe all of his commandments. In sum, when God raises the dead, brings his people back to the Promised Land, and restores the Davidic kingdom he will also come to dwell with his people in a new and eternal temple, and from there he will give perpetual life and righteousness to his people through the river of life and the sprinkling of water.

While Luke's infancy narrative implies the divinity of Jesus and so suggests the fulfilment of these themes, the prologue to John's Gospel states the divinity of Jesus explicitly.[31] The fourth Gospel begins with a mysterious description of God: "In the beginning was the Word, and the Word was with God, and the Word was God." The "Word" is *distinct* from "God" ("with God") and yet also *is* "God" ("was God"). How can this be? The answer is that the Word is the "only-begotten Son from the Father." Jesus is not the "son of God" merely in the sense of being the last Davidic king, nor even in the sense of being a mere human who was miraculously conceived in Mary's womb by God himself. Rather, Jesus is the only *eternal and divine* son of God. He is the Word who was in the beginning "with God" the Father and yet who also always "was God" the Son. The Father and Son are really *distinct as persons* yet both fully and equally possess the *one*

30 Ez. 36:24–29. See also Ez. 37:23–24.
31 For what follows, see Jn. 1:1–18.

divine nature of "God." As only-begotten Son, the eternal Word is the one through whom the Father creates all things: "all things were made through him, and without him was not anything made that was made." In addition, the Word is the one through whom the Father reveals himself to humanity: "No one has ever seen God; the only-begotten Son, who is in the bosom of the Father, he has made him known." How does the Word reveal the truth about the Father and his own divine Sonship?

As John's prologue makes clear, the eternal Son reveals the Father precisely by becoming the son of Mary in time. "The Word became flesh and *dwelt* among us, full of grace and truth; we have beheld his *glory*, glory as of the only-begotten Son from the Father."[32] The Word is the God who comes to dwell with his people in the new temple of his flesh; his divine glory fills his body and shines on the earth for all to see.[33] And God dwells among us in the flesh and shines forth his glory precisely in order to give us life: "to all who received him, who believed in his name, he gave power to become children of God; who were born, not of blood nor of the will of the flesh nor of the will of man, but of God."[34] The only-begotten Son gives people power to be born anew from God, and so to participate in his own divine sonship: "from his fulness have we all received, grace upon grace."[35] The Son is the Creator who opens the graves of the dead and restores them to life; his body is the sanctuary from which grace flows out like a river to give sinners new life as children of God. In sum, Jesus is not merely the Davidic king and shepherd prophesied by Daniel and Ezekiel. As the only-begotten Son of the Father, he is also the ancient of days and the divine shepherd; he is God in the flesh, and his coming among us is salvific: he comes to reveal the glory of God and to give eternal life to those who are dead in body and soul.

JESUS' PUBLIC MINISTRY: TEACHING AND MIRACLES

Having identified the meaning and salvific significance of the name "Jesus" and the titles "Christ" and "Son of God," we can now begin to

32 Jn. 1:14, emphasis added.   33 Ez. 43:2.
34 Jn. 1:12–13.   35 Jn. 1:16.

consider the saving *actions* which Jesus performed. The vast majority of the story of Jesus that is contained in the canonical Gospels consists of the presentation of his "public ministry." This ministry was the 3 year period in Jesus' adult life in which he travelled throughout Israel teaching, working miracles, gathering followers, and making enemies.[36] This was the period immediately prior to his Last Supper, crucifixion, and resurrection. The fact that the Gospels devote so many of their precious few pages to the public ministry of Christ should make us pause and consider the soteriological nature of this period of Christ's life.[37] In this section we will do just that. Our focus will be upon the major features of Christ's public ministry, namely, his teaching and miracles. Through his teaching and miracles, Jesus began to establish the eschatological kingdom of God and to reveal his identity as Son of Man and divine giver of life, law, and judgment.

At the outset of his public ministry Jesus claimed that the Kingdom of God had come. He went around "preaching the gospel of God, and saying, 'the time is fulfilled, and the kingdom of God is at hand; repent, and believe in the gospel.'"[38] We have already examined the ancient Jewish understanding of the Kingdom of God that is present in the prophecies of Daniel and Ezekiel. And we have seen how the infancy narratives and opening chapters of the Gospels identify Jesus as the Davidic king of this kingdom and also as God himself, the one who is ultimately responsible for the establishment of the kingdom. Now the question arises, did Jesus himself claim to be the Davidic king and divine Lord of this kingdom? And how exactly did Jesus describe the nature of this Kingdom?

We can identify three instances in Jesus' public ministry in which

---

36 Jesus' public ministry is commonly thought of as taking place over a 3 year period, from the time he was 30–33 years of age. This is due to the fact that John depicts him attending the annual festival of Passover in Jerusalem on multiple occasions. Conversely, the synoptic Gospels only mention one trip to Jerusalem, culminating in the crucifixion.

37 Put together, the four canonical Gospels consist of 89 total chapters: 4 chapters on the infancy and childhood of Christ, 67 chapters on the public ministry, and 18 chapters on the Last Supper, Passion, and Resurrection of Christ. Of the latter, 5 chapters are from the extended Last Supper discourses in Jn. 13–17.

38 Mk. 1:14–15.

he identified himself as the Davidic king of the newly arrived king-dom of God. First, a Samaritan woman tells Jesus that she knows "that the Messiah is coming," and in response Jesus says to her "I who speak to you am he." The woman then goes and describes her encounter with Jesus to others, saying "Can this be the Christ?"[39] Second, Jesus repeatedly referred to himself as the "Son of Man." As Son of Man, he would sit at God's right hand, come to earth upon the clouds of heaven, and cast evildoers "into the furnace of fire."[40] Through these descriptions, Jesus equated himself with the royal and heavenly "son of man" whom Daniel 7 describes as king of God's eschatological Kingdom. Third, Jesus asked his disciples, "who do men say that the son of man is?" In response, Peter professed that Jesus is "the Christ, the son of the living God." Jesus praises Peter as "blessed" for his an-swer and says that Peter's knowledge of Jesus' Messianic identity was revealed to him by God the Father himself.[41]

More dramatically, Jesus repeatedly claimed to be God himself. As a devout Jew and rabbi, Jesus emphasized the duty to exclusively worship the one God of Israel.[42] But he described the one God in new terms: he told his disciples to baptize everyone "in the name of the Father and of the Son and of the Holy Spirit."[43] He thus pointed to a plurality of persons who possess the one divine name. Most scandalously to his Jewish contemporaries, Jesus identified *himself* as the second of those three divine persons: he was the Son who is "one" with the Father and who needed to be "honored" in the same way as the Father is. And he can do whatever the Father does.[44] Jesus repeatedly emphasized his divine nature by using biblical language and referents: he referred to himself with the divine name that God revealed to Moses at the burning bush;[45] he claimed to have the au-thority to forgive the sins of strangers and to work on the sabbath,

39 Jn. 4:25–29.
40 Lk. 22:69, Mk. 13:26, and Mt. 13:41–42, respectively.
41 Mt. 16:13–17.   42 Mk. 12:28–34.
43 Mt. 28:19.   44 Jn. 10:30 and Jn. 5:19–29.
45 The initial revelation of God's name in Ex. 3 is "I AM HE WHO IS" (Gk. *ego eimi ho on*), but then Ex. 3 and subsequent biblical references use the abbrevi-ated form, "I AM" (*ego eimi*) or its reverent alternative, LORD (*kurios*). For Jesus' use, see, for instance, Mk. 6:50, Mk. 14:62, and Jn. 8:58.

things which only God had the right to do;[46] he equated his body with the Jerusalem Temple but then also claimed to be "greater than the Temple";[47] and he pointed to his eternal existence by saying that David had acknowledged him as his "lord" and that Abraham had seen him and rejoiced.[48]

As the God of Israel, Jesus claimed to be the source and giver of life after death. When Nicodemus asked Jesus what he must do to "enter the kingdom of God," Jesus told him to be "born of water and the Spirit."[49] Sitting by a well, he told a Samaritan woman that he could give her water which would become "a spring of water welling up to eternal life."[50] While at the Jerusalem Temple, he called the thirsty to come to him and drink from the "rivers of living water" which flowed from his heart.[51] Concretely, Jesus gives this life-giving water through the Sacrament of Baptism.[52] Teaching in a synagogue in Capernaum, he claimed to be able to give "food which endures for eternal life" and referred to this food as the "bread from heaven" and "bread of life." He then insisted that *he* was this bread, and consequently that people had to chew his flesh and drink his blood to have eternal life.[53] And the life that Jesus promised to give is not merely spiritual, for he also insisted that the bodies of the dead would rise and that he is the one who would resurrect them: "he who chews my flesh and drinks my blood has eternal life, and I will raise him up at the last day."[54] He told his friend Martha, "I am the resurrection and the life; he who believes in me, though he die, yet shall he live," and then he proceeded to raise her dead brother Lazarus to life.[55] Hence, Jesus claimed to be the temple from which the life-giving Spirit of God flowed; he claimed to be able to resurrect the dead; and just as God gave life to the Hebrews' bodies in the wilderness with bread from

46 Mk. 2:1–12, Jn. 5:1–18. Further, in Mk. 2:28 and Mt. 12:8, Jesus calls himself the "lord of the sabbath."
47 Jn. 2:13–22 and Mt. 12:6.
48 Mk. 12:35–37 (also Mt. 22:41–45) and Jn. 8:56–59.
49 Jn. 3:5.　　　　　　　　　　50 Jn. 4:14.
51 Jn. 7:37–39.　　　　　　　52 See Mt. 28:19 and Acts 2:37–41.
53 Jn. 6:25–59.　　　　　　　54 Mt. 22:32 and Jn. 6:54.
55 Jn. 11:17–44.

heaven and water from a rock, so now Jesus offers his disciples spiritual life through the Eucharistic bread and the waters of Baptism.

While Jesus offered eternal life and the resurrection of the body to all, he also affirmed that not everyone would receive these gifts and that he possessed the power to judge all people. In contrast to eternal life, Jesus referred to "eternal fire" and "eternal punishment."[56] He frequently used the Greek word *Gehenna* ("Hell") to describe this eternal state of body and soul.[57] In Jesus' own time, "Gehenna" was a valley outside of Jerusalem where garbage was dumped and burnt. In the Old Testament, that valley was a place of idolatry and child sacrifice.[58] Hence, Jesus was saying that there existed an eternal, repulsive and painful state of idolatry and sin. And he not only warned of the possibility of entering this eternal Gehenna, he also appeared to affirm the suggestion that the number of those who are "saved" would be "few."[59] Finally, Jesus made it clear that he is the judge who would determine whether a person entered eternal Gehenna or eternal life: he will separate the sheep from the goats, giving eternal life to the former and telling the latter, "depart from me, you cursed, into the eternal fire."[60]

What is the criteria which Jesus uses to judge people's eternal destination? Jesus' answer to this question was clear and consistent: people will be judged by their faith in him, and "faith" necessarily includes obedience to Jesus' commands.[61] Those who lack faith in Jesus reject his teachings and refuse to obey him: they are like the "many" who abandoned Jesus after he told them that he was the bread from heaven and commanded them to chew his flesh and drink his blood.[62] By spurning the bread of life, they have no life within them.[63] Conversely, Peter and the Apostles are examples of faith: they believed

---

56 Mt. 18:8 and 25:46.   57 For instance, Mt. 5:29 and 10:28.

58 See 2 Kgs 23:10 and "Gehenna," in *The Catholic Bible Dictionary*, ed. Scott Hahn (Doubleday, 2009), 305–6.

59 Lk. 13:22–24.   60 Mt. 25:43 and 41.

61 On the necessity of faith, see Jn. 3:15, Mk. 16:16, etc. In Jn. 3:36, the evangelist nicely summarizes the relation between faith, obedience, and salvation: "He who *believes* in the Son has eternal life; he who does not *obey* the Son shall not see life, but the wrath of God rests upon him" (emphasis added).

62 Jn. 6:41–66.   63 Jn. 6:53.

in the truth of Jesus' teaching about his flesh and blood, and consequently they obediently received his flesh and blood when he first offered it to them at the Last Supper.[64] As a result, they "abide" (*menei*) in Christ and so share in his eternal and risen life.[65] But sharing in Christ's life requires more than just reception of the Eucharist or even Baptism. At the Last Supper, Jesus reiterated the necessity of obedience to *all* of his commandments: "if you keep my commandments, you will abide (*meneite*) in my love." But those who do not keep his commandments and abide in his love are like branches which are cast away from the vine, wither, and are thrown into the fire.[66] Similarly, at the conclusion of the Sermon on the Mount Jesus emphasized that faith is not merely intellectual, but rather necessarily includes obedience: "Not every one who says to me, 'Lord, Lord,' shall enter the kingdom of heaven, but he who does the will of my Father who is in heaven."[67] For "every one who hears these words of mine and does them will be like a wise man who built his house upon the rock," whereas "every one who hears these words of mine and does not do them will be like a foolish man who built his house upon the sand." The house built on rock stands strong amidst the rain, floods, and winds, but the house built on sand falls.[68]

Jesus emphasized that salvific faith in him involved obedience to his commandments, and his commandments made clear distinctions between evil and good human acts. Jesus' fundamental moral command was to repent from sin, and he specified what sin looked like: "evil thoughts, fornication, theft, murder, adultery, coveting, wickedness, deceit, licentiousness, envy, slander, pride, [and] foolishness."[69] When a rich man asked what he must do to receive eternal

64 Jn. 6:66–71 and Mk. 14:22–24.   65 Jn. 6:56, etc.
66 Jn. 15:1–14.   67 Mt. 7:21.
68 Mt. 7:24–27. Jesus thus makes a soft allusion to the story of Noah and the flood: as Noah alone obeyed God's commands and so survived the flood, so too only those who do what Jesus commands will survive the flood.
69 Mk. 7:21–23. In 1 Cor. 6:9–11, Paul provided a similar list of sinful behaviors and tied them to eternal damnation: "Do you not know that the unrighteous will not inherit the kingdom of God? Do not be deceived; neither fornicators, nor idolaters, nor adulterers, nor the effeminate nor sodomites, nor thieves, nor the greedy, nor drunkards, nor revilers, nor robbers will inherit the kingdom of God." For

life, Jesus answered by telling him to observe the moral laws of the Ten Commandments: "You shall not kill, you shall not commit adultery, you shall not steal, you shall not bear false witness, honor your father and mother, and, you shall love your neighbor as yourself."[70] In the Book of Revelation, Jesus tells the prophet John that a lake of fire and brimstone awaits "the cowardly" and "murderers, fornicators, sorcerers, idolaters, and all liars."[71] On the positive side, Jesus commanded his followers to love one another as he loved them and to imitate his example. Concretely, this means serving others and laying down your life for them.[72] Those who do so will be the greatest in the Kingdom of God.[73] The duty to serve others includes care for the hungry, thirsty, stranger, naked, sick, and imprisoned as if they were Christ himself. Those who fail to do so "will go away into eternal punishment."[74] Similarly, to care for a child in the name of Christ is equivalent to caring for Christ himself, and those who cause children to sin would be better off dead at the bottom of the sea.[75] Perhaps most radically, Christ commanded us to love our enemies and pray for our persecutors.[76] Finally, one must persevere in obedience to Christ even when doing so results in family division, persecution, and even martyrdom.[77] For "If any man would come after me, let him deny himself and take up his cross and follow me. For whoever would save his life will lose it, and whoever loses his life for my sake will find it."[78]

Are those who refuse to obey Christ's commandments in a particular instance doomed to hell? The answer depends upon what the sinner does *after* they sin. Do they cling to their sin in pride or do they acknowledge the evil which they have done and ask the Lord for forgiveness? Jesus' exhorted people to "repent" and "sin no

---

Jesus' explicit commands to repent and sin no more, see Mk. 1:15 and Jn. 8:11.

70 Mt. 19:16–30.

71 Rev. 21:8: "As for the cowardly, the faithless, the polluted, as for murderers, fornicators, sorcerers, idolaters, and all liars, their lot shall be in the lake that burns with fire and brimstone."

72 Jn. 13:12–15 and 15:12–13.	73 Mk. 10:35–45.
74 Mt. 25:31–46.	75 Mt. 18:5–6.
76 Mt. 5:44.	77 Mt. 10:37 and 5:10–11.
78 Mt. 16:24–25.	

more."[79] He told his disciples, "if your brother sins, rebuke him; and if he repents, forgive him."[80] His parable of the prodigal son emphasized that God longs to forgive the sinner and welcome them back into his house, but that the sinner must first freely turn away from their sins and return in humility to the Father.[81] The Gospels record several instances in which Christ forgave people: the paralytic, the woman caught in adultery, the sinful woman who anointed his feet, the good thief, the Apostles who abandoned him during his Passion, and the various Romans and Jews who orchestrated his crucifixion.[82] These instances show that even the gravest sins are not beyond God's mercy, and that it is never too late *during this life* to repent and receive forgiveness. As God, Christ could forgive anyone, including strangers who had not sinned against him in his incarnate life.[83] Additionally, he gave his Apostles the power to forgive sins in his name, and he ordered them to forgive no matter how many times someone sinned against them.[84] So, while sin really casts the branches away from the vine, those branches may not immediately be thrown into the fire. Through repentance and forgiveness, the withering branches are regrafted onto the vine and begin to share in its life once again. Yet the branches must never presume upon these opportunities to be regrafted, nor pass upon them when they are presented. The living branch must continually cling with vigilance to the vine, for the judge will come like a thief in the night.[85]

What types of evidence did Jesus provide to support his bold claims to be the Christ, the Son of Man, and the divine lawgiver, judge, and giver of life? The first and most obvious evidence that we can identify are the miracles which occurred during the life of Christ. And here we must make an important distinction: the Gospels do not depict Jesus causing miracles by his *prayers*, that is, by asking God to perform a miracle; rather, they show Jesus performing miracles by

79 Jn. 5:14 and 8:11.   80 Lk. 17:3–4.
81 Lk. 15:11–32.
82 Mk. 2, Jn. 8, Lk. 7:36–50, Lk. 23, Jn. 21, and Lk. 23:34, respectively.
83 See Mk. 2:7: "Who can forgive sins but God alone?"
84 Jn. 20:22–23, Mt. 16:18–19, and Mt. 18:21–22.
85 1 Thess. 5:2. See also Mt. 24:43–44 and Rev. 16:15.

his own "authority" and "commands."[86] The man who claimed to be God did things which a human could not do by their own natural power: he walked on water, controlled the wind and waves, multiplied bread, transformed water into wine, drove out demons, healed the sick, and raised the dead.[87] Not everyone who encountered Jesus' miracles believed in him or concluded that he was God himself.[88] But for many, including Peter, James, and John, Jesus' miracles lead them to believe in his words and so to follow him obediently.[89] Hence, Christ used miracles as a means to draw people to saving faith in and obedience to himself.

The context provided by Jesus' teachings and miracles enables us to identify the basic meanings of his proclamation of the "Kingdom of God." First, the Greek word (*basileia*) underlying "kingdom" does not refer to a region but rather to "an active reality like our words 'reign' or 'command,'" and so Jesus is proclaiming "God's rule, his living power over the world."[90] By claiming that the kingdom of God is at hand, Jesus is saying that God's active reign in and over the world is now present. Second, God's active and present reign is "good news" (*euangelion*). The prophet Isaiah described the "good news" that God would come in the future to save his captive and oppressed people.[91] The Romans announced the "good news" of the birth or enthronement of new emperors. Along these lines, the angel announced to the shepherds at Bethlehem the "good news" of the birth of Jesus, "a savior who is Christ the Lord."[92] Hence, the "good news" of God's reign is bound up with the birth of Jesus, the king and savior through whom God will exercise his rule.

Third, God's reign is made present in the miraculous and life-giving activity of Jesus. Jesus actualizes God's conquest of evil by healing

---

86 Mk. 1:21–45.
87 See Mk. 4:35–41, Mk. 6:45–52, Mk. 6:30–44, Jn. 2:1–12, Mk. 1:21–28, Mk. 2:1–12, and Lk. 7:11–17, respectively.
88 Mk. 3:1–6 and 22.   89 See, for example, Luke 5:1–11.
90 Joseph Ratzinger, *Eschatology: Death and Eternal Life*, second ed., trans. Michael Waldstein (The Catholic University of America Press, 2007), 26.
91 Isa. 61:1–2. Jesus read this passage in a synagogue at Nazareth and claimed to be its fulfilment (Lk. 4:18–19).
92 Lk. 2:10–11.

the sick, raising the dead, and driving out demons: "if it is by the finger of God that I cast out demons, then the kingdom of God has come upon you."[93] Through Jesus' miracles "the ruler of this world" is "cast out."[94] Fourth, Jesus reigns through grace in the souls of his disciples who conform their lives to his will: "Thy kingdom come, thy will be done, on earth as it is in heaven."[95] God's kingdom is present in those who repent and receive his forgiveness, in the childlike and poor in spirit, and in those who endure persecution for the sake of righteousness.[96] Fifth, the Kingdom is the eternal and risen life which awaits those who conform their lives to Christ's commands.[97] God reigns especially in his saints and angels in heaven. Life in God's eternal kingdom of heaven is like possession of a treasure or pearl which surpasses the value of all other things.[98]

CONCLUSION

We can now conclude this chapter with a synthesis of the New Testament's depiction of the salvific value of Christ's being, teaching, and miracles. Christ saves us from error and unbelief by his teachings and by the miracles which he works in support of those teachings. As God, his teachings and commands possess ultimate authority and give those who believe in him certain knowledge of the truth. Believers can worship the true God and conform their lives to his commands because they have come to know him in Christ. And Christ cleanses us from sin and empowers us to do his will through the grace of forgiveness, the life-giving waters of Baptism, and the nourishing bread from heaven. He saves us from sickness and the devil in this world through his healings and exorcisms, and one day he will save us from ultimate physical and spiritual death through the gift of eternal life and the resurrection of the body. In these ways Jesus, as both God and royal Son of Man, establishes God's reign in this world and invites sinners to participate in that reign through reception of the gift

93 Lk. 11:20.   94 Jn. 12:31.
95 Mt. 6:10.
96 Mk. 1:15, Mt. 16:19, 19:14, 5:3 and 10, respectively.
97 Mt. 25:31–46.   98 Mt. 13:44–46.

of grace and the response of living faith which it enables. Those who repent and begin to live in Christ's kingdom here below will one day enter into the fulness of that kingdom in eternity.

∼

COMPREHENSION QUESTIONS

1. Why does the angel command Joseph to name Mary's child "Jesus" in Matthew 1:22–23?
2. What does *Yeshua* literally mean?
3. Why is the name "Jesus" associated with "YHWH" and "Emmanuel"?
4. How do the wise men's words to Herod and the angel's words to the shepherds indicate the function of "Christ?"
5. What is the literal meaning of the title "Christ" and who was it primarily applied to in the Old Testament?
6. What did God promise to David in 2 Samuel 7?
7. What were the following events and when did they occur? Division of the Davidic Kingdom; Assyrian Conquest; Babylonian Conquest and Exile; Greek and Roman conquests
8. What did Daniel Prophecy regarding pagan kingdoms and the Kingdom of God in Daniel 2 and 7?
9. Who is the "Son of Man" in Daniel 7?
10. What does Ezekiel prophecy regarding the saving work of God and the Christ in Ezekiel 34 and 37?
11. How is Jesus' identity as the Christ indicated by the angel's announcement to Mary and the shepherds in Luke 1 and 2?
12. What are two basic ways in which Jesus is the "Son of God?"
13. How do the Annunciation and Visitation stories in Luke 1 suggest that Jesus is God?
14. What does Ezekiel prophecy regarding the new temple in the kingdom of God?
15. What does John's prologue (Jn. 1:1–18) indicate about the divinity of Jesus and the saving function of the Incarnation?
16. What is the "public ministry" of Jesus and how is it presented in the Gospels?

17. How did Jesus identify himself as the Davidic king of the Kingdom of God?
18. How did Jesus claim to be God?
19. What are the two means by which Jesus claimed to give spiritual and physical life after death?
20. What is hell ("Gehenna")?
21. What does it mean to say that Jesus is a "judge" and what is the criteria by which he judges people?
22. What is "faith" and what must people do to "abide" in Jesus and "enter" the Kingdom?
23. What was Jesus' fundamental moral command?
24. What were some of Jesus' major negative and positive moral commands?
25. What did Jesus teach about repentance and forgiveness?
26. What evidence did Jesus provide in support of his claims about himself?
27. What are the five basic meanings of the "Kingdom of God" which Jesus proclaimed and actualized?

4

THE PASCHAL MYSTERY

W HAT *does Jesus save us from* and *how does he do so?* In the previous chapter we saw how Jesus saves us from idolatry, sin, death and hell through the gift of his Incarnate teaching and miracles. Through his teaching and miracles he draws us to believe in him, to know and do his will, and to receive the grace of sharing in his eternal and risen life. In this chapter we shift our focus from the New Testament's depiction of Jesus' public ministry to its account of the Paschal Mystery, namely, the Passion, Resurrection, and Ascension of Jesus. We will explore the New Testament's presentation of the saving value of Jesus' Paschal Mystery in itself and in relation to his public ministry. Our goal throughout will be to identify *how* the Paschal Mystery is a means through which God saves humanity from sin and its consequences and establishes his kingdom on earth.

This chapter is divided into three major sections. The first section examines the human and divine *causes* which led to Jesus' arrest and execution. The second section identifies the *ends* for which Jesus endured the Passion. It explores the saving value of the Passion in itself and in terms of its effects, which include the Resurrection and Ascension. The third section further reflects upon these themes by focusing upon the New Testament's depiction of the Paschal Mystery as a priestly and sacrificial act which brings about saving effects for humanity.

THE CAUSES OF THE PASSION

Why did Jesus suffer and die? This question concerns the *causes* of Christ's Passion. We can provide an initial answer to the question by identifying why some of Jesus' contemporaries chose to arrest and crucify him. The Gospels say that Jesus' crucifixion was orchestrated by some members of the Sanhedrin, the local Jewish governors of

Jerusalem, and by Pontius Pilate, the local Roman Governor of Samaria and Judea. The Sanhedrin had both religious and political reasons to execute Jesus, while Pilate's rationale was purely political. The Sanhedrin's *religious* concern was that Jesus was repeatedly accused by some of his Jewish contemporaries of blasphemy and violation of the Sabbath. Jesus elicited these charges by applying God's name (I AM) to himself and by claiming the authority to do things, such as forgive sins, which were considered to be the prerogative of God alone.[1] The accusations of blasphemy and violation of the Sabbath were serious given that the Old Testament prescribes the death penalty in response to both crimes.[2] Yet, Rome generally did not permit the Sanhedrin to execute people, and especially not in response to blasphemy or violation of the Sabbath.[3]

Hence, religious charges alone did not lead to Jesus' death. The Sanhedrin itself also had *political* concerns about Jesus: he had a large following who claimed that he was a king (the Messiah); Rome may see Jesus and the Jewish nation that supported him as rebels; hence, Rome may put an end to that perceived rebellion by simply destroying all of the Jewish people and their sacred Temple. The Sanhedrin determined that, if they initiated the execution of Jesus, this would assure Rome of their loyalty and hence assure the safety of the Jewish temple and nation.[4] The convergence of religious and political concerns is displayed in Mark's account of Jesus' trial before the Sanhedrin:

> Again the high priest asked him, "Are you the Christ, the Son of the Blessed?" And Jesus said, "I am; and you will see the Son of man sitting at the right hand of Power, and coming with the clouds of heaven." And the high priest tore his mantle, and said, "Why do we still need witnesses? You have heard his blasphemy. What is your decision?" And they all condemned him as deserving death.[5]

Jesus affirms that he is the royal Messiah, "the Son of the Blessed."

1 See, for instance, Mk. 2:24, Lk. 6:6–11, Jn. 5:16–18, Mk. 2:7, Jn. 8:58–59, Jn. 10:30–33.
2 Ex. 31:14–15 (Sabbath violation) and Lev. 24:16 (blasphemy).
3 Jn. 18:31.   4 Jn. 11:45–53.
5 Mk. 14:61–64.

But this claim in itself is not blasphemy, and here the Sanhedrin sentences Jesus to death because he has uttered blasphemy. As Brant Pitre has pointed out, Jesus' "blasphemy" consisted at least in his allusion to Daniel 7 and Psalm 110: he claimed that King David saw him a thousand years ago sitting at the right hand of God in heaven and that he was begotten of God before time began (Ps. 110); and that he is the Son of Man who will come on the clouds of heaven as only God can do (Dn. 7).[6] Further, Jesus' "I am" (*ego eimi*) statement may have been an allusion to God's name ("I AM WHO I AM," *ego eimi ho own*) which he revealed to Moses through the burning bush.[7]

Having condemned Jesus as a blasphemer deserving of death, the Sanhedrin now needed to convince Pilate to execute Jesus. They initially appear to have told Pilate that Jesus claimed to be "King of the Jews," thus indicating that Jesus was guilty of treason against Rome and so should be put to death.[8] But Pilate questions Jesus and does not find sufficient evidence of treason to execute him.[9] The Sanhedrin then returns to the underlying religious reason for which they want Jesus put to death: "We have a law, and by that law he ought to die, because he has made himself the Son of God."[10] Jesus has not claimed to be the Son of God in the merely Messianic and treasonous sense; he claims to be filially related to God in an additional, blasphemous sense. Upon hearing this, Pilate "was even more afraid" and so questioned Jesus again, asking "Where are you from?"[11] Jesus does not answer his question, and so Pilate resolves once again to release him. But then the Sanhedrin returns to the political: "If you

---

6 Brant Pitre, *The Case for Jesus: The Biblical and Historical Evidence for Christ* (Image, 2016), 157–63.

7 Ex. 3:14. Joseph Ratzinger makes this suggestion in *Jesus of Nazareth, Holy Week: From the Entrance Into Jerusalem to the Resurrection* (Ignatius Press, 2011), 180. Jesus clearly uses *ego eimi* in a divine way in reference to himself in Mk. 6:50 and Jn. 8:58.

8 Mt. 27:11–13; Mk. 15:1–5; Lk. 23:1–5; Jn. 18:28–33.

9 Lk. 23:4, etc.

10 Jn. 19:7. "Son of God" must here be meant in a way beyond a mere Messianic title, for their reference is to the law against blasphemy, and claiming to be the Messiah is not blasphemous.

11 Jn. 19:8–9.

release this man, you are not Caesar's friend; every one who makes himself a king sets himself against Caesar."[12] The Sanhedrin implies that they will inform Rome that Pilate is aiding and abetting a competitor to Caesar. Pilate realizes the threat and so asks them, "Shall I crucify your king?" They respond, "We have no king but Caesar."[13] The pressure which the Sanhedrin and their supporters placed upon Pilate ultimately prevailed over him.[14] The Gospels indicate that Pilate sentenced Jesus to death in order "to satisfy the crowd" which the Sanhedrin had "stirred up" against Jesus.[15] So, even though Pilate recognized that Jesus did not deserve to be crucified and even though "he perceived that it was out of envy that the chief priests had delivered him up," he nonetheless allows Jesus to be crucified.[16] Pilate chooses cowardice over justice: he hands an innocent man over to death in order to ensure his own safety and status.

While Pilate and some members of the Sanhedrin were the primary causes of Jesus' Passion, there is also a sense in which Jesus himself can be identified as a cause of the Passion. There are several reasons for this. First, Jesus repeatedly indicated that he knew he had enemies who sought to put him to death.[17] Yet he never ceased to teach and perform works which continued to elicit the ire of those enemies. Second, during his trials with the Sanhedrin and Pilate Jesus was given several opportunities to recant his blasphemous and treasonous claims. By doing so he could have escaped death. Instead he consistently reaffirmed the truth of what he taught or simply remained silent. Third, Jesus twice showed that he had the miraculous power to escape from anyone who attempted to physically harm him.[18] Yet he ultimately allowed himself to be seized and nailed to the cross. Hence, Jesus can be considered a cause of his Passion in the sense that he (1) *actively willed* to say and do certain things even though he knew those things would elicit the violent opposition of

12 Jn. 19:12.

13 Jn. 19:15–16.

14 Lk. 23:21–23.

15 Mk. 14:11–15.

16 Mk. 14:10.

17 Jesus explicitly predicts his Passion on three occasions in each of the Synoptic Gospels: Mt. 16:21–23, 17:22–23, 20:17–19; Mk. 8:31–32, 9:30–32, 10:32–34; and Lk. 9:21–22, 9:43–45, 18:31–34.

18 Lk. 4:30 and Jn. 18:1–6.

his contemporaries, (2) he *actively willed* to reaffirm the truth of his teachings even as he was on trial and was threatened with death for doing so, and (3) insofar as he *permitted* his enemies to violently harm him despite his divine power to escape their attacks. Jesus did not actively will people to arrest and execute him, for he made it clear that those who betrayed him and put him to death sinned by doing so.[19] And Jesus never commands or actively wills sin. Nonetheless, he did not use his miraculous power to defend himself from the violent sins of his enemies.

THE ENDS OF THE PASSION

Why did Christ freely choose to endure the Passion rather than use his divine power to save himself? This question requires us to reflect upon the *value* or *ends* of the Passion. What was the *good* which Jesus enacted or acquired by his free choice to suffer and die? The New Testament provides two basic answers to this question. The first is that Christ chose to endure the Passion out of *obedience* to the Father. Jesus said that his food was "to do the will of him who sent me" and he indicated that the Father's will included the command to die and rise again: "this command I have received from my Father." Jesus' obedience to that command was the "reason the Father loves me."[20] In Gethsemane, Jesus reiterated his willingness to suffer and die out of obedience to the Father even as he also expressed his natural repugnance at the prospect of pain and death.[21] Second, Christ endured the Passion *for* humanity. He told his disciples that they were his friends and that he would lay down his life out of love for them.[22] He compared himself to a good shepherd who lays down his life for his sheep.[23] He promised to give up his body and pour out his blood for his disciples.[24] And he taught them that greatness was measured

---

19 For instance, see Mt. 26:24, Jn. 19:11, and Lk. 23:34.
20 Jn. 4:24 and 10:17–18.   21 Mk. 14:36.
22 Jn. 15:12–13.   23 Jn. 10:11 and 15.
24 Lk. 22:19–20.

by service, and that he came to serve others even to the point of giving up his life for many.[25]

The New Testament's description of Christ's Passion as an act of obedience to the Father and love for humanity raises more questions. *Why* did the Father command Christ to suffer and die? And *how* was Christ's Passion of service to his disciples and to the many? The answer to the first question is largely dependent upon the answer to the second. For even if we say that the Father commanded Christ to endure the Passion *for the sake of humanity*, we still must explain how Christ's Passion is good for humanity. How is the Passion an act of love and service for us? How does Christ's Passion benefit and save us? We can answer these questions by considering the Passion in itself and in terms of its effects upon sinners and their relation to God.

The Passion in Itself

Regarding the Passion *in itself*, we can identify three ways in which Christ's endurance of suffering and death was salvific for humanity. First, Jesus' Passion gives sinners a *foundational witness* to the truth of his being and teaching. The Sanhedrin arrested Jesus and sentenced him to death because of what he claimed about himself, namely, that he was God (blasphemy) and that he was the Messiah. The Sanhedrin, Pilate, and Herod each gave Jesus opportunities to recant his teaching. But he did not. For, as he told Pilate, "For this I was born, and for this I came into the world, to bear witness to the truth."[26] Throughout his trials, Jesus bore witness to the truth by honestly answering the questions that were put to him and by remaining silent in response to others. And as his torture and crucifixion unfolded, he never recanted his teaching. He thus chose to testify to divine truth rather than to escape pain and death. Hence, Christ was a "faithful witness," a martyr.[27] If Jesus had recanted under torture and the threat of death then it is not clear why anyone would believe in him. But his willingness to die as a martyr, while not guaranteeing the veracity of his claims, nonetheless greatly increases the plausibility of those claims.

25 Mk. 10:45. 26 Jn. 18:37.
27 Rev. 1:5.

Second, Jesus' Passion gives us an *example* of moral righteousness and obedience. By refusing to lie even amidst the threat of torture and death, Christ exemplified moral fortitude. And his fortitude was further exemplified by the fact that he did not commit *any* sin during his Passion. Like Job, Jesus remained innocent even as the world fell apart around him. Despite his terrible pain, he did not curse his life, his enemies, or God.[28] Rather, like Isaiah's Suffering Servant, Jesus remained silent and non-violent as his enemies condemned him. Instead of returning evil for evil, he loved his enemies and prayed for those who persecuted him: "Father, forgive them, for they know not what they do."[29] He also expressed his dedication to and trust in God even as he approached his last breath: "Father, into thy hands I commit my spirit!"[30] The virtuous manner in which Jesus endured his crucifixion was a source of conversion for those who witnessed it: "Now when the centurion saw what had taken place, he praised God, and said, 'Certainly this man was innocent!' And all the multitudes who assembled to see the sight, when they saw what had taken place, returned home beating their breasts."[31] As Paul explained, Jesus was "obedient unto death, even death on a cross."[32] Jesus' endurance of the Passion shows us that humans can, with the help of God's grace, do what is right and obey God's commandments even amidst the most severe and tragic circumstances.

Third, and consequently, Jesus' Passion was the enactment and demonstration of his *conquest* and *reign* over the power of sin. During the Last Supper Jesus told his disciples to "take courage, I have conquered the world."[33] The Book of Revelation depicts Jesus as a lamb who "has conquered" and yet who is "standing, as if it had been slain."[34] But what has Jesus conquered, and how has he done so? The basic answer to this question is that Jesus has conquered sin. By his obedience unto death, even death on a cross, Jesus overcame any and all

---

28 For a thorough and moving account of the nature and extent of the pains which Christ endured in the Passion, see Thomas Aquinas, *ST* III, Q. 46, aa. 5–6.

29 Lk. 23:34; cf. Mt. 5:44. 30 Lk. 23:46.

31 Lk. 23:47–48. 32 Phil. 2:8.

33 Jn. 16:33. "Conquered" is my translation of the Greek *nenikeka* (νενίκηκα).

34 Rev. 5:5–6.

temptations which the devil, his enemies, and his own pain and passions placed before him. Jesus was "made like his brethren in every respect" and "in every respect has been tempted as we are, yet without sinning."[35] The severity of Jesus' temptations are displayed as he hung upon the cross:

> Those who passed by derided him, wagging their heads, and saying, "Aha! You who would destroy the temple and build it in three days, save yourself, and come down from the cross!" So also the chief priests mocked him to one another with the scribes, saying, "He saved others; he cannot save himself. Let the Christ, the King of Israel, come down now from the cross, that we may see and believe."[36]

Jesus's enemies tempt him to display his divine and Messianic rule by coming down from the cross. They tempt him to show his power over death. But Jesus chooses instead to endure death out of obedience to the Father, "that through death he might destroy him who has the power of death, that is, the devil."[37] The devil brought death into the world by successfully tempting Adam and Eve to sin. Adam and Eve disobeyed the Father in order to grasp at life and conquer death. But Jesus obeyed the Father in all things even as pain and death surrounded him. By doing so, Jesus enacted and displayed his conquest and reign over sin and temptation.

Christ's conquest of temptation and sin is the fundamental realization of the kingdom of God on earth. God's active rule and reign in human history is present above all in the free human decisions of Christ. The divine will and the human will are united in a supreme and unparalleled fashion in the person of Christ: Christ exclusively and consistently chooses, as a man, to do the will of the Father. In all things and in every instance, Christ wills as man in conformity with what he wills as God. This is displayed most radically in the Passion, when Christ was faced with innumerable reasons and temptations to curse God and neighbor. "The kingdom of heaven has suffered

---

35 Heb. 2:17 and 4:15, respectively.   36 Mk. 15:29–32.
37 Heb. 2:14.

violence, and men of violence take it by force."[38] Christ is the reign of God over and in the flesh; Christ suffered violence, and yet continued to conquer every temptation to sin anyway. His enemies claimed that they would believe in his kingship if he came down from the cross; but they failed to realize that his kingship, his reign, was realized most radically on the cross. For on the cross Christ conquered the most powerful temptations of the devil, the world, and the flesh. Christ's perfect love and obedience even unto death is the singular and exemplary actualization of God's active rule over a human heart, mind, and will. "The kingdom of God is in the midst of you" in the very being and action of Christ himself.[39]

The Effects of the Passion: Glorification

Having examined the Passion in itself as a witness to truth, moral example and conquest of sin, we can now examine the saving *effects* of the Passion. First, Jesus' conquest of sin results in his own *conquest of death and hell*. On Easter Sunday, Jesus conquered death by physically rising from the dead.[40] He then enjoyed a new, glorified bodily life which was not subject to natural constraints.[41] Forty days after his resurrection he ascended bodily into heaven, where he "sat down at the right hand of God" and received "all authority in heaven and on earth."[42] Jesus' resurrection and Ascension show that death and the underworld no longer have any power over him: he not only enjoys new and immortal bodily life, he does so eternally in heaven with God. Paul explains *why* Jesus was able to conquer death and hell:

> Christ Jesus, who, though he was in the form of God, did not count equality with God a thing to be grasped, but emptied himself, taking the form of a servant, being born in the likeness of men. And being found in human form he humbled himself and became obedient unto death, even death on a

---

38 Mt. 11:12.   39 Lk. 17:21.

40 See the accounts of the empty tomb and resurrection appearances in Mt. 28, Mk. 16, Lk. 24, and Jn. 20–21.

41 E.g., he appears and disappears at will, passes through locked doors, is unrecognizable, etc.

42 Mk. 16:19, Acts 1:3 and 9, and Mt. 28:18.

cross. *Therefore* God has highly exalted him and bestowed on him the name which is above every name, that at the name of Jesus every knee should bow, in heaven and on earth and under the earth.[43]

Jesus reigns in heaven over death and hell because he first emptied himself and was a servant on earth. His exaltation is a *result* of his humiliation: he rises from the dead and ascends into heaven precisely because he was first obedient unto death: "Whoever exalts himself will be humbled, and whoever humbles himself will be exalted."[44] Jesus practiced what he preached: "whoever seeks to gain his life will lose it, but whoever loses his life will preserve it."[45] He chose death over sin; he chose obedience to God over bodily life; and consequently he received new and unending bodily life from God.

Second, Jesus' conquest of death and hell are the *supreme witness* to the truth of his being and teaching. Jesus said that he would die and rise from the dead.[46] He said that he could raise others from the dead and give them eternal life.[47] But if he did not rise, how could anyone have believed in his teachings? A failure to rise would indicate that he was a lunatic or, worse, a liar. But when Jesus did rise this elicited faith in those who encountered him: Thomas the Apostle saw the risen Jesus and professed, "My Lord and my God!"[48] Saul violently persecuted Christians but then became Paul the Apostle after he encountered the risen Lord.[49] He then insisted upon the necessity of Christ's resurrection to Christian faith: "If Christ has not been raised, then our preaching is in vain and your faith is in vain."[50] And "If Christ has not been raised, your faith is futile and you are still in your sins. Then those also who have fallen asleep in Christ have perished. If for this life only we have hoped in Christ, we are of all men most to be pitied."[51] Christ's glorious resurrection from the dead and subsequent bodily Ascension into heaven are the supreme proofs in support of the truth of his teaching: they enable us

43 Phil. 2:5–10, emphasis added.
44 Mt. 23:11–12.
45 Lk. 17:33.
46 Jn. 2:19, etc.
47 Jn. 5:19–29, etc.
48 Jn. 20:28.
49 Acts 9:1–19.
50 1 Cor. 15:14.
51 1 Cor. 15:17–19.

to know the true God and his will with confidence. Like the Apostles who worshiped the risen Jesus as he ascended into heaven, we worship Jesus because his resurrection and Ascension prove that he is the resurrection and the life.[52]

Third, Jesus conquered death and hell not only for himself, but for humanity as well. When the good thief asked Jesus to remember him when he comes into his "kingdom," Jesus answers, "today you will be with me in paradise."[53] For Christ, crucified and risen, can now do what he promised to do during his public ministry: judge the nations, give eternal life, and raise the dead.[54] Death no longer has any power over Christ, who is "alive forevermore" and has "the keys to death and hades."[55] Following his death and before his resurrection, Jesus even "descended" in his human soul to the realm of the dead, where he "preached to the spirits in prison."[56] For no one is beyond the saving power of Christ: he opened paradise not only for the good thief, but even for the righteous who were long dead. For the risen Christ himself is the eschatological temple in heaven, the locus of divine presence and life, and he enables sinners to live forever in that temple.[57] He is the fountain of life, from which the river of life flows and gives eternal nourishment to the thirsty.[58] The tree of life grows and bears fruit on the sides of that river, and it is Christ himself who can "grant to eat of the tree of life, which is in the paradise of God."[59]

Our conquest of death and hell is simply a *participation* in Christ's conquest. Paul emphasizes that all have shared in the mortal and fallen life of Adam, but now we can share in the risen and glorified life of Christ: "Just as we have borne the image of the man of dust, we shall also bear the image of the man of heaven."[60] The risen bodies of the saints will be imperishable, glorious, powerful, and spiritual, just like the body of the risen Christ.[61] As Peter explained, Christ "called us to his own glory and excellence" and invited us to "become

---

52 Lk. 24:52–54 and Jn. 11:25–26. 53 Lk. 23:42–43, emphasis added.
54 Jn. 5:19–27, Jn. 6:40, 54, etc. 55 Rev. 1:17–18.
56 Eph. 4:9 and 1 Pet. 3:18–20. 57 Rev. 3:12 and 21:22.
58 Rev. 21:6, 22:1 and 17. 59 Rev. 22:2 and 2:7.
60 1 Cor. 15:49. 61 1 Cor. 15:42–49.

partakers of the divine nature."[62] The risen Christ gives us a share in his own divine life. He is our "forerunner" who has gone "into the inner shrine behind the curtain" in God's eternal temple.[63] He went into the Father's eternal house "to prepare a place for you," and he promised that he "will come again and will take you to myself, that where I am you may be also."[64] The eternal life and risen body which Christ gives us is simply a share in the eternal and risen life which he himself possesses. As Christ has Ascended into heaven and sits by the Father on his throne, so too those who conquer with Christ will ascend to where he is and sit by him on his eternal throne.[65] And from that throne they will rule with a rod of iron and trample their enemies, death and hell, under their feet.[66]

In order to participate in Christ's conquest of death and hell we must first participate in his conquest of sin. We have already seen how Jesus made repentance and obedience to his commandments the conditions for entrance into his eternal kingdom. For we can only abide in Christ and share in his life when we obey him: "If you keep my commandments, you will abide in my love, just as I have kept my Father's commandments and abide in his love."[67] To obey Christ's commandments is to live like him and thus conquer sin with him. In Revelation, Jesus says that "he who conquers" shall drink from the fountain of the water of life in heaven, "but as for the cowardly, the faithless, the polluted, as for murderers, fornicators, sorcerers, idolaters, and all liars, their lot shall be in the lake that burns."[68] The contrast is clear: those who conquer and receive eternal life are those who have avoided, or at least repented of, grave sins. This is further emphasized in the seven letters which Christ sends to the seven churches in Revelation 2–3. There Christ repeatedly promises to give eternal life as a reward to those who "conquer."[69] And those who conquer are those who "repent" from sin (2:5, 6, 16, 22; 3:2, 19),

---

62 2 Pet. 1:3–4.
64 Jn. 14:2–3.
66 Rev. 2:27; 1 Cor. 15:25–27; Ps. 110:1; Rev. 4:6, where God subdues the sea which represents temporal chaos.
67 Jn. 15:10.
69 Rev. 2:7, 11, 17, 26; 3:5, 12, 21.

63 Heb. 6:19–20.
65 Rev. 3:21.

68 Rev. 21:7–8.

who return to works of love (2: 4–5), who remain "faithful unto death" (2:10) and who "have kept my word and have not denied my name" (3: 8). In sum, "He who conquers" is he "who keeps my works until the end." And those who do so will receive "power over the nations, and he shall rule them with a rod of iron."[70] The one who repents and does the works of Christ shares in Christ's conquest of sin, and so they share in his conquest of death and hell as well: they reign with Christ in heaven because they have humbled themselves and become obedient with Christ on earth. They share in the complete victory of the Lion of the tribe of Judah who stands as though slain in the sanctuary of heaven: victory over sin, death, and hell.[71]

We can now conclude this section by considering the soteriological questions which it raises. First, why is eternal life only made accessible to sinners *after* Christ's Passion, resurrection, and Ascension? Second, how does the Paschal Mystery help sinners to conquer sin? We can understand why, from the standpoint of justice, Christ's perfect obedience and testimony even unto death on a cross resulted in *his own* eternal glorification. But why should this result in *our* opportunity for glorification? And if we grant that our reception of eternal life and bodily resurrection can only follow from our repentance and obedience, then *how* does the Paschal Mystery help to bring about that repentance and obedience in each person? The New Testament begins to answer these questions by depicting the Paschal Mystery as a saving sacrifice which was offered for sinners by Christ, our high priest. Our next section explores these topics.

THE PRIESTHOOD AND SACRIFICE OF CHRIST

What type of priest is Jesus? In Psalm 110, God speaks to the Davidic king who rules at his right hand, saying "You are a priest forever according to the order of Melchiz'edek."[72] So Davidic kings, and especially the future Christ, are like Melchiz'edek: they are both king *and* priest. And the Psalm indicates that this priesthood lasts *forever.* In the New Testament, the Letter to the Hebrews takes up these themes

70 Rev. 2:26–27.   71 Rev. 5:5–6.
72 Ps. 110:4.

explicitly. Jesus is a priest of the order of Melchiz'edek, not a Levitical priest of the order of Aaron.[73] And unlike Levitical priests, Jesus does not serve God in a man-made sanctuary on earth and his priesthood does not end when he dies. Rather, Jesus' priesthood continues in heaven, where he ministers to God in his eternal sanctuary.[74] And while the Levitical high priest could only enter into the holy of holies in Jerusalem once per year, Jesus is the high priest who has entered once and forever into the presence of God's glory in his heavenly holy place.[75]

How is Jesus' priesthood in heaven beneficial to sinners on earth? In order to answer this we first need to recall the purposes of Levitical priesthood and sacrifice. A priest's primary tasks are to minister to God in his temple and to mediate between God and humanity. Through the hands of the priest, sinners present offerings and sacrifices as gifts to God in his home. These gifts can be offered for different ends and their reception by God impacts the status of the relation between sinners and God.[76] Ultimately, when God is pleased by the sacrificial gifts which are given to him then he blesses the people and continues to remain with them through his glory in the temple. Sacrifices themselves represent gifts of food, and when the priest and/or person who offers the sacrifice eats a portion of the sacrificial flesh then they are sharing a fraternal meal with God. The pouring out of the blood upon God's altar represents God's dominion over all life and the handing over of one's life to God. When some of the blood is sprinkled upon the offerers, as in the covenant ratification ceremony at Mt Sinai, this further symbolizes the familial communion which the sacrifice establishes between God and the offerers. Sacrificial blood was also thought to have a purifying power, and hence on the annual Day of Atonement the high priest sprinkled blood on the Ark and throughout the holy of holies. This cleansed the area and objects from the defilements caused by human sin and ensured that the sanctuary remained a pure and pleasing place for God to dwell.

---

73 Heb. 5:6, 10 and 7:11–14.   74 Heb. 7:23–24 and 8:1–2.

75 Heb. 9:6 and 12.

76 See the analysis in Chapters 1 and 2 on the ends and effects of sacrifices in the
    Old Testament.

As our high priest, what sacrificial gift does Jesus give to God on our behalf? The answer is that Jesus *himself* is the gift: his body and blood are the sacrificial offering.[77] Jesus made this clear at the Last Supper when he took a chalice of wine and said "this is my blood of the covenant, which is poured out for many for the forgiveness of sins."[78] The reference to blood being "poured out" connects Jesus' death to the pouring out of the blood of sacrificial animals and to the pouring out of the life of the Suffering Servant in Isaiah 53.[79] The mention of "forgiveness" for "many" links the shedding of Jesus' blood to an atonement sacrifice and, specifically, to the atonement sacrifice of the Suffering Servant.[80] The "blood of the covenant" is a clear reference to the covenant ratification sacrifices which Moses conducted at the foot of Mt Sinai.[81] Finally, given that the Last Supper was a Passover meal, Jesus' institution of the Eucharist and reference to his death is compared to the sacrificial death and consumption of the Passover lamb.[82]

But how and why is Jesus' death a sacrificial *gift* to God? Put differently, why is God pleased by the death of his beloved Son? Ephesians 5 suggests an answer to this question: "Christ loved us and gave himself up for us, a fragrant offering and sacrifice to God."[83] The implication is that Christ's *love* and endurance of death *for sinners* is what is pleasing to God, not the pain and death in itself. God is pleased that Christ laid down his life *for his friends*, as a good shepherd lays down his life *for his sheep*.[84] Similarly, God was pleased by Christ's *obedience* unto death, even death on a cross.[85] The Letter to the Hebrews contrasts Christ's sacrifice of obedience with mere animal sacrifices:

> When Christ came into the world, he said, "Sacrifices and offerings thou hast not desired, but a body hast thou prepared

---

77 Heb. 7:27, 9:26, etc.   78 Mt. 26:28.

79 Ex. 29:12, Lev. 4:7, and Isa. 53:12.

80 Isa. 53:10–12.   81 Ex. 24.

82 1 Cor. 5:7: "Christ, our paschal lamb, has been sacrificed."

83 Eph. 5:2.   84 Jn. 10:15 and 15:13.

85 Phil. 2:8. See also Thomas Aquinas, ST III, Q. 47, art. 2 and Q. 48, art. 3, where Thomas argues that Christ's Passion was a pleasing sacrifice to God due to the charity and obedience with which he endured it. For Thomas's thorough treatment of the causes, nature, and effects of Christ's Passion, see ST III, QQ. 46–49.

for me; in burnt offerings and sin offerings thou hast taken no pleasure. Then I said, 'Lo, I have come to do thy will, O God.'"[86]

As a man, Christ does the will of God even amidst pain and impending death and even when God's will necessitates the endurance of pain and death. This is clear during Jesus' Agony in the Garden of Gethsemane, in which he asks the Father to deliver him from the Passion yet nonetheless resolves "not as I will, but as you will."[87] By enduring death out of obedience to God and love for sinners, and by remaining obedient to God's will even amidst pain and death, Christ gave God the pleasing gift of a *moral sacrifice*. By doing so, he followed in the footsteps of figures like Noah, Abraham, the confessors in Daniel 3 and 6, the Maccabean martyrs, and the Suffering Servant: he offers God the pleasing moral sacrifice of unconditional righteousness and obediential trust.

How does Christ's sacrifice of obedience impact the relation between sinners and God? Paul provides a basic answer to this question in Romans 5.[88] There he contrasts the saving effects of Christ's obedience with the destructive effects of Adam's disobedience. Adam's disobedience resulted in sin, condemnation, and death for all. But Christ's obedience brings about the offer of the *grace* of reconciliation, justification, acquittal, life, righteousness, and eternal life for all. Similarly, God saved Noah's entire family from the flood in response to the moral sacrifice of Noah. God then made a covenant with all of humanity as a result of Noah's ritual sacrifices. God blessed Abraham's descendants, and all of humanity, as a result of Abraham's obedience. And the seven martyred brothers of 2nd Maccabees prayed that, as a result of their obedience unto death, God would have mercy on the entire nation and release them from his wrath. These instances show that God often responds to the righteous sacrifice of an *individual* by showering blessings upon the *many*. In his infinite generosity, God gives back abundantly more than he has received. And so in response to the utterly unique, pleasing sacrifice of the one and only God-man, Christ, God showers all of humanity with infinite blessings. We can

---

86 Heb. 10:5–7.   87 Mt. 26:39.
88 For what follows see Rm. 5:1–21.

further appreciate the relation between Christ's sacrifice of obedience and our reception of God's gifts when we compare Christ's sacrifice to the three ritual sacrifices which he alluded to at the Last Supper: Passover, the covenant sacrifices at Sinai, and atonement sacrifices.

First, Jesus is the new Passover sacrifice. In Exodus God promised to "redeem" the Hebrews from Egypt.[89] But he tied their redemption to the Passover ritual: they had to kill a lamb "without blemish," smear its blood on the outside of their homes, and then eat its flesh.[90] This ritual was, in a sense, the redemption or ransom "price" which they had to pay for protection from the plague of death and for liberation from slavery. Analogously, Jesus referred to his death as a "ransom" price which he would pay for "many."[91] And 1 Peter says we were "ransomed" by "the precious blood of Christ, like that of a lamb without blemish or spot."[92] But Christ's sacrificial death does not redeem us from *physical death* or free us from *physical slavery*. Rather, Christ's sacrifice is the ransom price which results in our protection from the *spiritual death* of hell and the *spiritual slavery* of sin. And just as the Jewish people had to eat the Passover lamb in Egypt and every year afterward, so too Christ commanded his disciples to eat his flesh at the Last Supper and to do so repeatedly in remembrance of him.[93] For just as those who refused to eat the original Paschal lambs remained subject to death and slavery in Egypt, so too those who refuse to eat the flesh of Christ have no life within them.[94] But those who partake of Christ's flesh and who are marked with his blood receive the grace of communion with God: they are freed from slavery to sin and protected from the plague of eternal death.

Second, Jesus is the new covenant sacrifice. Upon leaving Egypt and arriving at Mt Sinai, the Hebrews were invited into a new covenant with God. God revealed his covenant laws to Moses, who wrote them down and read them aloud to the people at the base of Sinai. They then swore obedience to all of God's laws. Then Moses, after

---

89 Ex. 6:6.   90 Ex. 12:1–13.

91 Mk. 10:45.

92 1 Pet. 1:18–19. See also Rev. 5:8–10, where "ransom" and Passover language are connected to Christ's death.

93 Lk. 22:19, etc.   94 Jn. 6:53.

sacrificing oxen as holocausts and peace offerings, threw half of the sacrificial blood on God's altar and sprinkled the other half upon the people, saying "Behold the blood of the covenant which the LORD has made with you in accordance with all these words."[95] This sacrificial ritual sealed the new covenant relationship that existed between God and the people: the people are now one blood with God, they are his family. Hence, Moses and the elders ascend Sinai, see God, and eat the flesh of the peace offerings with him. Analogously, Jesus gave his entire self to God, in life and death, like a whole burnt offering. His blood, his very life, was poured out to God on the altar of the cross. Yet his blood is also sprinkled upon us in the Eucharistic chalice. And like a peace offering, Christ's flesh is given as a gift to God on the cross and to us in the Sacrament. The sprinkling of Christ's blood upon us and the consumption of his flesh makes us one flesh and blood with Christ, who is God himself: "He who eats my flesh and drinks my blood abides in me, and I in him."[96] Consequently, we are given the grace to obey God's new covenant commandments, just as Christ himself did. And we are enabled, through, with, and in Christ, to ascend God's eternal "mountain," look upon his "face," and "eat" with him.[97]

Third, Jesus' sacrifice can be compared to the Levitical sacrifices of atonement. These sacrifices resulted in the sinner's reconciliation to God, purification from ritual impurity, and assurance of continued access to God's glory in the temple. For the pouring forth of the animal's blood and placement of his flesh on God's altar represented the return of the offerer's life to the presence of God.[98] This was especially the case on the annual Day of Atonement, when the high priest sprinkled the sacrificial blood upon God's throne (the Ark) in his sanctuary and, outside, the scapegoat that symbolically bore the nation's sins was driven away from God's holy city. Similarly, Jesus' blood is poured out "for the forgiveness of sins."[99] He fulfills Isaiah's

---

95 Ex. 24:8.   96 Jn. 6:55–56.
97 See Rev. 21:10, 22:4, and 3:20, respectively.
98 See the helpful analysis by Khaled Anatolios, *Deification Through the Cross: An Eastern Christian Theology of Salvation* (William B. Eerdmans, 2020), 115–18.
99 Mt. 26:28.

prophecy of the Suffering Servant, for he "makes himself an offering for sin" and "poured out his soul to death" for the sake of the "many."[100] As a result of his sacrifice we are "healed" and "made whole" and he "makes many to be accounted righteous."[101] For the blood of Christ, sprinkled upon us, purifies us with the very life of Christ, and thus enables us to minister to God in his eternal presence: "They have washed their robes and made them white in the blood of the Lamb," the Book of Revelation says, and "therefore are they before the throne of God, and serve him day and night within his temple."[102] And as Hebrews explains, Jesus is the high priest who "entered once for all into the Holy Place, taking not the blood of goats and calves but his own blood."[103] Consequently, we now "have confidence to enter the sanctuary by the blood of Jesus, by the new and living way which he opened for us through the curtain, that is, through his flesh."[104] Those who consume Christ's flesh and blood are united to him and so participate in his sacrificial offering: they share in his life and abide in him as members of his body.[105] Hence, in Christ, their lives are poured out against, and presented upon, God's altar in heaven.

We can now conclude this section by returning directly to the questions which it sought to address. Why is access to eternal life only offered to sinners *after* Christ's Paschal Mystery? And how does Christ's Paschal Mystery contribute to *our* repentance and obedience? The New Testament answers these questions by emphasizing the incorporation of believers into Christ, the supreme sacrifice and priest. Christ, as man, merited to rise from the dead and live eternally as God's heavenly high priest. God, in his mercy, has allowed believers to share in the risen and glorified life of Christ just as, in justice, they shared in the pain and mortality of Adam. As God blessed the Chosen People in response to the pleasing sacrifices of figures like Noah and Abraham, so now he blesses believers with access to union with Christ as a result of Christ's pleasing sacrifice. And so

---

100 Isa. 53:10 and 12.   101 Isa. 53:5 and 11.

102 Rev. 7:14–15. Similarly, Rev. 22:14 states that those who wash their robes receive access to the tree of life.

103 Heb. 9:12.   104 Heb. 6:19–20 and 10:19–20.

105 1 Cor. 10:14–22 and Gal. 2:20.

where Christ is, there will believers be: united to him like branches on the vine, they will live in him and with him in the eternal house of the Father. But in order to share in Christ's eternal life, believers must first share in his victory over sin. They are empowered to do so by their union with Christ. As a branch draws life from the vine and bears fruit because of it, so believers are morally transformed by the grace of Christ and enabled to bear fruit in works of repentance, obedience, and love. Fed with Christ's divine flesh and marked with his divine blood, the crucified Christ lives in them and helps them to carry their crosses as he did. Christ's supreme moral sacrifice, offered in his Passion, is not merely an external example which the believer must strive to imitate by their own power. Rather, the crucified and risen Christ dwells in the believer and grants them a real share in his own power to do good, his own sacrificial love. We participate in Christ's perfect and eternal moral sacrifice to the Father.

CONCLUSION

How is the Paschal Mystery a means through which God saves us from sin and its consequences? Jesus could have escaped death if he recanted his "blasphemy" and his claim to be the "Christ." He did not, and so died as a *martyr* bearing witness to the truth about himself. Throughout this Passion, Jesus remained completely obedient to God and merciful towards those who persecuted him. He thus completely *conquered* every temptation and occasion of sin which he faced and provided a perfect *example* of moral righteousness. He had the power to escape his suffering, but freely chose to endure the attacks of his enemies out of *obedience* to the Father and *love* for sinners. His perfect witness, obedience, and love even unto death was a *sacrifice* which he offered to God. God was supremely pleased by this sacrificial gift, and as a result he rewarded Jesus with bodily resurrection from the dead and the glorification of his humanity in heaven. Hence, Jesus's conquest of sin resulted in his conquest of death and hell.

But Jesus' sacrifice was also offered to God on behalf of sinners, and it changes the relation between sinners and God. As high priest of the human race, the risen and glorified Jesus now perpetually ministers to God in his heavenly sanctuary. Jesus presents his own body and blood to the Father as a supreme gift of love and obedience on behalf of humanity. But Christ's body and blood are also given to sinners in the Eucharist. The sprinkling of Christ's sacrificial blood upon us purifies us from our wickedness and sanctifies us with the very life of the risen and glorified Christ. We become one blood, one family, with God Incarnate; we abide in Christ and Christ abides in us. By receiving the body of Christ in the Eucharist we become one body with him: we are members of his mystical body. And so where Christ is, we are: we are presented to the Father as a sacrificial gift through, with, and in Christ. In Christ, our blood is poured out against, and our flesh is placed upon, God's altar in heaven; we minister with Christ, our high priest, in the eternal sanctuary. Hence, as a result of Christ's sacrifice and our participation in that sacrifice through faith, repentance, obedience, and love, we have access to the grace of eternal life. We can now enter the heavenly paradise which was previously inaccessible. We can eat from the tree of life and drink from the river of the water of life in the new heavens and the new earth. By incorporation into Christ, we can share not only in Christ's conquest of sin, but also in his conquest of death and hell.

~

COMPREHENSION QUESTIONS

1. What were the religious and political reasons why some members of the Sanhedrin wanted Jesus put to death?
2. Why couldn't the Sanhedrin execute Jesus?
3. What is the meaning of Jesus' words to the high priest, and the high priest's reaction, in Mark 14:61–64?
4. What do the Sanhedrin imply will happen to Pilate if he does not execute Jesus? (Jn. 19:12)
5. Why does Pilate ultimately decide to execute Jesus?
6. What are the three ways in which Jesus can be identified as a cause of his Passion?

7. In what ways did Jesus actively will the Passion, on the one hand, and merely permit the Passion, on the other?
8. What are the two basic ends for which Jesus willed to endure the Passion?
9. How does Jesus' Passion give a foundational witness to sinners?
10. How does Jesus' Passion give us a moral example?
11. How is Jesus' Passion a conquest of sin?
12. How was Jesus tempted as he hung upon the cross? (Mk. 15:29–32)
13. What does it mean to say that Jesus conquered death and hell?
14. How is the Passion related to Jesus' conquest of death and hell? (Phil. 2:5–10)
15. How does Jesus' conquest of death and hell provide a supreme witness to sinners?
16. How does Jesus conquer death and hell for sinners?
17. How do we participate in Christ's conquest of sin, death, and hell?
18. What type of priest is Jesus, and how is his priesthood different from the Levitical priesthood?
19. What were the primary tasks of the Levitical priesthood?
20. What are the various meanings of Levitical sacrifice?
21. What is the sacrifice which Jesus gives to God?
22. What are the two reasons why Jesus' sacrifice is a pleasing gift to God?
23. How is Jesus' sacrifice a moral sacrifice?
24. According to Paul in Romans 5, what graces are given to sinners as a result of Christ's sacrifice?
25. At the Last Supper, how does Jesus allude to the ritual sacrifices of atonement, the Sinai covenant, and Passover?
26. How is Jesus' sacrifice and its effects like and unlike the following sacrifices: Passover; Sinai Covenant; and atonement/suffering servant?

PART II

SOTERIOLOGY IN SACRED TRADITION

5

FUNDAMENTAL PRINCIPLES OF MAGISTERIAL SOTERIOLOGY

THE PURPOSE of this chapter is to introduce readers to the fundamental principles of Catholic soteriology as expressed in the authoritative teachings of the Magisterium.[1] We will identify the positive content of those teachings as well as the questions which they raise. This chapter will be divided into two major sections. Section one provides a thorough overview of the soteriology of the early modern Council of Trent, which was called in response to the many soteriological objections and questions raised by the birth of Protestantism in Europe. Section two details the contemporary formulation of Catholic soteriology as contained in the *Catechism of the Catholic Church.*

SOTERIOLOGY IN THE COUNCIL OF TRENT

The Council of Trent (1545–1563) was called in response to the teachings of Martin Luther and the rise of Protestantism in Europe. Of all the ecumenical councils, Trent provides the most sustained treatment of central soteriological questions and issues. It did so in its decrees

---

1 "Magisterium" comes from the Latin *magister*, meaning "teacher." The Magisterium consists of the Pope and the bishops in union with him. They are the ordained and divinely empowered teachers of the Church. As successors of the Apostles, their task is to faithfully hand on, clarify, and apply the divinely revealed teaching of Christ in every age and in every place. Empowered by the Holy Spirit, the Magisterium is able to deliver infallible and definitive teachings on matters of faith and morals. When they do so, Catholics are to adhere to those teachings with absolute fidelity, as the teachings of Christ himself. The Magisterium can also deliver statements on faith and morals in an "ordinary," non-definitive way. Catholics are also bound to receive these teachings with humility and trust, while also recognizing that such teachings are non-definitive and, consequently, capable of revision. See the Second Vatican Council, *Lumen Gentium* (1964), §25 and the Congregation for the Doctrine of the Faith, *Donum Veritatis* (1990), especially §§21–31.

and canons on Original Sin, Justification, and Penance. We will examine the major soteriological contents of these Council statements.[2]

Trent's teaching on original sin clarifies *what* Christ came to save us from.[3] Adam's sin in Eden brought about destructive effects upon himself and all of his descendants: the loss of the grace of original justice, the anger and displeasure of God, physical death, and captivity to the devil.[4] These destructive effects are passed onto Adam's descendants "by propagation and not by imitation." Hence, even newborn babies who have never freely chosen to do evil nonetheless possess the state of original sin, and, consequently, should be baptized. Free will remains in the descendants of Adam, but their wills have been "weakened."[5] And humans are now plagued by "concupiscence," an innate inclination to do evil.[6] Neither natural human power alone nor perfect observance of the letter of the law of Moses enables humans to overcome their fallen condition.[7] Hence, God sent Jesus so that "all might receive adoption as sons" and in order to provide a "propitiation through faith in his blood."[8]

Christ saves us from original sin and our personal sins through the grace of "justification." "Justification" is the "transition from that state in which a person is born as a child of the first Adam to the state of grace and of adoption as children of God through the agency of the second Adam, Jesus Christ."[9] Justification occurs in the sacrament of baptism or, at least, through the desire for it: the baptized enter "the waters of rebirth." Sinners do not in any way "merit" the grace of justification, but rather they receive it completely "as a free gift."[10]

2 Next chapter we will examine Trent's decrees on the Eucharist and the Sacrifice of the Mass.

3 All references to the texts of the Council of Trent are from the versions provided by Tanner, *Decrees of the Ecumenical Councils*, Volume II: *Trent-Vatican II* (Georgetown University Press, 1990). I cite the Council session, canon and/or chapter, and the page number from Tanner.

4 For this and the following two sentences see Trent session 5, canons 1–4, 666–67.

5 Trent session 6, ch. 1, 671.   6 Trent session 5, canon 5, 667.

7 Trent session 6, ch. 1, 671.

8 Trent session 6, ch. 2, 671. My translation, from "*proposuit Deus propitiatorem per fidem in sanguine ipsius*," a citation of Rom. 3:25.

9 For this and the following quotation, see Trent session 6, ch. 4, 672.

10 Trent session 6, ch. 8, 674.

And it is even by God's grace that a sinner is "roused and helped" to approach baptism in the first place: grace prompts the sinner to believe in divine revelation, repent, and commit themselves to the observance of God's commandments. Yet the sinner must freely respond to this grace and could reject it at any time. Hence, the process of conversion which leads to justification involves "cooperation" between God's grace and human freedom.[11] The grace of justification itself really removes all sin and guilt from the recipient and makes them innocent and beloved by God, such that "nothing at all impedes their entrance into heaven."[12] Concupiscence remains in those who are justified, but they now have the grace which they need to resist that tendency to sin. Trent explicitly condemns the view that "justification" means only that God ceases to "impute" sin and guilt to a person. That is, God does not "justify" a person in the sense that a judge may arbitrarily declare a criminal to be "innocent" in spite of their crime. Rather, those who are justified by baptism have been "reborn" like a "new person," they really "become innocent, stainless, pure blameless and beloved children of God, *heirs indeed of God and fellow heirs with Christ (Rm. 8:17)."*

The grace of justification is made accessible to us as a result of Christ's Passion. Christ, *"out of the great love with which he loved us (Eph 2:4),* merited justification for us by his most holy passion on the wood of the cross, and made satisfaction to God the Father on our behalf."[13] Christ endured the passion out of *love* for sinners, and this made the passion an act of *merit* and *satisfaction* before God on our behalf. While Christ laid down his life on the cross for all sinners, nonetheless "not all receive the benefit of his death, but only those to whom the merit of his Passion is communicated."[14] Christ's merits are communicated or "applied" to sinners through baptism.[15] Hence, Trent makes a distinction between the *objective* work of Christ in the Passion and our *subjective* appropriation of that work: Christ's

---

11 Trent session 6, ch. 6, 672.
12 For this and the quotations that follow in this paragraph see Trent session 5, canon 5, 667.
13 Trent session 6, ch. 7, 673.   14 Trent session 6, ch. 3, 672.
15 Trent session 5, canon 3, 666.

passion is an objective fact which in and of itself satisfies for our sins and merits the grace of justification for us; but we must still freely choose, as individual subjects, to receive that grace.

What exactly does Trent mean when it refers to Christ's Passion as an act of "merit" and "satisfaction?" Thomas Aquinas's *Summa Theologiae* helps to answer this question.[16] As Pope Leo XIII observed, the Council of Trent began by placing the *Summa* upon the altar alongside of the Bible and papal decrees.[17] Hence, the *Summa* is a reliable and insightful guide to the proper understanding of Trent's teaching. For Aquinas, a person merits a reward from God when they freely perform a good work.[18] The gift of the Holy Spirit in the soul enables a person to perform supernatural works of charity which merit the supernatural reward of eternal life.[19] Christ's Passion was meritorious because he endured it freely, out of charity: "Whoever suffers for justice's sake," Aquinas explains, "merits his salvation by doing so, according to Mat. 5:10: 'Blessed are they that suffer persecution for Justice's sake.'"[20] Aquinas also points to Philippians 2:9, which indicates that Christ merited his own resurrection and Ascension as a reward for his service, humiliation, and obedience unto death.[21] And Christ also merited for sinners, as Aquinas explains: "Grace was bestowed upon Christ, not only as an individual, but inasmuch as he is the head of the Church, so that it might overflow into his members; and therefore Christ's works are referred to himself and to his members."[22] As mediator between God and man, Christ's charity unto death merits not only for himself, but also for all those for whom he suffered; and these merits are applied to us when we receive the grace of justification.[23]

16 See also Anselm of Canterbury, *Why God Became Man* (*Cur Deus Homo*), in *The Major Works*, ed. Brian Davies and G.R. Evans (Oxford University Press, 2008); Daniel Waldow, "A Love Greater Than Which Cannot Be Imagined: Divine Goodness and Mercy in Anselm's *Cur Deus homo*," *The Heythrop Journal* 62.4 (2021): 703–18.
17 Leo XIII, *Aeterni Patris* (1879), §22.
18 Thomas Aquinas, *ST* I-II, Q. 114, art. 1.
19 *ST* I-II, Q. 114, art. 3 and 4.   20 *ST* III, Q. 48, art. 1.
21 *ST* III, Q. 48, art. 1, sc.   22 *ST* III, Q. 48, art. 1.
23 See also Anselm, *Cur Deus Homo*, bk. 2, ch. 19, where he argues that justice

Aquinas treats satisfaction as an element of the virtue of penance. Justice requires that a repentant sinner do penance, which includes sorrow for one's past sins, the resolution to sin no more, and the free offering of recompense to the victim of your sin. This free payment of recompense is what Aquinas calls "satisfaction."[24] Satisfaction fulfills the demands of justice, restores the relationship between an evildoer and their victim, and so releases the evildoer from any further need to be punished. Aquinas applies these principles to Christ's Passion and to humanity's relationship with God: "He properly satisfies for an offense who offers something which the offended one loves equally, or even more, than he detested the offense. But by suffering out of love and obedience, Christ gave more to God than was required to compensate for the offense of the whole human race."[25] Christ's Passion was a "superabundant" satisfaction for all human sin due to the "magnitude of charity" with which he suffered, the dignity of his divine and human life, and the extent of his pain and sorrow.[26] All repentant sinners who receive the gift of justification are united to Christ as members of his body, and therefore they are the beneficiaries of Christ's work of satisfaction: their relation to God is restored, and so they will not suffer the punishment of perpetual death and the loss of eternal life.[27]

Trent teaches that the grace of justification is itself a real participation in the life of Christ. Through justification, Christ himself comes to live in us:

> Though no one can be just unless the merits of the passion of our lord Jesus Christ are communicated to him; nevertheless, in the justification of a sinner this in fact takes place when, by the merit of the same most holy passion, the love of God is poured out by the agency of the holy Spirit in the hearts of those who

demands that the Son, who is perfect and does not need a reward, can share his reward with whomever he chooses.

24 *ST* III, Q. 85, art. 3.   25 *ST* III, Q. 48, art. 2.

26 *ST* III, Q. 48, art. 2.

27 *ST* III, Q. 48, art. 2, ad 1. See also Daniel Waldow, "Aquinas on the Nature of Christ's Punishment and its Role in His Work of Satisfaction," *New Blackfriars* 103.1103 (2022): 7–28.

are being justified, and abides in them. Consequently, in the process of justification, together with the forgiveness of sins a person receives, through Jesus Christ into whom he is grafted, all these infused at the same time: faith, hope, and charity. For faith, unless hope is added to it and charity too, neither unites him perfectly with Christ nor makes him a living member of his body. Hence it is very truly said that faith without works is dead and barren.[28]

Christ's merits are shared with us, and as a result we come to possess the very source of those merits: God's love, the power of the Holy Spirit, and the infused virtues of faith, hope, and charity. Christ's merits enable us to become members of Christ's body, and thus to share in his divine love and infused virtues. Consequently, "the reborn are immediately ordered to preserve the justice freely granted to them through Jesus Christ in a pure and spotless state," and to do so by keeping the commandments: "If you would enter life, keep the commandments" (Mt. 19:7)" The baptized are empowered with the very life of Christ and so can and must imitate Christ's obedience: they must practice "faith united to good works" and the "observance of the commandments of God."[29] By doing so, they not only continue to abide in Christ, but the life of grace within them continues to "grow and increase."

The grace of Justification can be lost after baptism but then restored again. Those who are justified are obligated to observe God's commandments, and no one must think "that the commandments of God are impossible of observance by one who is justified. For God does not command the impossible."[30] Rather, God "gives his aid to enable you" to keep his commands, and all "can do [so] with the divine help." Nonetheless, in this life people "will sometimes fall into sin, at least light and everyday sins which are also called venial," yet such sins do not destroy the grace of justification. Rather, justification is only lost through a mortal sin. Those who commit mor-

28 For this and the two quotations that follow, see Trent session 6, ch. 7, 673–74.
29 For this and the following quotation, see Trent session 6, ch. 10, 675.
30 For this and the following two quotations, see Trent session 6, ch. 11, 675.

tal sins "are severed from the grace of Christ."[31] This is the case even if they still possess faith, in the sense of continuing to intellectually acknowledge the truth of revelation. Fortunately, though, those who are justified have the capacity, "with the help of divine grace," to freely "refrain" from committing mortal sin. Yet even if someone does commit mortal sin, they can be justified again through the sacrament of penance. Once again, it is the "merit of Christ" which enables this "restoration of the fallen."[32] The sacrament is the means "by which the benefit of Christ's death is applied to those who have fallen away after baptism."[33] God's grace prompts sinners to approach the sacrament, and the sacrament requires contrition, the resolution to sin no more, verbal confession of one's mortal sins to a priest, and the willingness to perform the work of satisfaction assigned by the priest. Satisfaction consists of prayer, fasting and almsgiving.[34]

The grace of justification ultimately results in the gift of eternal life. To those who possess the grace of justification, "eternal life should be held out, both as a grace promised in his mercy" and "as a reward to be faithfully bestowed, on the promise of God himself, for their good works and merits."[35] God gives eternal life as a grace of *mercy* and *reward* to those who "die in a state of grace." Yet even understood as a reward, eternal life is not given to us on account of our merely natural works and merits. Rather:

> Jesus Christ himself continually imparts strength to those justified, as the head to the members and the vine to the branches, and this strength always precedes, accompanies and follows their good works, and without it they would be wholly unable to do anything meritorious and pleasing to God … what is called our justice, because we are justified by its abiding in us, is that same justice of God, in that it is imparted to us by God through the merit of Christ.

31 For this and the following two quotations, see Trent session 6, ch. 15, 677.
32 Trent session 6, ch. 14, 677.   33 Trent session 14, ch. 1, 703.
34 Trent session 6, ch. 14, 677.
35 For this and all the quotations that follow in this paragraph, see Trent session 6, ch. 16, 678.

Any good work that a justified person does is because God's grace has preceded, accompanied, and followed that good work. Christ's strength is what empowered them to do the good that they did. Hence, in his goodness, God "desires his own gifts to be their merits." And so those who cooperate with God's grace in this life and die in that grace "have truly deserved to gain eternal life in their time."

Our conformity to Christ through grace and good works includes our works of satisfaction. In the sacrament of penance, Priests are to impose works of satisfaction upon penitents because such works deter from sin, heal the effects of sin which remain after sacramental absolution, and remove evil habits.[36] When penitents carry out these works of satisfaction, they "become like Christ Jesus who made satisfaction for our sins." Yet, crucially:

> This satisfaction which we offer in payment for our sins is not so much ours that it is not also done through Christ Jesus; for we can do nothing of ourselves as of ourselves; with his co-operation we can do everything in him who strengthens us. Thus we have nothing of which to boast; but all our boasting is in Christ, in whom we live, in whom we merit, in whom we make satisfaction and yielded fruits that will benefit repentance, which have their worth from him, are offered by him to the Father, and through him are accepted by the Father.

Hence, in no way is "the value of the merit and satisfaction of our lord Jesus Christ" ever "obscured or in some way diminished as a result of acts of satisfaction on our part." Rather, any works of prayer, fasting and almsgiving which we voluntarily undertake, and any involuntary suffering which we bear "with patience," is all done "through Jesus Christ," in whom "we are able to make satisfaction before the Father."[37]

---

36 For this and all the quotations that follow in this paragraph, see Trent session 14, ch. 8–9, 709.

37 Trent session 14, Canons on the Sacrament of Penance, canon 13 (Tanner, 713) specifies that Christian works of satisfaction are offered "for temporal punishment for sins." We will clarify the nature of temporal punishment below as taught in the *Catechism of the Catholic Church*.

Having considered the main lines of Catholic soteriological teaching as expressed in the early modern Council of Trent, we can now examine the contemporary synthesis of Catholic soteriology that is contained in the *Catechism of the Catholic Church* (henceforth CCC). The CCC was published during the pontificate of Pope John Paul II, who identified it as a "sure norm for teaching the faith" and a "sure and authentic reference text for teaching Catholic doctrine."[38] We now turn to the text of this sure norm in order to see how it affirms and expands upon the essential soteriological teaching of Trent.

SOTERIOLOGY IN THE CATECHISM OF THE CATHOLIC CHURCH

The CCC emphasizes that "Original Sin" is an inherited and fallen state of being. Adam "transmitted" the condition of original sin to his descendants, a condition "with which we are all born afflicted."[39] Given the "unity of the human race" in Adam, all of humanity is "implicated in Adam's sin, as all are implicated in Christ's justice."[40] Adam and Eve's decision to sin in Eden "affected *the human nature* that they would then transmit *in a fallen state*." Original sin is thus "a state and not an act." Every person who is created experiences this fallen state, for they have "a human nature deprived of original holiness and justice." Adam and Eve had this grace in Eden prior to their sin, and by this grace they shared in the divine life, lived in virtuous harmony with one another and the rest of creation, and were preserved from bodily death.[41] But the loss of original justice resulted in the following destructive effects:

> The control of the soul's spiritual faculties over the body is shattered; the union of man and woman becomes subject to tensions, their relations henceforth marked by lust and domination.

38 Pope John Paul II, *Fidei Depositum* (1992), §3, as contained in *The Catechism of the Catholic Church: With Modifications From the Editio Typica* (Doubleday, 1997), 6–7.
39 CCC, §403.
40 This quotation as well as the next three quotations in this paragraph are from CCC, §404.
41 CCC, §§375–379.

Harmony with creation is broken: visible creation has become alien and hostile to man. Because of man, creation is now subject "to its bondage and decay." Finally, the consequence explicitly foretold for this disobedience will come true: man will "return to the ground," for out of it he was taken. *Death makes its entrance into human history.*[42]

In this fallen state of original sin, "human nature has not been totally corrupted," but "it is wounded in the natural powers proper to it; subject to ignorance, suffering, and the dominion of death; and inclined to sin—an inclination to evil that is called 'concupiscence.'"[43] And in this fallen state humans suffer the experience of domination under the power of the devil.[44] "Original sin," therefore, refers to the fallen state of human nature which every person experiences as a result of Adam and Eve's disobedience in Eden, and this state involves damage and privation to the mind, the will, and the body.

But God became incarnate in order to save us from Original Sin and from the personal sins to which it leads. Following the Council of Nicaea, the CCC affirms that God became human "for us and for our salvation."[45] There are four basic ways in which the Incarnation saves sinners: (1) by reconciling them to God, (2) helping them to know God's love, (3) giving them Christ as the model of holiness, and (4) making them partakers of the divine nature.[46] Christ reconciles us to God precisely by serving as a "'propitiation' for our sins (1 Jn. 4:10)."[47] "Propitiation" or "expiation" are used in Scripture to refer to sacrifices of atonement as well as to the mercy seat where God dwelled atop the Ark of the Covenant.[48] These two cultic realities were linked on the Day of Atonement, when the blood of sin offerings was sprinkled

---

42 CCC, §400, quoting Rm. 8:21 and Gn. 3:19.

43 CCC, §405. 44 CCC, §407.

45 CCC, §456. 46 CCC, §§457–60.

47 CCC, §457. My translation from the Latin *propitiationem pro peccatis nostris.*

48 "Propitiation" or "expiation" translates the New Testament's Greek nouns *hilasmos* (1 Jn. 2:2, 4:10) and *hilasterion* (Rom. 3:25, Heb. 9:5) as well as the verb *hilaskomai* (Heb. 2:17; cf. Lk. 18:13). See the helpful analysis of these words by Gerald O'Collins, *Jesus Our Redeemer: A Christian Approach to Salvation* (Oxford: Oxford University Press, 2007), 15–17.

on the mercy seat. Hence, Christ is our "propitiation" who reconciles us to God precisely by being the presence of God's glory to us and by pouring out his blood to God as a sacrifice of atonement for our sins.[49] Christ's entire life was also a "revelation" of the truth about God and a "redemption" from sin and its consequences.[50] It was also a "recapitulation" by which Jesus reversed the history of human sin and repaired human nature in himself.[51] And while Christ's life is an external model, it is one to which we can be conformed: "Christ enables us *to live in him* all that he himself lived, and *he lives it in us*."[52] Christ enables us and calls us simply to be united with him as members of his body and thus "to share in what he lived for us."[53] To illustrate this point, the CCC provides an extended commentary on the nature of, and our participation in, the mysteries of Christ's birth and childhood, baptism, temptations, proclamation of the kingdom of God, transfiguration, and entrance into Jerusalem.[54]

The CCC then proceeds to examine the mystery of Christ's Passion. While particular people executed Christ for religious and political reasons, Christ's death is ultimately caused by *all* sinners, not just those who were involved in the historical event of the Passion.[55] And the Passion was not the result of mere historical chance but rather was part of God's plan and was foretold by Scripture.[56] Christ died in solidarity with sinners, for whom death is a punishment, yet he "did not experience reprobation as if he himself had sinned."[57] Jesus *freely* chose to die out of obedience and love for the Father and love for sinners.[58] His *obedience* to the Father, enacted throughout his entire life and Passion, is the *sacrifice* which he offers to the Father on our behalf.[59] He is the Suffering Servant, the "lamb of God who takes

---

49 Pope Benedict XVI, *Jesus of Nazareth: Holy Week: From the Entrance into Jerusalem to the Resurrection* (Ignatius Press, 2011), 39–40.

50 CCC, §§516–17.

51 CCC, §518. "Recapitulation" is further explained by two quotations from Irenaeus's *Against Heresies*, bk. 3, ch. 18.

52 CCC, §§520–21.

53 CCC, §521.

54 CCC, §§522–29.

55 CCC, §§572–91 and 598.

56 CCC, §§599–601.

57 CCC, §§602–3.

58 CCC, §§609 and 612.

59 CCC, §606.

away the sin of the world."[60] He is also the Passover sacrifice which redeems sinners and the "sacrifice of the new covenant" which restores us to communion with God.[61] Christ's sacrifice of obedience is in "substitution" and "reparation" for "our disobedience," and by his obedience he "made satisfaction for our sins to the Father."[62] Christ is the "'New Adam' who, because he 'became obedient unto death, even death on a cross,' makes reparation (*reparat*) superabundantly for the disobedience of Adam."[63] His sacrifice also "merited justification for us."[64] And the salvific and universal effects of Christ's sacrifice are due to the love with which he offered himself as well as because of the divinity of his personhood.[65] Finally, all are called to participate in Christ's sacrifice by taking up their cross and following him.[66]

Christ's descent to the dead, resurrection, and ascension are also for our salvation. As his dead body lay in the tomb, Christ descended in his soul as savior to the realm of the dead. There he proclaimed the good news to the righteous and "opened heaven's gates for the just who had gone before him."[67] Then, Christ's physical resurrection from the dead provided a "confirmation" of the truth of his teachings and works, especially of his divinity, and fulfilled his own promise to rise.[68] His resurrection is also the "principle," the cause, of the grace of justification for our souls and of the future resurrection of our bodies.[69] Through the grace of justification we receive "filial adoption," become Christ's brothers, and receive "a real share in the life of the only Son."[70] Through grace, the risen Christ "lives in the hearts of his faithful" such that "their lives are swept up by Christ into the heart of divine life."[71] Our share in the life of Christ includes a participation in the glorified, heavenly life which he enjoys through his

---

60 CCC, §§608, quoting Jn. 1:29.   61 CCC, §613.
62 CCC, §614–15.
63 CCC, §411, quoting 1 Cor. 15:21–22 and Phil. 2:8 and referring to Rm. 5:19–20. My translation of *reparat*.
64 CCC, §617, quoting the Council of Trent.
65 CCC, §616.   66 CCC, §618.
67 CCC, §§632–37. Christ "did not descend into hell to deliver the damned, nor to destroy the hell of damnation" (§633).
68 CCC, §§651–53.   69 CCC, §658.
70 CCC, §654.   71 CCC, §655.

Ascension. The members of Christ's body are able to follow their head into the Father's eternal house and sanctuary.[72] There Christ eternally intercedes for us as our high priest and is "the center and the principal actor of the liturgy that honors the Father in heaven."[73] Finally, Christ's Ascension into heaven and seat at the right hand of the Father both manifests his divinity and establishes his universal and eternal kingdom. As God and Messianic king, Christ rules over all things in heaven, on earth, and under the earth.[74]

From his divine throne in heaven, the risen Christ gives life to his mystical body on earth through the gift of the Holy Spirit.[75] The Spirit grafts us like branches unto the vine which is Christ, and consequently we are "divinized," meaning, "we become communicants in the divine nature."[76] The CCC uses the phrase *sanctifying grace* to refer to this divinizing presence of the Spirit within us: sanctifying grace is "a habitual gift, a stable and supernatural disposition that perfects the soul itself to enable it to live with God, to act by his love."[77] Through sanctifying grace we are healed from sin and sanctified, such that we participate in the very life of God.[78] Through the gift of the Spirit we share in the power of divine love: "God's love has been poured into our hearts through the Holy Spirit that has been given to us."[79] The initial reception of sanctifying grace occurs through Baptism and is called *Justification.*[80] The moment of justification is the completion of the conversion process: we have turned away from sin, come to believe, and so now cling to God in faith, hope, and charity. This conversion process is initiated and sustained by God's actual grace but also requires the "cooperation" of man's freedom.[81] The justified sinner is not *merely declared* "righteous" by God, but rather is actually made righteous by the healing and sanctifying presence of the Holy Spirit

72 CCC, §661.   73 CCC, §662.
74 CCC, §§664 and 668.   75 CCC, §739.
76 CCC, §1988, quoting Athanasius, *Ep. Serap.* 1, 24.
77 CCC, §2000.   78 CCC, §§1997–99.
79 CCC, §733, quoting Rm. 5:5.
80 CCC, §§1266 and 1992. The grace of justification can also be received through baptism by blood or, in extraordinary circumstances, baptism by desire. See CCC §§1258–61.
81 CCC, §§1993 and 2001–2.

within them: "with justification, faith, hope, and charity are poured into our hearts, and obedience to the divine will is granted us."[82]

Faith, hope, and charity are theological virtues which empower us to live like Christ. *Virtues* are "firm attitudes, stable dispositions, [and] habitual perfections of intellect and will."[83] They "govern our actions, order our passions, and guide our conduct." While many virtues can be cultivated by natural human effort, the *theological virtues* are supernatural gifts which God must infuse into the soul.[84] The theological virtues are "the pledge of the presence and action of the Holy Spirit in the faculties of the human being." *Faith* enables us to believe in God, revelation, and the teaching of the Church. Faith is not merely intellectual assent to a proposition; it is also the choice to obey God and to bear witness to the truth of the faith.[85] *Hope* inclines us to desire eternal life as our happiness, to trust in God's promises, and to rely upon the help of his grace and the power of the Holy Spirit.[86] By hope we order all of our actions towards eternal life.[87] *Charity* empowers the will to "love God above all things for his own sake, and our neighbor as ourselves for the love of God."[88] Citing Thomas Aquinas, the CCC defines "love" as "to will the good of another."[89] Hence, charity inclines us to *act* for the good which God wills, including the good of our neighbors, in order to please God. Charity enables us to love as Christ loves: to obey God's commands, to do good to our enemies, and to serve the poor and children as if they were Christ himself.[90] Faith, hope and charity live together in all those who possess sanctifying grace, and "faith apart from works is dead."[91] The union of faith, hope and charity gives us "living faith" by which we know God and do his will out of love for him.[92]

The life of grace is destroyed through mortal sin but can be restored through the sacrament of Reconciliation. A *mortal sin* "results in the loss of charity and the privation of sanctifying grace," or, "the

82 CCC, §1991. See also §§1989–92, etc.
83 For this and the following quotation, see CCC, §1804.
84 CCC, §§1805, 1810, and 1813.   85 CCC, §§1814–16.
86 CCC, §§1817.   87 CCC, §1818.
88 CCC, §1822.   89 CCC, §1766.
90 CCC, §§1823–25.   91 CCC, §1815, quoting James 2:26.
92 CCC, §1814.

state of grace."[93] A sin is mortal when it involves "grave matter" and is chosen with "full knowledge" and "complete consent."[94] If any of these three conditions are lacking, then the sin is merely venial. A *venial sin* "weakens," but does not destroy, charity; those who commit merely venial sins remain in communion with God and will receive eternal life.[95] Conversely, "those who die in a state of mortal sin descend into hell."[96] *Hell* is the result of "a willful turning away from God (a mortal sin)" followed by "persistence in it until the end."[97] Hell is "eternal separation from God," the "state of definitive self-exclusion from communion with God and the blessed."[98] In order to avoid hell, anyone who commits a mortal sin must repent and accept God's merciful love.[99] The forgiveness of mortal sin "is normally accomplished" through the *Sacrament of Reconciliation*.[100] Reconciliation causes the sinner to "recover the grace of justification" and so is like a "second plank after the shipwreck which is the loss of grace."[101] This sacrament requires that the sinner confess their mortal sins with sincere contrition to a priest or bishop and promise to carry out the penance (satisfaction) which they impose upon them. The priest or bishop then forgives the sinner and restores them to the state of grace with the following words: "I absolve you from your sins in the name of the Father, and of the Son, and of the Holy Spirit."[102]

Heaven awaits those who receive forgiveness and die in the state of grace. "By his death and resurrection, Christ has 'opened' heaven to us."[103] But what exactly does "heaven" or "eternal life" consist of? Put in general terms, "to live in heaven is 'to be with Christ.'"[104] Sim-

---

93 CCC, §1861.
94 CCC, §§1857–59.
95 CCC, §§1862–63.
96 CCC, §1035.
97 CCC, §1037.
98 CCC, §§1035 and 1033, respectively.
99 CCC, §1033.
100 CCC, §1856. Forgiveness of mortal sin can also occur outside of the Sacrament through the grace of perfect contrition, though this form of repentance includes the intention to receive sacramental absolution as soon as possible. See CCC, §1452.
101 CCC, §1446.
102 For the essential components of this sacrament, see CCC, §§1440–70. For the words of absolution, see §1449.
103 CCC, §§1026. See also §§1023–25.
104 CCC, §1025.

ilarly, "this perfect life with the Most Holy Trinity—this communion of life and love with the Trinity, with the virgin Mary, the angels and all the blessed—is called 'heaven.'"[105] Heaven is the end for which we were created, the "fulfillment of the deepest human longings," and "the state of supreme, definitive happiness."[106] Specifically, heaven consists of two spiritual elements: the Beatific Vision and the communion of saints. The "Beatific Vision" refers to our intimate relation with God in heaven: we will receive the grace to know and love God "as he is," to "see the divine essence with an intuitive vision, and even face to face, without the mediation of any creature."[107] On this earth we really know and love God, but his presence and being remains shrouded to us; it is as if he speaks to us from beyond a veil. But in heaven the veil is drawn back: then, alongside the risen Jesus, we will look directly upon the face of the Father forever with the love of the Holy Spirit. In this Beatific Vision, God "opens himself in an inexhaustible way" to the saints, and he gives himself to them as their "ever-flowing well-spring of happiness, peace, and mutual communion."[108] The "communion of saints" refers to the fact that all of the saints in heaven will know and love God together, and consequently will also know and love one another with the love of Christ.[109]

Those who die in the state of grace are "assured" of entrance into heaven, but before receiving eternal life they must first be "purified" and acquire the "holiness" which is "necessary."[110] If this purification is not completed by the time a person dies then it is accomplished after death in the spiritual state called "Purgatory."[111] Mortal sin destroys the life of grace in our soul. The Church calls this the "eternal punishment" of sin, because this loss of grace results in hell if that grace is not restored.[112] But all sin, even merely venial sins, also produces "temporal punishment," namely, "an unhealthy attachment to creatures" which follows "from the very nature of sin." The sacraments of Baptism and Penance restore us to the state of grace and so free us

---

105 CCC, §1024.   106 CCC, §1024.
107 CCC, §§1028 and 1023, respectively.
108 CCC, §1045.   109 CCC, §§1026, 1029, etc.
110 CCC, §§1023 and 1030.   111 CCC, §1031.
112 For this and the following three quotations, see CCC, §1472.

from eternal punishment, but temporal punishment often remains. For instance: a man who binge drinks for decades will be restored to the state of grace if he sincerely repents and goes to Confession; but after his Confession he may still experience disordered, strong, and recurring inclinations for alcohol. In order to enter into the joy of heaven, he needs to be purified from those disordered inclinations to sin. This purification can be acquired in this life, with the help of God's grace, through the practice of charity, mercy, prayer and penance.[113] Finally, we can contribute to the purification of the souls in Purgatory by offering the sacrifice of the Mass for them as well as through our prayers, good works, penances, and indulgences.[114]

Heaven is primarily and initially spiritual, but it will eventually include physical reality as well. The soul of a person who dies in the state of grace, and then undergoes any necessary purification in Purgatory, *immediately* enters into the Beatific Vision and the communion of saints. Eternal life is thus principally a *spiritual state of being*, not a physical place—it is the purified soul's enjoyment of communion with God and the saints. Right now, the only physical, human bodies in heaven are those of Jesus and Mary. Yet things will not continue this way forever—when Christ returns to earth in the future for the last judgment, at a time which only God knows, then he will resurrect the physical bodies of the saints and exalt the material universe.[115] God "will definitively grant incorruptible life to our bodies by reuniting them with our souls," and he "will 'change our lowly body to be like his glorious body.'"[116] We will then live in our risen and glorified bodies within "the new heavens and the new earth."[117] In this new state, "the visible universe" will "be transformed" and "restored to its original state."[118] Not only our physical bodies, but the entire physical universe itself "will be set free from

---

113 CCC, §1473.
114 CCC, §1032. See also 2 Macc. 12, where Judas Maccabeus offers prayer and sacrifice for the dead. On indulgences, see CCC, §1471.
115 CCC, §§1001, 1038 and 1040. The souls of the damned in hell will also receive their physical bodies again (CCC §§998 and 1038).
116 CCC, §§997 and 999, respectively, quoting 1 Cor. 15: 44.
117 CCC, §1043, quoting Rev. 21:1.
118 CCC, §1047, quoting Irenaeus of Lyons, *Against Heresies* 5.32.1.

its bondage to decay."[119] Hence, while the joy of heaven consists primarily and foundationally in the Beatific Vision, this vision will one day include the joy of looking upon the risen Christ and our risen neighbors with our bodily eyes.

CONCLUSION

This chapter has introduced readers to the fundamental soteriological principles of Catholic Magisterial teaching. We have examined the fallen human experience: original sin, concupiscence, venial and mortal sin, and hell. We have also considered the gifts of grace which God provides to fallen humanity: sanctifying grace and the theological virtues of faith, hope, and charity; justification; Purgatory; and eternal life. Finally, we have examined the relationship between the Incarnation and Paschal Mystery of Christ and our access to these gifts of grace. Trent speaks of Christ's Passion as an act of love for sinners which provides satisfaction for sin and merits justification and eternal life. The CCC adds that Christ's life was a revelation of the truth about God, a recapitulation of human nature, and a model of holiness. The Passion was a paschal and covenant sacrifice which Christ freely endured out of love for sinners and obedience to the Father. The divinity of Christ and the love with which he offered himself is the source of his merits.

Christ's merits are applied to sinners in baptism, by which we are justified. We are led to Baptism by God's grace and our free cooperation with that grace. This conversion process includes repentance from sin, recognition of the truths of the faith, and a commitment to observe Christ's commandments. Justification really changes the sinner by filling them with the Holy Spirit and the gift of sanctifying grace. The person is now grafted onto the vine which is Christ, given the theological virtues, and empowered by grace to observe Christ's commandments. Yet we can freely lose the grace of justification by committing a mortal sin. We are made just again through sincere repentance and reception of the sacrament of penance. God's

---

119 CCC, §1046, quoting Rom. 8:21.

grace empowers us to perform works of satisfaction, by which we become more conformed to Christ and overcome the lingering disorders caused by sin. Those who remain faithful to Christ and die in the state of grace will receive eternal life as a merciful gift and as a reward for their cooperation with God's grace. As Christ conquered death and entered into heavenly glory through his resurrection and Ascension, so now those who dwell in Christ share in the eternal life which he possesses.

~

COMPREHENSION QUESTIONS

The Council of Trent

1. What is original sin and how is it transmitted?
2. What is concupiscence and what is the status of human free will following the fall?
3. What is justification and what is mere "imputed" justification?
4. How does Christ merit our justification and how are his merits communicated to us?
5. How is justification received, lost, and restored?
6. What is the relation between God's grace and human free will in the process of conversion which culminates in justification?
7. How do we preserve and increase the grace of justification?
8. Can the justified keep God's commandments and refrain from mortal sin?
9. Can those who have faith commit mortal sin?
10. What is the nature and purpose of works of satisfaction?
11. Why did Christ's Passion satisfy for all human sin?
12. What is the relationship between our good works, satisfactions, and the grace of God?

The Catechism of the Catholic Church

13. According to the CCC §§516–17, what are the four ways in which the Incarnation saves sinners?

14. How is Christ a revelation, example, and source of grace?
15. What were the religious and political causes of Christ's Passion?
16. What are the causes, nature, and effects of Christ's Passion?
17. What was Christ's descent to the dead?
18. What are the two salvific effects of Christ's resurrection from the dead?
19. What does the Ascension of Christ manifest and establish?
20. What graces are offered to sinners as a result of Christ's Paschal mystery?
21. What is divinization and sanctifying grace?
22. What are the theological virtues of faith, hope, and charity?
23. What are mortal and venial sin?
24. What are eternal and temporal punishment?
25. What is the Sacrament of Penance and what is the purpose of works of satisfaction?
26. What are hell, Purgatory, and heaven and how do you enter them?

6

THE SACRIFICE OF THE CROSS
AND THE ALTAR

I N T H E previous chapter we examined the fundamental principles of Catholic soteriology as contained in the Council of Trent and the *Catechism of the Catholic Church*. We focused upon the saving value of Christ's Paschal Mystery, the Sacraments of Baptism and Penance, and the relationship between grace and human choices. In this chapter we will build upon those foundational doctrines by exploring the teachings of the Magisterium on the saving significance of the Eucharist. We will focus upon the sacrificial and life-giving nature of the Eucharist. As we examine various Magisterial texts, we will do so with an eye to the following soteriological questions: *What does it mean to say that the Eucharist is a "sacrifice"? What is the relationship between the Eucharist and the "sacrifice" of Christ on the cross? How does the Eucharist contribute to our salvation?* This chapter consists of four related sections. The first section examines the foundational teaching of the Council of Trent on the sacrificial and life-giving nature of the Eucharist. The second and third sections focus upon the meaning of the Eucharist as a saving "sacrifice" as explained in the papal writings of Pius XII, John Paul II, and Benedict XVI. The fourth section treats contemporary Magisterial teaching on the centrality, worthy reception, and saving effects of the Eucharist.

THE COUNCIL OF TRENT ON THE EUCHARIST

Trent depicts Jesus as a priest who offers himself as a sacrifice on the cross and in the Mass. Given the "powerlessness" of the Levitical priesthood, God sent Jesus as a priest of the order of Melchisedech.[1]

---

1 Council of Trent session 22, ch. 1, 732. All citations from the texts of the Council of Trent are to the texts provided by Norman P. Tanner, ed. *Decrees of the Ecumenical Councils*, Volume 2: *Trent-Vatican II* (Georgetown University Press, 1990). I

Christ "was to offer himself once to God the Father" upon the cross, and by doing so he brought about an "eternal redemption" for sinners.[2] Yet "his priesthood was not to be eliminated by death." For Christ left the church "a visible sacrifice (as human nature requires), by which that bloody sacrifice carried out on the cross should be represented, its memory persist until the end of time, and its saving power be applied to the forgiveness of the sins which we daily commit." This visible sacrifice is the Eucharist, which "is a true and singular sacrifice."[3] The Eucharist is a true "sacrifice" insofar as it *recalls* the sacrifice of the cross, makes the sacrificial victim *present*, and *applies* the power of the cross today. Christ instituted this sacrifice of the Eucharist at the Last Supper when he "offered his body and blood to God the Father under the forms of bread and wine," and then he commanded his apostles and their successors "to offer them" as "priests of the new covenant."[4] The sacrifice of the Eucharist is "a new Passover, namely the offering of himself by the church through its priests under visible signs." The reason for this new paschal sacrifice is "in memory of his own passage from this world to the Father, when he redeemed us by the shedding of his blood, rescued us from the power of darkness and transferred us to his kingdom." The sacrifice of the Eucharist is the "fulfilment and consummation" of all of the legitimate sacrifices which were offered under the natural and Mosaic law.

Trent specifies that the Eucharist is both a sacrificial object and action. The Eucharist is a "divine sacrifice which is *performed (peragitur)* in the mass."[5] In this sacrificial action "the very same Christ is *contained* and *offered* in bloodless manner who made a bloody sacrifice of himself once for all on the cross." The difference between the cross and the Eucharist is not the object that is offered, but rather the *way in which* that same object is offered: "For it is one and the same victim here *offering himself* by the ministry of his priests, who

cite the council session, chapter and/or canon, and the page in Tanner.

2 For this and the following two quotations, see Trent session 22, ch. 1, 733.

3 Trent session 22, opening, 732. "*Verum et singulare sacrificium est.*"

4 For this and all following quotations in this paragraph, see Trent session 22, ch. 1, 733.

5 For this and all following quotations in this paragraph, see Trent session 22, ch. 2, 733.

then *offered himself* on the cross: it is only the manner of offering that is different." Both on the cross and in the Eucharist, Jesus is the object which is offered to God. And it is obvious how the cross is a sacrificial action—Jesus is offered on the cross just as all sacrificial victims are offered, namely, he is killed and his blood is poured out. But it is less obvious how the Eucharist is a sacrificial action—how does Jesus offer himself to God in the Eucharist? And what exactly is the relation and difference between Christ's bloody offering of self on the cross and his unbloody offering of self in the Eucharist? Put more simply, what and how does Christ give of himself to the Father on the cross and in the Eucharist?

It is helpful to consider these questions in light of the biblical elements of sacrifice which we have examined in earlier chapters. Recall the six features of all ritual sacrifices which we first identified in the context of Genesis 14's description of the oblation of Melchizedek and which we saw further illustrated in the various forms of Levitical sacrifice. A "sacrifice" features: (1) *who* offers; (2) *what* they offer (the object, e.g., a bull); (3) the *manner in which* they offer the object (what is done to the object); (4) *to whom* they offer—God; (5) *the spiritual ends* for which they offer; and (6) the person *for whom* they offer. How do these features apply to the "sacrifice" of Christ on the cross and in the Eucharist? In particular, how is the third feature (the manner in which the object is offered) realized by Christ, the ordained minister, and the faithful assembled at Mass? What is the "unbloody" action which Christ is both the agent and object of in the Mass? What is done to Christ or by Christ in the Mass?[6] We will return to these questions throughout this chapter. For now, we proceed to consider how the teaching of Trent addresses the fourth–sixth features of sacrifice listed above.

As a sacrifice, the Eucharist produces saving effects for sinners. Christ's bloody offering of self on the cross results in "benefits" for

---

6 For a survey of post-Tridentine responses to this question, and largely critical assessments of those responses, see Charles Journet, *The Mass: The Presence of the Sacrifice of the Cross*, trans. Victor Szczurek (St Augustine's Press, 2008), 252–67, and Lawrence Feingold, *The Eucharist: Mystery of Presence, Sacrifice, and Communion* (Emmaus Academic, 2018), 355–60.

mankind, and those benefits "are received in the fullest measure through the bloodless offering."[7] The sacrifice of the Eucharist, Trent explains:

> Brings it about that if we approach God with sincere hearts and upright faith, and with awe and reverence, *we receive mercy and find grace to help in time of need.* For the Lord is placated (*placatus*) by this oblation (*oblatione*), he gives the gracious gift of repentance, [and] he absolves even enormous offences and sins.[8]

The Eucharist should be offered for the "sins, penalties, satisfactions and other needs" of the living and the dead. In response to the sacrifice of the Eucharist, God gives the grace of forgiveness, frees from punishments and the duty of satisfaction, and showers gifts upon us. Christ's sacrifice is "pleasing" or "delightful" (*placatus*) to God, but this does not mean that God's being or will towards us is changed in any way by Christ's sacrifice. Rather, it simply means that Christ's sacrifice is objectively good in God's judgment, and that it results in sinners being changed by God.[9] Yet Trent does not specify the reason(s) why the Eucharist is a "pleasing" (*placatus*) gift to God and, consequently, why exactly this gift merits the outpouring of graces upon sinners. While Trent makes it clear that Christ gives himself to the Father in the Eucharist, it is not entirely clear what that means—how is the being and action of Christ upon the altar a gift to God? We will return to this question momentarily, but for now proceed to consider the relation between the sacrifice of the Mass and reception of the Eucharist.

Trent distinguishes yet also relates the sacrificial and saving nature of the Eucharist to sacramental holy communion. The "fruits of this sacrifice" of the Mass are received "more fully" when the faithful

---

7 For this and all following quotations in this paragraph, see Trent session 22, ch. 2, 733–4.

8 My translation of *placatus* and *oblatione.*

9 See the concerns expressed by Gerald O'Collins, *Jesus Our Redeemer: A Christian Approach to Salvation* (Oxford University Press, 2007), 138–39, and the response by Brandon Peterson, "Paving the Way? Penalty and Atonement in Thomas's Aquinas's Soteriology," *The International Journal of Systematic Theology* 15.3 (July 2013): 278–80.

receive holy communion.[10] On the one hand, this means that the sacrifice of the Mass is *not reducible* to the lay reception of holy communion: an act of sacrificial offering takes place and bears fruit even if none of the laity receive holy communion.[11] On the other hand, the fruits of the sacrificial action are more fully received by the laity through sacramental communion, by which they consume the flesh of the sacrificial victim. Hence, Trent exhorts Catholics "to receive frequently that life-supporting bread" which is "the life of the soul" and "the unending health of the mind."[12] In order to receive the Eucharist worthily, those who have committed mortal sin must first repent, confess their sins and receive absolution in the sacrament of penance.[13] Upon being reconciled to God, the newly justified can partake of Christ's sacrificial flesh and so receive the strength that they need to "reach the heavenly fatherland."[14]

Having examined the Council of Trent's foundational teaching on the sacrificial and life-giving nature of the Eucharist, we can now proceed to explore how subsequent Magisterial teaching has affirmed and expanded upon this teaching.

CONTEMPORARY PAPAL TEACHING ON THE SACRIFICE OF THE MASS

In this section we examine how the contemporary papal writings of Pope Pius XII, Pope John Paul II, and Pope Benedict XVI have explained the sacrificial nature of the Eucharist.

Pope Pius XII

What exactly does the Church mean when it calls the Eucharist a "sacrifice?" Pope Pius XII addressed this question in paragraphs 66–79 of his 1947 encyclical on the liturgy, *Mediator Dei*. Pius first clarifies that the Eucharist "is no mere empty commemoration of the passion," but rather is "a true and proper sacrifice, whereby the high priest by an unbloody immolation offers himself as a most acceptable victim

---

10 Trent session 22, ch. 6, 734.
12 Trent session 13, ch. 8, 697.
14 Trent Session 13, ch. 8, 697.
11 Trent session 22, canon 1, 735.
13 Trent Session 13, ch. 7, 696.

to the eternal Father, as he did upon the cross."[15] What does it mean to say that Christ "offers himself" as an "unbloody immolation" and "acceptable victim" just as "he did upon the cross?" Before explicitly addressing this question, Pius insists that the cross and the Eucharist feature the same priest and victim, Christ himself.[16] Hence, on the cross and on the altar, the one *who* offers (the priest) and *what* is offered (the victim) are the same. But he then reiterates the teaching of the Council of Trent: "the manner, however, in which Christ is offered is different."[17] This indicates that *what is done to* Christ on the cross and on the altar, or *what Christ himself does* on the cross and on the altar, differs in some way.

Pius distinguishes and relates the two manners in which Christ is offered as a sacrifice on the cross and on the altar, respectively. He explains:

> On the cross He completely offered Himself and all His sufferings to God, and the immolation of the victim was brought about by the bloody death, which He underwent of His free will. But on the altar, by reason of the glorified state of His human nature, "death shall have no more dominion over Him," (Rm. 6:9) and so the shedding of His blood is impossible.

Jesus died once and for all. He will not and cannot die again. Hence, the Eucharist as a "sacrifice" does *not* involve the physical immolation of Jesus' body and blood. And yet, Pius continues:

> The sacrifice of our Redeemer is shown forth in an admirable manner by external signs which are the symbols of His death. For by the "transubstantiation" of bread into the body of Christ and of wine into His blood, His body and blood are both really present: now the eucharistic species under which He is present symbolize the actual separation of His body and blood. Thus

---

15 Pope Pius XII, *Mediator Dei* (1947), §68. Unless otherwise noted, throughout this chapter I cite the English and Latin versions of papal texts, Vatican II documents, the *Catechism of the Catholic Church*, and the 1983 *Code of Canon Law* as provided on the Vatican's website, www.vatican.va.

16 Pius XII, *Mediator Dei*, §§69–70.

17 For this and the following two quotations, see Pius XII, *Mediator Dei*, §70.

the commemorative representation of His death, which actually took place on Calvary, is repeated in every sacrifice of the altar, seeing that Jesus Christ is symbolically shown by separate symbols to be in a state of victimhood.

The Eucharist is a "sacrifice" in the sense, at least, that it is a *symbol* of the sacrifice of the cross. The double consecration of bread, on the one hand, and wine, on the other, into the body and blood of Christ symbolizes the lethal separation of Christ's body and blood (their immolation) that occurred on the cross. Every time Christ's body and blood become present upon the altar in the two distinct species of bread and wine, the separation of Christ's body and blood upon the cross is symbolically commemorated. Crucially, Christ's body and blood are *not actually separated* in the Eucharist: rather, the full Christ is present, body and blood, in each of the two separate visible species of bread and wine.

Pius also describes the Eucharist as a "sacrifice" in the sense that it shares the same ends and acts as the sacrifice of the cross. The first end of the cross and the Eucharist is to "give glory to the heavenly Father."[18] Pius explains:

> From His birth to His death Jesus Christ burned with zeal for the divine glory; and the offering of His blood upon the cross rose to heaven in an odor of sweetness. *To perpetuate this praise,* the members of the Mystical Body are united with their divine Head in the eucharistic sacrifice, and *with Him, together with the Angels and Archangels, they sing immortal praise to God* and give all honor and glory to the Father Almighty.

As a man, Christ praised the Father throughout his life on earth and even during his Passion. And he continues to actively praise the Father from his presence in the Eucharist upon our altars. The faithful who participate in the liturgy of the Eucharist share, along with the angels, in Christ's eternal offering of praise to the Father. The implication is that the Eucharist not only makes present the praise which Christ offered in the past, during his temporal life, but also

18 For this and the following quotation, see Pius XII, *Mediator Dei*, §71.

makes present the praise which the risen Christ offers now, eternally in heaven. So, the Eucharist not only makes Christ's sacrificial body and blood present; it also makes his sacrificial *act* of praise, temporally past and eternally now, present upon our altars.

The second end of the cross and the Eucharist is "to give thanks to God."[19] Pius says that only Christ, as the divine Son of the Father, "whose immense love he knew, could offer Him a worthy return of gratitude." He did so "at the Last Supper when He 'gave thanks.'" And "He did not cease to do so when hanging upon the cross, nor does He fail to do so in the august sacrifice of the altar, which is an act of thanksgiving or a 'eucharistic' act; since this 'is truly right and just, our duty and our salvation.'" Christ gives thanks and gratitude to God at the Last Supper, on the cross, and in the Eucharist. The Eucharist is a sacrificial "act" [*actionem*] of thanksgiving by Christ himself. So, again, the Eucharist does not merely make Christ's body and blood present; it also makes present his eternal *act* of gratitude to the Father. In the Eucharist, upon our altars, Christ offers thanksgiving to the Father.

The third end of the cross and the Eucharist is "expiation, placation, and reconciliation."[20] Pius states, "no one was better fitted to make satisfaction to Almighty God for all the sins of men than was Christ. Therefore, He desired to be immolated upon the cross 'as a propitiation for our sins, not for ours only but also for those of the whole world' (1 Jn. 2:2)." Pius then adds: "And likewise He daily offers Himself upon our altars for our redemption, that we may be rescued from eternal damnation and admitted into the company of the elect," and he does the same for the faithfully departed. Christ's voluntary self-offering on our behalf continues day in and day out through his presence in the Eucharist upon our altars: there Christ perpetually offers himself in an unbloody manner to the Father for the sake of our liberation from sin and communion with God and the saints.

19 For this and the following quotations in this paragraph, see Pius XII, *Mediator Dei*, §72.

20 For this and the following quotations in this paragraph, see Pius XII, *Mediator Dei*, §73. Here I translate "*placationis*" literally as "placation" rather than the Vatican translation's "propitiation."

The fourth end of the cross and the Eucharist is what Pius calls "impetration," which means "petition" or "supplication" on our behalf.[21] Each and every sinner has "made bad use of and dissipated the goods which he received from his heavenly Father. Accordingly, he has been reduced to the utmost poverty and to extreme degradation." But Christ has come to our aid "on the cross," where he was "offering prayers and supplications with a loud cry and tears, [and] has been heard for His reverence" (Heb. 5:7). As a man, Christ prayed for us on the cross, and the Father heard his prayers. And "Likewise upon the altar He is our mediator with God in the same efficacious manner, so that we may be filled with every blessing and grace." Christ continues to be our mediator and pray for us in the Eucharist. The Eucharist is the perpetuation of the same prayers which he offered for us on the cross. And as a result of those prayers, God showers fallen humanity with grace. Hence, once again, the Eucharist is not merely the presence of Christ's body and blood; it is also the presence of Christ's *acts* of prayer, his sacrifices of intercession on our behalf.

We can now apply Pius XII's teaching to our questions regarding *what is done* to Christ or by Christ in the Eucharist and why what is done to or by him is *pleasing* to the Father. What is done *to* Christ on the cross is that he is physically immolated. This historical event is pleasing to the Father insofar as Christ freely chose to endure it out of praise and thanks to God and in satisfaction and supplication for sinners. What is done *by* Christ in the Eucharist is that he becomes present to us under the distinct accidents of bread and wine. By doing so, he gives us a memorial of the immolation of his body and blood which occurred upon the cross. And under the accidents of bread and wine, Christ continues to act on our behalf just as he did upon the cross: he offers prayers in praise and thanks to God, in satisfaction for our sins, and in supplication for our needs. The Eucharist is a pleasing sacrifice to the Father insofar as, by the double consecration of bread and wine, the Passion of Christ is recalled, Christ becomes present to us for our sakes, and Christ acts on our behalf from our altars. And all of this is done in an unbloody manner.

21 For this and the following quotations in this paragraph, see Pius XII, *Mediator Dei*, §74.

Pope John Paul II and Pope Benedict XVI

Pope John Paul II emphasizes that the Eucharist is a sacrificial action of Christ which is one with his sacrifice of the cross. The liturgy of the Eucharist is "a holy and sacred action" which is performed by Christ himself.[22] This liturgy features "the continual presence and action of Christ" who is "the high priest of the new covenant." It is Christ, sacramentally "represented" by the ordained priest, who enters the sanctuary and is "the offerer and the offered, the consecrator and the consecrated." Hence, while the ordained priest "offers the holy Sacrifice *in persona Christi*," it is Christ himself who "is the author and principal subject of this sacrifice of His." Through his ordained priest, Christ performs "a true sacrificial act that brings creation back to God."[23] Crucially, the sacrifice of the Eucharist is "one and the same sacrifice" as the sacrifice of the cross, and it makes "this single sacrifice" of the cross "present." But how exactly does the Eucharist make present the sacrifice of the cross?

John Paul II teaches that the Eucharist makes present the saving *victim* and *work* of Christ's cross and resurrection. The Eucharist is the "sacramental re-presentation" of "the event of the Lord's passion and death" and "is the sacrifice of the cross perpetuated down the ages."[24] The Eucharist "is the gift of [Christ] himself, of his person in his sacred humanity, as well as the gift of his saving work." Christ's death and resurrection are the "central event of salvation," and in the Eucharist these events "becomes really present and 'the work of our redemption is carried out.'" The passover sacrifice of Christ "includes not only his passion and death, but also his resurrection."[25] And so "the Eucharistic sacrifice makes present not only the mystery of the Saviour's passion and death, but also the mystery of the resurrection which crowned his sacrifice." The Mass is "the sacramental re-presentation of Christ's sacrifice, crowned by the resurrec-

---

22 For this and the quotations in the following three sentences, see Pope John Paul II, *Dominicae Cenae* (1980), §8.

23 For this and the following two quotations, see John Paul II, *Dominicae Cenae*, §9.

24 For this and the quotations in the following two sentences, see Pope John Paul II, *Ecclesia de Eucharistia* (2003), §11.

25 For this and the following quotation, see John Paul II, *Ecclesia de Eucharistia*, §14.

tion."[26] Hence, Christ is present in the Eucharist as "the living and risen one."[27] Christ's death and resurrection "is so decisive for the salvation of the human race that" he "offered it and returned to the Father only *after he had left us a means of sharing in it* as if we had been present there."[28] The Eucharist is thus the sacramental presence and perpetuation of the sacrificial event and work of Christ's death and resurrection.

But how does the Eucharist make present the sacrificial event and work of Christ's passion and resurrection? John Paul explains that when Christ instituted the Eucharist at the Last Supper, "he did not merely say: 'This is my body,' 'this is my blood,' but went on to add: 'which is given for you,' 'which is poured out for you.'"[29] This means that "Jesus did not simply state that what he was giving them to eat and drink was his body and his blood; he also expressed *its sacrificial meaning* and made sacramentally present his sacrifice which would soon be offered on the Cross for the salvation of all." John Paul is saying that the event or work of the cross which the Eucharist makes present is precisely the sacrificial love of Christ which led him to offer his body on the cross and take it up again in the resurrection. The Eucharist is not only the presence of Christ's physical body and blood. It is also the presence of Christ's "love which goes 'to the end' (cf. Jn 13:1), a love which knows no measure."[30] John Paul explains:

> By virtue of its close relationship to the sacrifice of Golgotha, the Eucharist is *a sacrifice in the strict sense*, and not only in a general way, as if it were simply a matter of Christ's offering himself to the faithful as their spiritual food. The gift of his love and obedience to the point of giving his life is in the first place a gift to his Father. Certainly it is a gift given for our sake, and indeed that of all humanity, yet it is *first and foremost a gift to the Father*: "a sacrifice that the Father accepted, giving, in return for this total self-giving by his Son, who 'became obedient

26 *Ecclesia de Eucharistia*, §15.   27 *Ecclesia de Eucharistia*, §14.
28 *Ecclesia de Eucharistia*, §11.
29 For this and the following quotation, see John Paul II, *Ecclesia de Eucharistia*, §12.
30 *Ecclesia de Eucharistia*, §11.

unto death' (Phil 2:8), his own paternal gift, that is to say the grant of new and immortal life in the resurrection."[31]

Christ's death on the cross is above all else a gift to the Father. But this is the case only because Christ freely chose to die out of love for and obedience to the Father. The *physical sacrifice* of Christ's body and blood upon the cross is only pleasing to God because it flows from Christ's *moral sacrifice* of love and obedience. The gift which is pleasing to the Father is therefore not Christ's death in and of itself; rather, it is Christ's love and obedience even unto death. The pleasing sacrifice which Christ offers on our behalf is his total self-giving love even to the point of and amidst his passion. The Father accepts this pleasing sacrifice and responds to it by showering grace not only upon Christ, but upon all of those for whom Christ died. The Eucharist makes present not only the sacrificial body and blood which were immolated on the cross, but also the sacrificial love and obedience which made Christ's immolation pleasing to the Father.

Pope Benedict XVI also described the Eucharist as the presence of Christ's sacrificial love and obedience. Benedict says, "Jesus is the true paschal lamb who freely gave himself in sacrifice for us, and thus brought about the new and eternal covenant."[32] This covenant was established through "the mystery of Christ's obedience unto death, even death on a Cross (Phil. 2:8)." On the cross, Christ "gives himself in order to raise man up and save him. This is love in its most radical form." Christ's free endurance of the cross is the "supreme act of love and mankind's definitive deliverance from evil."[33] And the cross was an act of love and obedience precisely because Jesus freely chose to endure it, and anticipated doing so at the Last Supper: "In instituting the sacrament of the Eucharist, Jesus anticipates and makes present the sacrifice of the cross and the victory of the resurrection." Benedict explains how the Eucharist makes the sacrifice of the cross and resurrection present:

31 *Ecclesia de Eucharistia*, §13, quoting his own *Redemptor Hominis* (1979), §20.
32 For this and the quotations in the following two sentences see Pope Benedict XVI, *Sacramentum Caritatis* (2007), §9.
33 For this and the following quotation, see Benedict XVI, *Sacramentum Caritatis*, §10.

Jesus gave this act of oblation an enduring presence through his institution of the Eucharist at the Last Supper. He anticipated his death and resurrection by giving his disciples, in the bread and wine, his very self, his body and blood as the new manna (*Jn* 6: 31–33). The ancient world had dimly perceived that man's real food—what truly nourishes him as man—is ultimately the *Logos*, eternal wisdom: this same *Logos* now truly becomes food for us—as love. The Eucharist draws us into Jesus' act of self-oblation. More than just statically receiving the incarnate *Logos*, we enter into the very dynamic of his self-giving. The imagery of marriage between God and Israel is now realized in a way previously inconceivable: it had meant standing in God's presence, but now it becomes union with God through sharing in Jesus' self-gift, sharing in his body and blood.[34]

The Eucharist makes present the same body and blood of Christ that was immolated on the cross and taken up again in the resurrection. But the Eucharist is also the presence of the self-giving love and obedience of Christ, the free action and choice which make his death and resurrection a *pleasing* sacrifice to God. And through sacramental holy communion we receive not only his flesh and blood as our food but also, and more importantly, his self-giving love and obedience. Nourished by the sacrificial victim, we share in his life and are offered to the Father through him, with him, and in him. The Eucharist enables us to participate in Christ's sacrificial offering of self to the Father on the cross, an event in which "God's freedom and our human freedom met definitively in an inviolable, eternally valid pact."[35]

There is an additional and secondary way in which we can speak of the Mass as a true act of sacrifice. Recall that in the Old Testament a ritual "sacrifice," strictly speaking, is an act by which the object which is offered to God is destroyed. We have already seen how the Church insists that Christ is not killed, harmed or changed in any way in the Eucharist. Yet there is something else which *is* changed in the liturgy

---

34 Pope Benedict xvi, *Deus Caritas Est* (2005), §13.
35 Benedict xvi, *Sacramentum Caritatis*, §9.

of the Eucharist, namely, the substance of the bread and wine.[36] The consecration causes this natural substance to be converted into the substance of Christ, as John Paul II explains:

> The sacramental re-presentation of Christ's sacrifice, crowned by the resurrection, in the Mass involves a most special presence which—in the words of Paul VI—"is called 'real' not as a way of excluding all other types of presence as if they were 'not real,' but because it is a presence in the fullest sense: a substantial presence whereby Christ, the God-Man, is wholly and entirely present." This sets forth once more the perennially valid teaching of the Council of Trent: "the consecration of the bread and wine effects the change of the whole substance of the bread into the substance of the body of Christ our Lord, and of the whole substance of the wine into the substance of his blood. And the holy Catholic Church has fittingly and properly called this change transubstantiation."[37]

The laity bring bread and wine to the priest so that he may offer them to the Father in thanksgiving for the gift of creation.[38] And in return the laity receive a far greater gift: for Christ himself, through the ordained minister, converts the bread and wine into his body and blood, just as he did at the Last Supper. Every Mass makes present the miraculous power which Jesus exercised at the Last Supper. And so as Mary Magdalene thought she was looking upon a gardener, but was actually looking upon the risen Jesus (Jn. 20:11–18), so now in the Eucharist we continue to see what looks like bread and wine, but which is actually the substantial presence of the crucified and risen Jesus.

Before concluding our treatment on the sacrificial nature of the Mass, we can briefly mention one additional way in which the Mass is a sacrifice: the laity offer themselves to God in the liturgy. John Paul

---

36 For a similar analysis, see Reginald Garrigou-Lagrange, *Reality: A Synthesis of Thomistic Thought*, trans. Patrick Cummins (Ex Fontibus Co., 2006), 223–24.
37 John Paul II, *Ecclesia de Eucharistia*, §15, quoting Trent session 13, Decree on the Eucharist, ch. 4.
38 *Catechism of the Catholic Church*, §§1357 and 1359.

II taught that the presentation of the gifts of bread and wine are "a symbol of all that the eucharistic assembly brings, on its own part, as an offering to God and offers spiritually."[39] As the priest consecrates the bread and wine into the sacrificial flesh and blood of Christ, the laity "offer with him ... their own spiritual sacrifices represented by the bread and wine." The Second Vatican Council also affirmed the sacrificial nature of the laity's participation in the Mass: along with the priest, the laity "offer the divine victim to God, and offer themselves along with it."[40] And "by offering the Immaculate Victim, not only through the hands of the priest, but also with him, they should learn also to offer themselves."[41] For "together with the Lord's body," the faithful offer their good works as "spiritual sacrifices acceptable to God."[42] They do so in union with the ordained priest who consecrates the Eucharist and presides at the liturgy: he "unite(s) the prayers of the faithful with the sacrifice of their Head" in the Eucharist.[43] Hence, the Mass is a sacrifice in which Christ and the prayers and good works of the faithful are offered up to God through the ministry of the ordained priest. Through the Mass, Christ our high priest becomes present in the Eucharist and gives himself in love to the Father in praise, thanks, satisfaction and supplication on behalf of sinners. For their part, the faithful provide the bread and wine which becomes the body and blood of Christ, and they offer their own prayers and good works to the Father through, with, and in Christ and by the ministry of the ordained priest. Hence, the entire liturgy of the Eucharist is a participation, on earth, in the liturgy of heaven: the faithful, through and alongside Christ, their eternal high priest, offer a sacrifice of praise and worship to the holy Trinity and intercede for the salvation of sinners.

We can now synthesize the teaching of Trent, Pius XII, John Paul II and Benedict XVI regarding the sacrificial nature of the Eucharist. What does it mean to say that the Mass is a "sacrifice?" Especially,

---

39 For this and the following quotation, see John Paul II, *Dominicae Cenae*, §9.
40 Second Vatican Council, *Lumen Gentium* (1964), §11.
41 Second Vatican Council, *Sacrosanctum Concilium* (1963), §48.
42 Vatican II, *Lumen Gentium*, §34, emphasis added.
43 Vatican II, *Lumen Gentium*, §28.

how does Christ offer himself to God in an unbloody manner in the Eucharist? *What is done* to or by Christ in the Eucharist? And why is what is done to or by Christ *pleasing* to the Father, such that it results in his salvific gifts to sinners? The answers to these questions are multi-layered and best understood in light of the aspects of biblical sacrifice which we have previously examined in this book. Recall that in Scripture the word "sacrifice" refers to actions that are ritual or moral. A ritual "sacrifice" always involves the destruction of the object: the animal is killed and then at least partially burnt; the grain is burnt, the wine is poured out. The sacrifice of an animal can include the consumption of some of the animal's flesh by the priest and even by the people. A moral "sacrifice" consists of good works such as repentance, gratitude, obedience, service to the needy, and heroic witness and martyrdom. Such a sacrifice can involve literal physical death (martyrdom) or just metaphorical death (death of self-will, death to sin). Given this context, we can now understand how the Eucharist is a "sacrifice." We organize this treatment in terms of questions which address the six major features of biblical sacrifice mentioned above.

Who offers? To whom do they offer? What is the object or victim which they offer? The faithful and the ordained priest offer bread and wine as well as their prayers and good works to God. Christ works through the ordained priest to transform the oblation of bread and wine into himself, such that *he* becomes the object which is offered. Christ then offers himself, along with the prayers and good works of the ordained priest and faithful, to God. This communal offering in Christ is realized especially through the worthy reception of holy Communion, by which our union with Christ is realized to the greatest degree. Christ is the principal priestly actor in the liturgy of the Eucharist, but the ordained minister and the faithful participate in his priestly action in their own proper ways, and in virtue of their union with Christ they too become objects which are offered to God. Christ himself, as true God and true man, is the mediator between God and man: he is both the offerer, the object offered, and the one to whom it is offered.

What is the manner in which the victim is offered, i.e., what is done to or by the victim? There are several levels to this answer: (a) Christ himself is not destroyed, harmed, or changed in anyway, but the substances of bread and wine are—they are converted into the substance of Christ's body and blood, soul and divinity; this event occurs through the collective agency of the faithful who provide the bread and wine, the ordained priest who performs the consecration, and above all by Christ who gives the consecration efficacy and makes himself present to us upon our altars; (b) the separate consecration of bread and wine, and the real presence of Christ under both accidents, symbolizes the real separation of Christ's body and blood on the cross; (c) the sacrificial *being* of Christ, the same being who was crucified and risen, is now present upon our altar, and so too are his sacrificial *actions*, for he continues to give of himself in love and obedience to the Father; in this sense, the *event* or *work* of Christ's passion and resurrection is made present in the Mass, for the crucified and risen Lord is present and so is the perfect moral sacrifice which he offered on the cross and offers eternally in heaven; (d) the ordained priest who presides at Mass *must consume* Christ's flesh and blood in the Eucharist, and the present faithful who are sufficiently prepared are encouraged to do the same—hence, what is done to Christ includes, but is not reducible to, his consumption by the priest and, at minimum once per year, by the faithful. In all of these ways, what is done to the victim by the ordained priest, the faithful, and by the victim himself (for he makes himself present and acts therein) is done in an unbloody manner.

What are the spiritual ends for which the victim is offered? Trent specifies that the sacrifice of the Mass is offered in satisfaction for our sins and punishments, for deliverance from evil, and in supplication for all of our needs. It can be offered for the living and the dead. In response to this pleasing sacrifice, God showers sinners with mercy and gives the grace of repentance, forgiveness and deliverance. Pius XII adds that Christ offers himself upon the altar in praise of God, in thanksgiving, in satisfaction for our sins, and in supplication for all of our needs. And when the offering of the victim includes our sacramental reception of his flesh and blood in holy communion, we perform this act in order to be nourished with spiritual life in our soul, health of mind, and strength for the journey to eternal life.

Why is what is done to the victim pleasing to God? God is pleased that: (a) the faithful present bread and wine and pray for it to become the body and blood of Christ; (b) the ordained priest performs the double consecration in remembrance of Christ's Passion and, above all, so as to convert the bread and wine into the flesh and blood of Christ; (c) Christ works through the ordained priest to make the double consecration efficacious and hence to actually become present under the accidents of bread and wine; (d) present in the Eucharist, Christ gives of himself in love and obedience to the Father, and in praise, thanks, satisfaction and supplication on behalf of sinners; (e) the faithful offer their personal prayers and good works in union with the bread and wine and, above all, in union with Christ's love and prayers on their behalf; (d) Christ allows himself to be sacramentally consumed by the priest and faithful for the spiritual nourishment of their souls and in greater actualization of their life-giving communion with God.

Now that we have provided a basic account of how the Eucharist is a "sacrifice" which contributes to our salvation, we can now consider Magisterial teaching regarding the central place of the Eucharist in the life of the Christian as well as the requirements for worthy and fruitful reception of the Eucharist.

THE CENTRALITY, WORTHY RECEPTION, AND EFFECTS OF THE EUCHARIST

The contemporary Magisterium has repeatedly emphasized the centrality of the Eucharist to the life of grace. Vatican Council II referred to the Eucharistic sacrifice as the "font and summit [*fontem et culmen*] of the whole Christian life."[44] This means that everything a Christian does is empowered by, and strives for, the Eucharist. The Council's decree on the priesthood explains:

The other sacraments, as well as with every ministry of the

44 Vatican II, *Lumen Gentium*, §11.

Church and every work of the apostolate, are tied together with the Eucharist and are directed toward it. The Most Blessed Eucharist contains the entire spiritual boon of the Church, that is, Christ himself, our Pasch and Living Bread, by the action of the Holy Spirit through his very flesh vital and vitalizing, giving life to men who are thus invited and encouraged to offer themselves, their labors and all created things, together with him.[45]

Every Sacrament and evangelical work of the Church—everything that the Church does for her members and for the world, is directed to the Eucharist, for the Eucharist is Christ himself. The Eucharist is "the source and the apex of the whole work of preaching the Gospel" and "the font and summit of all evangelization, since its goal is the communion of mankind with Christ."[46] The life of grace which we initially receive in baptism "is constantly renewed and consolidated by sharing in the Eucharistic Sacrifice, especially by that full sharing which takes place in sacramental communion."[47] As John Paul II explained, the Eucharist puts us into life-giving union with Christ himself: "It is because of him that we have life: 'He who eats me will live because of me' (*Jn* 6:57). Eucharistic communion brings about in a sublime way the mutual 'abiding' of Christ and each of his followers: 'Abide in me, and I in you' (*Jn* 15:4)." As the Second Vatican Council explained, the Eucharist is the "paschal banquet in which Christ is eaten, the mind is filled with grace, and a pledge of future glory is given to us."[48] Through the Eucharist, above all, "charity toward God and man" is "communicated and nourished."[49] The Eucharist is the supreme source and end of charity, the supernatural virtue which empowers us to imitate the sacrificial love of Christ and seek eternal union with God. By worshipping and clinging to the Eucharistic

---

45 Second Vatican Council, *Presbyterorum Ordinis* (1965), §5.
46 Vatican II, *Presbyterorum Ordinis*, §5 and John Paul II, *Ecclesia de Eucharistia*, §22, respectively.
47 For this and the following quotation, see John Paul II, *Ecclesia de Eucharistia*, §22.
48 Vatican II, *Sacrosanctum Concilium*, §47.
49 Vatican II, *Lumen Gentium*, §33.

Lord, "we already unite ourselves with the heavenly liturgy and anticipate eternal life."[50]

Reception of the Eucharist requires the observance of two basic conditions. The first condition is a contingent matter of discipline which varies depending upon the specific rite within the Church. In the Roman rite, the requirement is to fast from food and drink (other than water) for one hour prior to the reception of the Eucharist. An exception exists for priests who say multiple Masses per day and for the elderly, infirm, and their caregivers.[51] The second condition is a universal requirement which is based on the very nature of the act of holy communion: the recipient must be baptized, in communion with the Church, and in the state of grace. The reason for this is that receiving Jesus in the Eucharist *does not establish* a life-giving relationship with him, but rather expresses and strengthens a spiritual communion which *already exists*.[52] This prior communion is both "invisible" (the person who approaches the Sacrament is already united to the holy Trinity through possession of sanctifying grace) and "visible" (they are a baptized and professing member of the Church in union with the Pope and their local bishop).[53] Receiving Jesus in the Eucharist is like saying, "Jesus, I thank you for the gift of yourself to me; I wish to receive all that you are and all that you give me—all of your grace, commandments, teachings and ordained shepherds; and I give my whole self back to you in faith, hope, and love." Those who cannot say such words with honesty, due to a lack of invisible or visible communion with the Church, cannot receive the Eucharist worthily. If they choose to receive the Sacrament anyway, then they commit the grave sin of sacrilege and "will be guilty of profaning the body and blood of the Lord."[54]

Sacramental absolution of grave sins is normally required for worthy reception of the Eucharist. A baptized and believing Catholic

---

50 *Catechism of the Catholic Church*, §1326. Henceforth referred to as "ccc."
51 *Code of Canon Law* (1983), §919 and ccc §1387. The Code will henceforth be referred to as "cic."
52 John Paul II, *Ecclesia de Eucharistia*, §35.
53 John Paul II, *Ecclesia de Eucharistia*, §§35–39.
54 ccc §1385, quoting 1 Cor. 11:27–29.

removes themselves from invisible communion with Christ (the state of grace) through a mortal sin. As we have seen, a mortal sin occurs "when a person knowingly and willingly, for whatever reason, chooses something gravely disordered."[55] Given this definition, it is theoretically possible for a person to commit an act which is gravely evil and yet to remain in the state of grace due to a lack of knowledge and/or consent in regards to their evil act. In such a situation, their sin would be "grave" in the objective sense but not "mortal" because it did not destroy charity in their soul.[56] Nonetheless, the Church does not say that those who commit *merely* grave sins can worthily receive the Eucharist. Rather, "in the church's doctrine and pastoral action, grave sin is in practice identified with mortal sin."[57] The Church teaches that anyone who has committed an objectively grave sin, even if they are not subjectively certain that their sin was mortal, must receive absolution in the sacrament of Penance prior to receiving the Eucharist. For instance, the *Catechism* states: "Anyone conscious of a grave sin (*peccati gravis*) must (*debet*) receive the sacrament of Reconciliation before coming to communion."[58] Likewise, the Code of Canon Law: "A person who is conscious of grave sin (*peccati gravis*) is not to celebrate Mass or receive the body of the Lord without previous sacramental confession."[59] Pope John Paul II repeatedly stated that anyone who is conscious of having committed "grave sin (*peccati gravis*)" must receive sacramental absolution before receiving the Eucharist.[60]

---

55 Pope John Paul II, *Reconciliatio et Paenitentia* (1984), §17. Similarly, John Paul states that a mortal sin is a "sin whose object is grave matter and which is also committed with full knowledge and deliberate consent."

56 This may occur, for instance, with children who are below the age of reason or with adults who are mentally handicapped, experience hallucinations, or who are given errant moral direction from a priest, etc.

57 Pope John Paul II, *Reconciliatio et Paenitentia*, §17.

58 CCC, §1385. 59 CIC, §916.

60 "The *Catechism of the Catholic Church* rightly stipulates that 'anyone conscious of a grave sin must receive the sacrament of Reconciliation before coming to communion.' I therefore desire to reaffirm that in the Church there remains in force, now and in the future, the rule by which the Council of Trent gave concrete expression to the Apostle Paul's stern warning when it affirmed that, in order to receive the Eucharist in a worthy manner, "one must first confess one's sins,

The reality of this norm is especially evident when we consider the situation of people who publicly and persistently commit grave sins. Canon law requires that sacramental communion be *refused* to those who "obstinately persist in manifest grave sin."[61] John Paul II specified that this law applies "in cases of *outward conduct* which is seriously, clearly and steadfastly contrary to the moral norm."[62] From the standpoint of those who administer the Eucharist, the question of whether or not a particular person should be given the Eucharist is exclusively concerned with the objective and visible nature of the person's actions. Have they committed grave sins in a public and persistent way, or not? The additional question of whether the grave sinner has the knowledge and consent necessary to render their sins "mortal" is not relevant to the question of whether they should receive the Eucharist. For instance, imagine a scenario in which a small town contains a medical clinic which sells contraception and administers surgical and chemical abortions. They explicitly advertise for these services and everyone in the town knows that they provide them. Everyone has also known for years that the owner and manager of the clinic is a man who identifies as "Catholic." Moreover, the local Catholic priest has reached out to the man on numerous occasions and challenged him to give up his gravely sinful occupation, but to no avail. One Sunday morning the priest is out for a walk and sees the man open up the clinic for the day. A few hours later the clinic owner is at Mass. As he approaches the sanctuary and extends his hands to receive the Eucharist, what ought the priest to do? Must he strive to determine whether or not this man has committed mortal sins and thus whether he is in the state of grace? No. He knows that the man obstinately persists in manifest grave sin. He must refuse

when one is aware of mortal sin" (*Ecclesia de Eucharistia*, §36); "If a Christian's conscience is burdened by grave sin (*peccati gravis*), then the path of penance through the sacrament of Reconciliation becomes necessary for full participation in the Eucharistic Sacrifice" (*Ecclesia de Eucharistia*, §37); "it must be remembered that the church, guided by faith in this great sacrament, teaches that no Christian who is conscious of grave sin (*peccati gravis*) can receive the Eucharist before having obtained God's forgiveness" (*Reconciliatio et Paenitentia*, §27).

61 *CIC* §915.

62 *Ecclesia de Eucharistia*, §37, emphasis added.

to give him the Eucharist, lest he lead the man to be one who "eats and drinks judgment upon himself."[63] And the clinic owner, for his part, must not present himself for reception of the Eucharist again until he has firmly repented of his sins and received absolution in the Sacrament of Penance.

There is one scenario in which those who are conscious of having committed grave sins can worthily receive the Eucharist prior to the reception of the Sacrament of Penance. Canon 916 states:

> A person who is conscious of grave sin is not to celebrate Mass or receive the body of the Lord without previous sacramental confession unless there is a grave reason and there is no opportunity to confess; in this case the person is to remember the obligation to make an act of perfect contrition which includes the resolution of confessing as soon as possible.[64]

What "grave reason" could permit a person who is conscious of grave sin to receive the Eucharist without first confessing their sins? The answer is when a person is in imminent danger of death (e.g., a soldier about to march into battle) or when, through no fault of their own, they may be prevented long term or even permanently from encountering a priest who can hear their confession (e.g., a person who lives in a country where there are no priests or where Catholicism has been outlawed). Yet even in these situations, the penitent who is given the opportunity to receive the Eucharist can only do so if they first make an act of "perfect contrition." The reason for this is that perfect contrition *restores the person to the state of grace*, thus restoring them to invisible communion with Christ and rendering them objectively worthy to receive the Eucharist. What is perfect contrition? All contrition involves "detestation for the sin committed" and "the resolution not to sin again."[65] But perfect contrition results in "forgiveness of mortal sins" because "it arises from a love by which God is loved above all else," a "contrition of charity."[66] Whereas "imperfect" contrition results from a fear of hell and other punishments,

---

63 CCC, §1385, quoting 1 Cor. 11: 27–29.
64 CIC, §916.   65 CCC, §1451.
66 For this and the following quotation, see CCC, §1453.

perfect contrition is a turning away from sin out of supernatural love for God. God infuses theological charity as a grace into the soul of the sinner, and the sinner cooperates with this grace. By doing so, they are absolved of their sins and rendered worthy to receive the Eucharist even before they are able to receive the Sacrament of Penance.

Those who are able to receive the Eucharist worthily are encouraged to do so frequently. Catholics are required to attend Mass every Sunday and holy day of obligation and to receive the Eucharist at least once per year, during the Easter season.[67] Failure to do so is a grave sin.[68] But the requirement of weekly participation in the sacrifice of the altar and annual reception of holy Communion is a minimum which we must not fall below, not an ideal which we ought to strive towards. For "the Church strongly encourages the faithful to receive the holy Eucharist on Sundays and feast days, or more often still, even daily."[69] Pope Pius x taught that "frequent and daily communion" is "a practice most earnestly desired by Christ our Lord and by the Catholic Church."[70] He identified two ways in which Christ indicated his desire for the faithful to receive the Eucharist daily: first, when he compared the Eucharist to the manna from heaven which was given each day as nourishment to the Hebrews in the desert; second, when he taught us "to ask for 'our daily bread,' by which words, the holy Fathers of the Church all but unanimously teach, must be understood not so much that material bread which is the support of the body as the Eucharistic bread which ought to be our daily food." Pius also identified the various salvific and life-giving effects of frequent, worthy reception of the Eucharist: "that the faithful, being united to God by means of the Sacrament, may thence derive strength to resist their sensual passions, to cleanse themselves from the stains of daily faults, and to avoid these graver sins to which human frailty is liable"; and, "It is plain that by the frequent or daily reception of the Holy Eucharist union with Christ is strengthened, the spiritual life

67 CCC, §1389.   68 CCC, §2181.
69 CCC, §1389.
70 For what follows, see the Decree by the Sacred Congregation of the Council, *On Frequent and Daily Reception of Holy Communion* (1905), issued with the approval of Pope Pius x.

more abundantly sustained, the soul more richly endowed with virtues, and the pledge of everlasting happiness more securely bestowed on the recipient." In sum, we should receive the Eucharist each day if we are able to do so worthily. By doing so, we are saved from our sinfulness and sanctified with the life of the crucified and risen Lord.

CONCLUSION

What is the relationship between the passion and resurrection of Christ and the Eucharist? How is the Eucharist a Sacrifice? How does the Eucharist contribute to the salvation of sinners? This chapter has examined the answers to these questions that are provided in the Magisterial teachings of the Council of Trent, Vatican Council II, and the contemporary papacies of Popes Pius X, Pius XII, John Paul II, and Benedict XVI. We can now synthesize the Eucharistic teaching of these sources. The Church teaches that the Eucharist is a sacrament which is administered by an ordained priest or bishop. Christ works through these ministers to transform bread and wine into his own flesh and blood. This transformation is itself a sacrifice— the substance of bread and wine ceases to exist precisely by being converted into the substance of the body and blood of Christ. Only the accidents of bread and wine remain. And the double consecration of bread and wine, respectively, symbolizes the immolation of Christ's body and blood upon the cross: as his body and blood were separated on Golgotha, so now the risen Christ comes to us under two separate visible forms in the Eucharist.

The Eucharist is a true sacrifice which perpetuates the memory, presence, and saving fruits of the bloody sacrifice of the cross as well as of Christ's glorious resurrection from the dead. The Eucharist is a sacrifice which is offered by Christ to the Father through the ordained priest. The Eucharist is the same sacrifice as the sacrifice of the cross: the priest who offers, the victim which he offers, and that for whom he offers is the same. The only difference is the manner of offering, namely, bloody and unbloody. Since it involves an offering and that which is offered, the Eucharist is the presence of both a sacrificial victim and a sacrificial event and work: it is the sacrificial being and action of Christ. From the moment of consecration, the visible sacrificial victim that is Christ's body and blood is present; but so too is the invisible sacrifice of Christ's love, obedience, praise, gratitude, satisfaction and supplication. Just as on the cross Christ offered himself in love to the Father for us even unto the shedding of his blood; just as he intercedes for us now in his risen body in heaven; so now, upon the altar, the same Christ offers himself in an unbloody manner with the same love to the Father for us. The one sacrifice of Christ, in both its bloody and unbloody manner, pleases God, satisfies for sin and punishments, and merits our access to forgiveness, divinization, and eternal life. Following the consecration, the faithful at Mass offer the body and blood, love and obedience, praise, thanks, satisfaction and supplication of Christ, through the hands of the priest, to the Father along with their spiritual sacrifices of prayer and good works. The ordained priest and people offer themselves to the Father at Mass through, with, and in Christ.

The completion of the sacrifice of the Mass consists in sacramental holy Communion. Christ does not offer himself to the Father in the Eucharist merely as a whole burnt offering. He is also a sin offering from which the priest must partake. And he is the paschal lamb, peace offering and covenant ratification offering of which even the people can partake. This means that those who are properly disposed can receive Christ's sacrificial body and blood. Reception of the Eucharist is the most effective way to participate in and receive the saving fruits of Christ's cross: the gifts of grace which he merits for us by his sacrifice are poured out upon us in an unparalleled way in holy Communion. By receiving the Eucharist, the risen Christ comes to abide more fully within us and grants us a greater share in his sacrificial love. He cleanses us from the stains of sin and strengthens us in charity. Any baptized Catholic can receive the Eucharist so long as they have observed the required fast and received sacramental absolution for any grave sins which they committed. Those who are not in visible and invisible communion with Christ, but who insist upon receiving the Eucharist anyway, commit the grave sin of profaning the body and blood of the Lord. Conversely, worthy participation in the liturgy of the Eucharist is the source and summit of the entire Christian life—through the Eucharist, Christ divinizes us and empowers us with his own charity. This charity impels us to seek ever greater union with him and to draw others into that union. And the culmination of our discipleship and evangelization always leads back to the Eucharist, in which we continually renew and deepen our union with the divine bridegroom and experience a foretaste of the marriage of the lamb.

～

COMPREHENSION QUESTIONS

1. According to Trent, what is the relationship between the priest, victim, offering and effects of the sacrifice of the cross and the sacrifice of the Mass?
2. Who offers the sacrifice of the Mass, to whom do they offer, and for whom do they offer?
3. What is the object(s) or victim which is offered in the Mass?
4. What is the manner in which the object is offered in Mass?
5. Is anything done to or by Christ at Mass?
6. How does the Eucharist involve the being and action of Christ as well as the event/work of the passion and resurrection?
7. How is the manner of offering in Mass distinct from the manner of offering on the cross?
8. What are the spiritual ends for which the sacrifice of the Mass is offered?
9. What does it mean to say that God is *placatus* by the sacrifice of the Mass, and what does God do in response to this sacrifice?
10. What is the fullest way to receive the fruits of the sacrifice of the Mass?
11. What do Trent and Pius x teach regarding the frequency of sacramental holy communion?
12. What are the two ways in which Christ indicated how often we ought to receive the Eucharist?

13. How is the sacrifice of the Mass similar to, and distinct from, whole burnt offerings, sin offerings, the passover, peace offerings, and the Sinai covenant ratification sacrifice?
14. How and why is the Eucharist the font and summit of the entire Christian life?
15. What are the two basic conditions for worthy reception of the Eucharist?
16. What are the requirements of visible and invisible communion for worthy reception of the Eucharist?
17. Under what circumstances can a person who is conscious of grave sin receive the Eucharist without prior reception of the Sacrament of Penance?
18. What does canon 915 require regarding those who "obstinately persist in manifest grave sin?"
19. What sin is committed when a person receives the Eucharist unworthily?
20. What is the minimum requirement regarding Mass attendance and reception of holy Communion?

7

SOTERIOLOGY AND THE LITURGY
OF THE EUCHARIST

T HE PREVIOUS chapter explicated the teachings of the Magisterium upon the true presence, sacrificial nature, and consequent saving power of the sacrament of the Eucharist. We saw how
the Magisterium insists that the Eucharist is the source and summit
of the Christian life—it is the fundamental means through which
Christ saves us and the end to which this salvation leads in this life.
The centrality of the Eucharist to the Catholic faith has resulted in
the generation, in the history of the Church, of a plethora of liturgical prayers and rituals which lead up to, and follow, the consecration
of the bread and wine into the flesh and blood of Christ and the reception of holy Communion.[1] The purpose of this chapter is to explore the rich soteriological content of these Eucharistic liturgies.
We will show how these liturgies depict the following central soteriological truths: the fallen human condition; the incarnate work and
sacrifice of Christ; the sacrificial nature and divinizing power of the
Eucharist; and the primacy of God's grace along with the necessity
of the free human response to that grace. This chapter unfolds over
two major sections. Section one explores the two Eucharistic liturgies within the Roman rite of the Church, namely, the Traditional
Latin Mass and the Mass of Pope Paul VI. Section two examines the
two most prominent liturgies within the eastern rites of the Church,
namely, the Byzantine divine liturgies of John Chrysostom and Basil the Great, respectively.

Before proceeding to examine these liturgical texts, we should first
briefly explain our reasons for doing so. Why look to the liturgy as

1 "Liturgy" literally means "service" and is used in reference to the official and public acts of worship in the Church, especially those acts of worship which include
the administration of the Sacraments. The primary non-sacramental liturgy is
the "Divine Office" (also called the "Liturgy of the Hours").

a source of soteriology? First, because of the mutually enriching relationship between Magisterial teaching and the sacred liturgy. Liturgical rites which are approved by the Magisterium are a concrete expression of her doctrinal and moral teaching.[2] Consequently, the practice and study of these rites contributes to the Church's ongoing proclamation, defense and insight into the revealed mysteries of the faith.[3] Second, because the composition and long historical development of the Eucharistic liturgies bears witness to the unity of the Church's soteriological principles across time and space. All of these rites, Roman and Byzantine, patristic and medieval, are saturated with Scripture and express the same faith in the sacrificial and saving work of Christ on the cross and in the Eucharist. Third and finally, studying the soteriological content of the Eucharistic liturgy can enhance our participation in the liturgy and reception of its divinizing grace. What is the purpose of the various prayers and actions of the Mass? How are these rituals meant to contribute to our salvation? Answering these questions, even only partially, can help us to better direct our mind, heart and will in accord with the purpose of the liturgy and towards its end: life-giving worship of God.

SOTERIOLOGY IN THE TRADITIONAL ROMAN RITE

The Roman Eucharistic rite which is commonly referred to today as the "Traditional Latin Mass" (henceforth, TLM) has a long and rich history.[4] It is typically celebrated today using either the missal of Pope

2 See Pope Pius XII, *Mediator Dei*, §§47–48: "The entire liturgy, therefore, has the Catholic faith for its content, inasmuch as it bears public witness to the faith of the Church…the venerable maxim, *Legem credendi lex statuat supplicandi*—let the rule for prayer determine the rule of belief…. But if one desires to differentiate and describe the relationship between faith and the sacred liturgy in absolute and general terms, it is perfectly correct to say, *Lex credendi legem statuat supplicandi*—let the rule of belief determine the rule of prayer."

3 The Soteriological content of Byzantine liturgy, especially the divine office and prayers from the Eucharistic liturgies of specific seasons and feasts, has recently been examined by Khaled Anatolios, *Deification Through the Cross: An Eastern Christian Theology of Salvation* (William B. Eerdmans Publishing Company, 2020), 43–93 (Chapter 1: Doxological Contrition in Byzantine Liturgy).

4 See the concise overview provided by Michael Fiedrowicz, *The Traditional Mass:*

John XXIII (1962) or of Pope Pius XII (1955), both of which are largely identical to the missal of Pope Pius V (1570). That missal was codified in response to the request of the Council of Trent for a standard, universal missal for the Roman rite. Yet many aspects of the 1570 rite were in use far earlier, and the basic form of the Roman Canon goes back at least to Pope Gregory the Great in the sixth century. Hence, the TLM provides ancient and medieval liturgical testimony to the soteriology of the Church. In this section, we will examine the major soteriological content of the "Ordinary of the Mass," namely, the standard prayers and rituals which are performed at every TLM said using the 1955 or 1962 Missals. We will begin with a consideration of the soteriological significance of the basic liturgical direction, movements and structure of the TLM. We will then examine the soteriological content of the specific parts of the Ordinary: first, the "Mass of the Catechumens," which consists of the "Preparation" and "Instruction"; second, the "Mass of the Faithful," consisting of the "Offertory," "Canon," "Communion," and "Thanksgiving."

Soteriological Direction, Movements and Structure of the TLM

The direction in which the priest and people face during the TLM emphasizes the Christocentric and eschatological nature of the liturgy and Christian life. The altar is the standard focal point throughout the liturgy, and consequently the entire assembly (priest and laity) are positioned on the same side of the altar and look towards it together.[5] Traditionally, this meant that the entire assembly faced towards the

---

History, Form, and Theology of the Classical Roman Rite, trans. Rose Pfeifer (Angelico Press, 2020), 3–41 (Ch. 1, "Phases of Development"). For a concise history of the ways in which Mass has been prayed in Rome, see Uwe Michael Lang, *A Short History of the Roman Mass* (Ignatius Press, 2024). For a more thorough treatment see Lang's *The Roman Mass: From Early Christians Origins to Tridentine Reform* (Cambridge University Press, 2022).

5 Some refer to this as the priest "having his back to the people," but this would be akin to saying that a quarterback has his back to the running back or that a shortstop has his back to the left fielder. Rather, these players are all facing the same direction because they are united in action and focus upon the same object and event before them.

east (*ad orientem*) throughout the liturgy.[6] The reasons for this practice were symbolic. As the sun rises in the east and drives away the
darkness, so now we look east to the risen Son who gives light to the
world. Christ has ascended into his sanctuary in heaven (Ps. 68:32–
35) but has promised to one day return like lightning from the east
(Mt. 24:27); and so in the liturgy we look east towards his eternal
sanctuary and in preparation for his return. And the garden of Eden,
the pristine paradise and locus of communion between God and humanity, was "in the east" (Genesis 2:8). Now, we look east to the new
paradise, the new meeting place between God and humanity: the altar, where God becomes present to us in the Eucharist. In sum, by
worshipping God together towards the east, the assembly adores the
risen and glorified Christ and prays for the light of his grace. They
beg for communion with him in his eternal Eden. And they repent
of their sins and ask for forgiveness and strength in preparation for
Christ's return as judge of the nations.

Even when the altar is not literally in the east, the united direction of the assembly towards it (known as "liturgical *ad orientem*" or
"*ad Deum*") remains theocentric and stresses the sacrificial nature of
the Mass. The entire assembly prays together to God in his sanctuary. They all hear the risen Christ speak to them through the words
of Scripture, just as he opened up the Scriptures to the disciples on
the road to Emmaus and to his Apostles on Easter Sunday (Lk. 24).
And through the priest, the assembly presents gifts of bread and wine
to God upon his altar. The priest consecrates the bread and wine into
Christ's body and blood and then raises the Eucharist up towards
heaven in the sight of all: Christ, the high priest and sacrificial victim,
offers himself as a gift of love and obedience to the Father, in praise,
thanksgiving, satisfaction, and supplication for all sinners. The priest
and people then offer their own prayers of praise, thanks, contrition
and supplication to the Father through, with, and in Christ.

After begging to be made worthy to participate in Christ's sacrifice, the laity approach the sanctuary and kneel at the communion

---

6 For a thorough account of the history and meaning of *ad orientem* liturgical
orientation, see U.M. Lang, *Turning Towards the Lord: Orientation in Liturgical
Prayer* (Ignatius Press, 2004).

rail. The priest then turns towards them and descends to the rail in order to give them a share in the sacrificial feast. They become like the Apostles at the Last Supper as they face, are fed by, and fed with the body of Christ. While kneeling, they receive the Eucharistic host directly into their open mouths in a posture of adoration and humble receptivity: the Eucharist is Christ himself, a divine gift, not a merely created good or human achievement to be grasped at. Following communion, the priest and laity face the altar together again: they adore God and thank him for enabling them to feast with him upon the flesh of the paschal lamb and to be sprinkled with the blood of the new covenant. Having examined how the basic direction, movements and structure of the TLM highlights its Christocentric, eschatological, and sacrificial focus, we can now examine the soteriological content of its particular prayers and rituals.

The Preparation and Instruction

The Mass of the Catechumens begins with a penitential rite which manifests our need for divine mercy and our desire to enter into God's presence. The vested priest processes into the sanctuary and prays an antiphon ("I will go in to the altar of God") while standing at the foot of the altar.[7] He prays Psalm 42, in which he asks God to bring him into his "holy mountain" and "tabernacle," and then repeats the antiphon. He then prays the *Confiteor* ("I confess..."), acknowledging his sins of thought, word, and deed. He begs God to have mercy upon him, forgive him of all his sins, and bring him to eternal life. He then finally ascends the steps to the altar itself. There he once more asks God to take away their sins, "that we may enter with pure minds into the Holy of Holies." He makes this prayer "through Christ our Lord." Hence, the beginning of the TLM features central and clear references to the cultic realities of salvation history: the altar, the mountain of God, the tabernacle and the inner sanctuary of

---

7 All citations in this section are from the Latin text and English translation of the Ordinary of the 1962 Missal as contained in the classic and widely accessible *Saint Joseph Sunday Missal*, ed. Hugo Hoever, S.O.Cist. (Catholic Book Publishing Co., 1964), 19–78. I occasionally make slight modifications to the English translation in order to adhere more literally to the Latin text.

God. The priest prays for mercy for himself and the people so that they may enter God's presence in his sanctuary and serve him at his altar. The beginning of the Mass is thus a microcosm of the entire Christian life: we pray to God for mercy and forgiveness so that we may be able to enter into his presence and serve him in his eternal sanctuary of heaven.

The Mass of the Catechumens continues with prayers and readings which testify to the saving power of Christ. The priest does a reading (the *Introit*) from Scripture on the right side of the altar and then returns to the center to pray the *Kyrie*: "*Kyrie, eleison*" (Lord have mercy), "*Christe, eleison*" (Christ have mercy), each said a total of three times. He then leads the people in the *Gloria*: they praise Christ as the one who sits "at the right hand of the Father" and as the "Lamb of God" who "takes away the sins of the world"; and they once more ask Christ to have mercy on them and to grant their prayers. The priest proceeds to read a biblical *epistle* on the right side of the altar and then the *Gospel* at the left side. He departs from the altar to the ambo to deliver a homily. The Mass of the Catechumens concludes with the *Credo* (the Nicene-Constantinopolitan Creed), which affirms that God the Son became human "for us men, and for our salvation." The priest and laity confess their faith that Christ died, rose, and is glorified in heaven; that he will return to judge all peoples; that the Holy Spirit, the "giver of life," proceeds from the Father and the Son; that there is "one baptism for the remission of sins"; and that they hope for the "resurrection of the dead and the life of the world to come." In sum, Christ speaks to us through the words of Scripture in the *introit*, *epistle* and *Gospel*, and we prepare for and respond to his word in prayer: the *kyrie*, *Gloria*, and *Credo* adore and petition Christ as the divine judge, giver of life, and sacrificial lamb who takes away the sins of the world.

The Offertory and the Canon

The Mass of the Faithful begins with the *Offertory*, in which the priest offers bread and wine to God on behalf of the people and for their salvation. Standing at the center of the altar, the priest lifts the host and asks God to "accept" it. He offers the bread for his sins and for the sins of all Christians, so that it will "profit" them "as a means of salvation to life everlasting." He adds a drop of water to the chalice of wine, praying: "through the mystery of this water and wine, may we be made partakers of his divinity, who has condescended to become partaker of our humanity." This prayer reflects a common patristic theme: the Son of God becomes man in order to make men sons of God; and this divinizing exchange is accomplished through our reception of Christ's sacrificial blood. Lifting the chalice, the priest prays that the wine will become the pleasing sacrifice that is Christ's blood: "We offer you, O Lord, the chalice of salvation, humbly begging of your mercy that it may arise before your divine majesty, with a pleasing fragrance, for our salvation and for that of the whole world." Bowing, he prays that God will accept everyone present and that their "sacrifice be so offered in your sight this day as to please you." He asks the Holy Spirit to bless "this sacrifice" which they have "prepared." The priest continues: "Accept, Most Holy Trinity, this oblation, which we offer in memorial of the Passion, Resurrection, and Ascension" of Christ and to "aid our salvation." The priest turns to the people and asks them to pray "that my sacrifice and yours may become acceptable" to God. They respond, "May the Lord accept this sacrifice from your hands, to the praise and glory of his name, to our advantage and that of all his holy Church."

What is the "sacrifice" that the assembly has offered for the sake of their salvation, and which they repeatedly pray will be "accepted" by God? The assembly has offered the merely natural goods which they have, and which are themselves *gifts from God* in the first place. But they have done so with the prayer that these natural offerings will become the crucified and risen offering, Christ himself. The prayers of the *Offertory* thus show that the Mass is the God given opportunity for sinners to *actively cooperate with and unite themselves to* Christ's sacrificial gift of self to the Father. God gives sinners the goods of the earth and the capacity to form them into bread and wine; they can then freely bring this bread and wine to God; and in response, God miraculously converts the bread and wine into another gift, a supernatural and divine gift: the crucified, risen, and glorified Christ in the Eucharist. This same Christ eternally praises, thanks, and petitions

157

the Father on our behalf in the heavenly sanctuary. This Christ is a gift from God to man, but then also a gift from man to God: Christ gives himself to the Father along with all those who have united themselves to him through their participation in the liturgy.

The Offertory is followed by the *Sanctus* and the *Roman Canon*. The *Sanctus* mimics the prayers of Jesus' disciples during his entrance into Jerusalem on Palm Sunday: "Blessed is he who comes in the name of the Lord. Hosanna in the highest!" This prayer anticipates the coming of Jesus in the Eucharist which will occur in the prayer known as the *Canon*. During the *Canon*, the priest performs the sign of the cross over the bread and wine and asks God "to bless these gifts, these offerings, these holy and unblemished sacrifices." He specifies that he offers the bread and wine for believers living and dead: for their protection, peace, unity in the faith, "the redemption of their souls" and the "hope of salvation." After venerating the saints and asking for their intercession, he again prays that God be "pleased to accept" (*placatus accipias*) the oblation which they offer and to bless them in return with peace and eternal life. He then prays: "O God, bless, acknowledge, and approve this oblation which we offer, and make it reasonable and acceptable, that it may become for us the body and blood of your most beloved Son, our Lord Jesus Christ." The ultimate reason for the oblation of bread and wine to God is made clear: so that God may change it into the true and living sacrifice of Christ's flesh and blood. This change occurs in the ensuing ritual of "consecration," in which the priest takes first the bread and then the chalice into his hands and repeats the words of Jesus: "Take this, all of you, and eat of it: for this is my body," and "Take this, all of you, and drink from it: for this is the chalice of my blood." The priest genuflects after each of these words of consecration, for the gifts of bread and wine have been accepted and sacrificed: their substance was converted into the substance of Christ's flesh and blood. The substance of bread and wine no longer exists; the crucified and risen Lord, the living sacrifice, is now sacramentally present and active upon the altar under the accidents of bread and wine.

The proceeding prayers of the *Canon* emphasize the sacrificial nature of the Eucharist and the assembly's plea to be included in that sacrifice. After recalling Christ's Paschal Mystery, the priest performs the sign of the cross five times over the Eucharist and prays to the Father: "we offer to your supreme majesty, from the gifts which you have given to us, this pure victim, this holy victim, this immaculate victim, the holy bread of eternal life and the chalice of everlasting salvation." These prayers are not meant to suggest that Christ needs the assembly to "offer" him to the Father. For Christ is the high priest who has already offered himself in his Paschal Mystery, an offering of love and prayer which continues eternally in heaven and which is now present and active upon the altar independent of other human activity. Rather, these prayers manifest the priest and laity's attempt to *unite themselves to Christ's offering*, so that *Christ's offering will be counted as their own*, and consequently that they may share in the saving fruits of Christ's self-offering. This context enables us to better appreciate the priest's ensuing petitions to the Father regarding the Eucharistic gifts: "accept them, as you accepted the gifts of your child Abel, the just, the sacrifice of our patriarch, Abraham, and the offering of your high priest, Melchiz'edek, a holy sacrifice, an immaculate victim." God was pleased by these Old Testament sacrifices and blessed those who offered them and those for whom they were offered. Similarly, the priest prays that, in response to the pleasing sacrifice of Christ in the Eucharist, God will shower blessings upon the assembly who unites itself to that sacrifice and upon those for whom they offer it. Christ is thus like a whole burnt offering, a gift which is given entirely to God and which results in blessings for those for whom and by whom it is offered. The priest then continues:

> Command that these gifts be brought by the hands of your holy angel to your altar on high, in the sight of your divine majesty: so that all of us, who through this participation at the altar receive the most holy body and blood of your Son, may be filled with every grace and heavenly blessing, through the same Christ our Lord.

This prayer depicts the Eucharist like a peace offering in which a portion of the flesh of the sacrificial victim is offered to God upon his altar while the remaining portion is consumed by the offerers. As

Moses and the elders ascended Mt Sinai, saw the Lord, and ate the peace offering with him (Ex. 24), so now humanity ascends into the presence of God and shares a feast with him in the Eucharist. God and his chosen people are united around the altar of Christ's flesh: the crucified and risen Lord is the mutual delight of, and source of communion between, heaven and earth.

Communion and Thanksgiving

The union between God and the faithful upon the peace offering of Christ's flesh is accomplished in the *Communion* rite which follows the *Canon*. After leading the assembly in the "Our Father," the priest places a particle of the host into the chalice and prays that the "body and blood of our Lord Jesus Christ help us who receive it to eternal life. Amen." The entire assembly then prays, "Lamb of God, who takes away the sins of the world, have mercy on us" and "grant us peace." The priest says several prayers in preparation for his own reception of the Eucharist: "Let not the partaking of your body, O Lord Jesus Christ, which I, though unworthy, presume to receive, turn to my judgment and condemnation; but through your goodness, may it become a safeguard and an effective remedy of both soul and body"; "May the body of our Lord Jesus Christ keep my soul unto eternal life"; "What return shall I make to the Lord for all he has given me? I will take the chalice of salvation, and I will call upon the Name of the Lord"; "May the blood of our Lord Jesus Christ keep my soul unto eternal life." The faithful who are properly prepared to receive the Eucharist then approach the sanctuary and kneel at the altar rail; the priest places the body of Christ directly onto their tongues while audibly praying, *"Corpus Domini nostri Jesu Christi custodiat animam tuam in vitam aeternum. Amen."*[8] He then returns to the altar to wash the chalice and his fingers while praying, "What has passed our lips as food, O Lord, may we possess in purity of heart, that what is given to us in time, will be our healing for eternity"; and "May your body, O Lord, which I have eaten, and your blood which I have drunk, cleave to my very soul, and grant that no trace of sin

---

8 "May the body of our Lord Jesus Christ keep your soul unto eternal life. Amen."

be found in me, whom these pure and holy mysteries have renewed." The prayers surrounding the reception of sacramental holy Communion thus indicate the healing and life-giving quality of the Eucharist: through this Sacrament Jesus fills us with his grace, cleanses us from our sinfulness and prepares us for eternal life.

The Mass of the Faithful concludes with the "Last Gospel," which reaffirms the saving presence of the Incarnate Lord in our midst. The priest goes to the left side of the altar and reads John 1: 1–14. This Gospel identifies the Word of God as God himself and the one through whom all things were made. The Word is the source of life and light for the world. The Word came into the world, and to those who believe in him and receive him "he gave the power of becoming sons of God." Those who believe in the Word "are born not of blood, nor of the will of the flesh, nor of the will of man, but of God." The priest and faithful then kneel when the priest reads, "AND THE WORD BECAME FLESH and dwelt among us." After everyone rises, the priest concludes the passage: "And we saw his glory, the glory as of the Only-Begotten of the Father, full of grace and of truth." Everyone says "Thanks be to God," and the Mass ends. The reading of this Gospel passage at the conclusion of Mass reiterates the central event of salvation history, an event that has been experienced sacramentally in the Mass: God the Son has become human in order to give us new birth, by his divine power, as sons of God. Through the Word incarnate, the Word who died, rose, ascended, and who is now present to us in the Eucharist, we have life-giving and eternal access to the glory of God himself.

SOTERIOLOGY IN THE MODERN RITE OF PAUL VI

In 1969 Pope Paul VI published a new Missal for use within the Latin-rite Church.[9] While rarely done, Paul VI's Mass can still be celebrated *ad orientem*, in Latin, with an altar rail, and with the faithful receiving Communion directly on the tongue as they kneel. So the Christocentric and sacrificial meaning of those practices can con-

---

9 He promulgates this missal and discusses some of its elements in his 1969 Apostolic Constitution, *Missale Romanum*.

tinue to be present in Paul's liturgy. But the 1969 Missal does contain significant changes. For our purposes, the most relevant are that the *Offertory* was replaced with the "Presentation and Preparation of the Gifts," the *Roman Canon* was renamed "Eucharistic Prayer I," and three other Eucharistic prayers were provided as alternatives. In this section we will draw out the soteriological and sacrificial content of these new aspects of the Mass of Paul VI.

The Presentation and Preparation of the Gifts

While briefer than the classical *Offertory*, the presentation and prepa-ration of the gifts still emphasizes the sacrificial nature of the Mass. Unlike in the TLM, in the Mass of Paul VI the members of the laity can process to the sanctuary with the gifts of bread and wine and hand them over to the priest. He then brings the laity's gifts to the altar. This ritual is meant to symbolize the fact that the gifts of bread and wine which the priest offers to God are offered on behalf of the laity and in union with their prayers and good works. At the altar, the priest raises the host and thanks God for "the bread we offer you," bread which "will become for us the bread of life."[10] After sprinkling some water into the wine, the priest raises the chalice and thanks God for "the wine we offer you," wine which "will become our spiritual drink." After setting the chalice down, the priest bows and prays: "may we be accepted (*suscipiamur*) by you, O Lord, and may our sacrifice in your sight this day be pleasing (*placeat*) to you." The priest then faces the assembly and says, "Pray, brethren, that my sacrifice and yours may be made acceptable (*acceptabile*) to God." The assembly then re-sponds: "May the Lord accept (*suscipiat*) the sacrifice at your hands, for the praise and glory of his name, for our good and the good of all his holy Church." Hence, like in the *Offertory*, here the priest and laity pray that the gifts they offer will become the sacrificial gifts of Christ's flesh and blood, and that the assembly will be accepted by

---

10 All references to the Mass of Paul VI are from the Latin text and English trans-lation provided in *Daily Roman Missal* (Midwest Theological Forum, 2012). I occasionally make minor revisions to the English translation for the sake of a more literal rendering of the Latin. All references in this paragraph are to the "Presentation and Preparation of the Gifts," 727–29.

God along with the sacrifice of Christ. The presentation and preparation of the gifts is then followed by one of the four Eucharistic prayers. Each of these Eucharistic prayers contains the same essential rite of consecration as well as a prayer called the "Mystery of Faith." We will examine this common portion of the Eucharistic prayers and then proceed to a consideration of their distinct elements.

The Consecration in the Eucharistic Prayers

In the Mass of Paul vi the consecration involves two distinct steps. First, the priest takes the host of bread in his hand and states audibly, "Take this, all of you, and eat of it, for this is my body, which will be given up for you." Second, he takes the chalice of wine and says: "Take this, all of you, and drink from it, for this is the chalice of my blood, the blood of the new and eternal covenant, which will be poured out for you and for many for the forgiveness of sins. Do this in memory of me." At this point the bread and wine become the body and blood of Christ. Following the consecration, the assembly prays one of the following versions of the "Mystery of Faith":

> We proclaim your death, O Lord, and profess your resurrection, until you come again.

> When we eat this bread and drink this cup, we proclaim your death, O Lord, until you come again.

> Save us, savior of the world, for by your cross and resurrection you have set us free.

The Eucharist is thus a "proclamation" and "profession" of Christ's death and resurrection, the means by which he has "set us free." The words used for the consecration, taken from the Last Supper, give a basic indication of *how* Christ's death contributes to our salvation: he freely gives up his body and pours out his blood for us as an atonement and covenant ratification sacrifice. The Eucharist is the presence of Christ's physical and moral sacrifice, his body and blood and the sacrificial love by which he offered his body and blood on the cross for us. We will now examine how the distinct elements of Paul vi's three new Eucharistic prayers, both before and after the consecration, further depict the sacrificial and saving nature of the Eucharist.

Eucharistic Prayer II[11]

Eucharistic Prayer 11 is the shortest and simplest of the Eucharistic prayers. It begins with the priest praying that the Holy Spirit will descend upon the gifts of bread and wine to "sanctify" them "so that they may become for us the body and blood" of Christ. The priest then promptly proceeds to perform the consecration and mystery of faith. He then refers to the Eucharistic liturgy as a "memorial" of Christ's death and resurrection and prays: "we offer you, Lord, the Bread of life and the Chalice of salvation, giving thanks that you have held us worthy to be in your presence and minister to you." Continuing, he says: "we pray that, partaking of the body and blood of Christ, we may be gathered into one by the Holy Spirit." Eucharistic Prayer 11 concludes with the priest praying for an increase of charity for the Church, eternal life for the faithful departed, and for "mercy on us all," that along with the saints "we may merit to be coheirs to eternal life, and may praise and glorify you through your Son, Jesus Christ." These elements of Eucharistic Prayer 11 convey the following soteriological points: first, our natural offerings of bread and wine can only become sources of salvation when they are accepted and transformed by the grace of God; second, the Church unites herself to Christ's offering in the Eucharist and prays for the salvation of the living and dead in response to Christ's sacrifice; third, Christ's body and blood give the Holy Spirit, and thus divinizing life, to those who partake of them worthily.

Eucharistic Prayer III[12]

At the outset of Eucharistic Prayer 111, the priest affirms God's creative and sanctifying gifts to humanity: "through your son our Lord Jesus Christ, by the power and working of the Holy Spirit, you give life to and sanctify all things." He then alludes to Malachi 1:11 by thanking

---

11 All references in this paragraph are to *Daily Roman Missal*, "Eucharistic Prayer 11," 783–89.

12 *Daily Roman Missal*, "Eucharistic Prayer 111," 791–99.

God for assembling "a people to yourself, so that from the rising of the sun to its setting a pure oblation (*oblatio*) may be offered to your name." He asks God to send the Holy Spirit upon the "gifts" (*munera*) of bread and wine, so that "they may become the body and blood" of Christ. The consecration and profession of the Mystery of Faith follows, and then the priest says "we offer you in thanksgiving this holy and living sacrifice (*sacrificium*)." Continuing, he prays:

> Look, we pray, upon the oblation (*oblationem*) of your Church and, recognizing the sacrificial victim (*Hostiam*) by whose immolation you willed to be pleased (*cuius voluisti immolatione placari*), grant that we, who are nourished by the body and blood of your Son and filled with his holy Spirit, may become one body, one spirit in Christ.

The Eucharist is thus clearly identified as Christ himself, the victim whose sacrificial death (immolation) was pleasing (*placari*) to God. This victim is now offered to the Father in the Eucharist *as the oblation of the Church*, and at the same time is received by the Church as a source of divinizing nourishment. The priest prays that both the offering and reception of the Eucharist will contribute to the "faith and charity" of the Church and the "peace and salvation of all the world." He says: "May he make of us an eternal gift (*munus*) to you, so that we may obtain an inheritance with your elect." Christ, the pleasing sacrificial gift, makes those for whom he is offered and those who receive him pleasing gifts to God in their own right.

Eucharistic Prayer IV[13]

Eucharistic Prayer IV begins with a Preface which praises God for his majesty and goodness as well as a summary of the history of salvation. "When through disobedience man had lost your friendship, you did not abandon him to the domain of death," the priest recalls, for "you came in mercy to the aid of all, so that those who seek might find you." God reached out to his people through covenants and through the prophets, and ultimately he sent Jesus "to be our Savior." Christ

---

13 *Daily Roman Missal*, "Eucharistic Prayer IV," 801–9.

"shared our human nature in all things but sin," and "to the poor he proclaimed the good news of salvation, to prisoners, freedom, and to the sorrowful of heart, joy." Then, "to accomplish your plan, he handed himself over (*tradidit semetipsum*) in death, and, rising from the dead, he destroyed death and restored life." Finally, "that we might live no longer for ourselves but for him who died and rose again for us, he sent the Holy Spirit from you, Father, as the first fruits for believers, bringing to perfection his work in the world, he might complete the sanctification of all." Having completed this summary, the priest calls upon the Holy Spirit to "sanctify" the "gifts" (*munera*) of bread and wine so that "they may become the body and blood" of Christ, a great "mystery" which Christ himself left us "as an eternal covenant." The consecration and mystery of faith follow.

After referring to the liturgy as the memorial of Christ's Paschal Mystery, the priest prays: "we offer you his body and blood, the sacrifice acceptable to you and to save the whole world." He continues, "Look, O Lord, upon this victim (*Hostiam*), which you yourself have provided for your Church, and grant" that "to all who partake of this one bread and one chalice that, gathered into one body by the Holy Spirit, they may become in Christ a living victim (*hostia*), to the praise of your glory." Hence, the priest offers Christ in the Eucharist as a sacrifice to God for the salvation of the world, and at the same time he prays that those who receive the Eucharist become a living sacrifice to the Father in Christ and the Holy Spirit. He then prays again for "all for whom we offer this oblation (*oblationem*)," living and dead, including "those who take part in this offering (*offerentium*)." Eucharistic Prayer IV concludes by praying that "we may enter into a heavenly inheritance" with Mary and all of the saints "in your kingdom," so that "there, with the whole of creation, freed from the corruption of sin and death," we may "glorify you through Christ our Lord, through whom you bestow on the world all that is good." Hence, Christ saves us by offering himself to the Father for us in the Eucharist, and by giving his sacrificial flesh and blood to us in holy Communion: by doing so he sanctifies us with the Holy Spirit, liberates us from sin and death, and feeds us for eternal life.

The Communion Rite[14]

The Communion Rite which follows the Eucharistic Prayer highlights the life-giving power of the Eucharist. After saying the Lord's Prayer and prayers for deliverance and peace, the priest places a particle of the consecrated host into the chalice and prays "May this mingling of the Body and blood of" Christ "bring eternal life to us who receive it." The assembly prays the "Lamb of God," and then the priest quietly prays either of the following:

> Lord Jesus Christ, son of the living God, who by the will of the Father and the work of the holy Spirit, through your death gave life to the world, free me by this, your most holy body and blood, from all my sins and from every evil; keep me always faithful to your commandments, and never let me be parted from you.

> May the reception of your body and blood, Lord Jesus Christ, not bring me to judgment and condemnation, but through your loving mercy be for me protection in mind and body and a healing remedy.

He genuflects to the Eucharist and then, taking the host and chalice in his hands, turns towards the people and says: "Behold the Lamb of God, behold him who takes away the sins of the world. Blessed are those called to the supper of the Lamb." The people respond by acknowledging their unworthiness to receive Christ and professing his saving power: "I am not worthy that you should enter under my roof, but only say the word, and my soul shall be healed." The priest faces the altar again and quietly prays that the body and then the blood of Christ will "keep him safe for eternal life." After distributing holy communion to the faithful, the priest returns to the altar and prays: "What has passed our lips as food, O Lord, may we possess in purity of heart, that what has been given to us in time may be our healing for eternity." All of these prayers leading up to and following the reception of holy Communion focus upon the divinizing power of the Eucharist: the flesh and blood of Christ are medicine and food for

---

14 *Daily Roman Missal*, "The Communion Rite," 811–17.

the soul which heal from sin, give strength to keep the commandments, and preserve the soul for eternal life.

SOTERIOLOGY IN BYZANTINE EUCHARISTIC LITURGIES

As a universal church and faith, Catholicism features numerous Eucharistic liturgies and traditions that are not contained in the Roman
Missals of 1969 or 1962. Most of these are "eastern rites," as they are
commonly called.[15] These rites all express the same Catholic faith
in the Eucharist and are all approved by the Pope. Yet, because the
prayers and rituals of the eastern Eucharistic liturgies differ from
the Roman rites, they provide a distinct source for contemplating
the soteriological teaching of the Church and her faith in the Eucharist. The Roman and eastern Eucharistic rites are thus comple-
mentary sources of theological reflection. As Pope John Paul II put
it, these two wings of the Church are like the two lungs by which we
breathe.[16] In this section we examine the soteriological teaching of
the two most prominent eastern Eucharistic liturgies, namely, the
Byzantine liturgies of John Chrysostom and Basil the Great. Basil
lived from about 330–379 AD and was the bishop of Caesarea. John
lived about 347–407 AD and was archbishop of Constantinople. Both
are important patristic voices and are recognized as doctors of the
Church. The Byzantine liturgies which bear their name do so because
the "Anaphora" prayers (i.e., Eucharistic prayers) within those liturgies, which we shall examine below, are thought to have been written
by these saints or at least inspired by their theology.[17]

The Liturgy of John Chrysostom

The Liturgy of John Chrysostom features numerous prayers which
testify to the need for cooperation between God's grace and

---

15 There are also approved Eucharistic rites which are neither Eastern nor contained in the Roman Missals, such as the Dominican rite, the Ambrosian rite,
  the Ordinariate, etc.
16 Pope John Paul II, *Ut Unum Sint* (1995), §54.
17 On the history of these liturgies and the actual texts of the Anaphoras, see Ste-
  fanos Alexopoulos and Maxwell E. Johnson, *Introduction to Eastern Liturgies*
  (Liturgical Press Academic, 2022), xxx–xxxiv, 63–64 and 86–92, respectively.

human choices. Before reading a biblical epistle, the priest prays the "Trisagion":

> From nothingness you brought all things into being. You created man in your own image and likeness and adorned him with all your graces. You give wisdom and understanding to all who ask. You do not turn your face from the sinner but offer repentance as a way for salvation. You have made us, your humble and undeserving servants, worthy to stand before the glory of your holy altar at this very time, and bring you due worship and praise… Forgive us all our offenses, voluntary and involuntary. Sanctify our souls and bodies, and grant that we, in holiness, may serve you all the days of our lives.[18]

This prayer shows that God creates each person, showers them with grace, and gives them the opportunity to serve him in their lives and at the liturgical altar. God offers us the grace of forgiveness after we sin, but in order to be forgiven we must repent of our sins and resolve to serve him in holiness. He sanctifies us with his grace to empower our efforts to follow him. Similar themes are shown in a prayer just before the Gospel is read: "Make the pure light of your divine knowledge shine in our hearts, O loving Master. Open the eyes of our minds that we may understand the message of your Gospel. Instill in us the fear of your blessed commandments that we may subdue all carnal desires and follow a spiritual way of life, thinking and doing all that pleases you."[19] God's grace is primary yet human cooperation is necessary: God enables us to know him and empowers us to resist our sinful desires and keep his commandments; yet we must freely choose to do so.

The prayers which precede the Anaphora acknowledge the priestly and sacrificial nature of the Eucharistic liturgy. Christ is the "high

---

18 See "The Divine Liturgy of Saint John Chrysostom," page 5. I cite the English version approved by the 1987 Synod of the Hierarchy of the Ukrainian Catholic Church and available online: www.saintstephencalgary.ca/uploads/8/1/6/5/81651318/sunday_divine_liturgy_-_english.pdf. I henceforth cite this as "LJC" ("Liturgy of John Chrysostom") along with the page number.

19 LJC, 6.

priest" who "handed down to us the priestly ministry of this liturgical and unbloody sacrifice."[20] The sacramental priest petitions
God: "by the power of your Holy Spirit enable me, who am clothed
with the grace of the priesthood, to stand before this, your holy table, and offer the sacrifice of your holy and most pure body and
precious blood." He begs not be rejected, but rather that God will
"allow these gifts to be offered to you by me, your sinful and unworthy servant. For it is you who offer and you who are offered; it
is you who receive and you who are given, O Christ our God." The
ordained priest adds nothing to the sacrifice of Christ: Christ is the
one who offers, and the one who is offered. The sacramental priest
simply prays that he, and the prayers of the liturgical assembly, will
be offered and accepted with Christ's offering: "Accept also the petitions of us sinners and bring them to our holy altar. Enable us to
offer you gifts and spiritual sacrifices for our sins and for the sins of
ignorance of the people."[21] The priest and assembly pray that their
participation in Christ's sacrificial offering will result in the outpouring of grace upon them: "Make us worthy to find favour with you
so that our sacrifice may be acceptable to you and so that the good
Spirit of your grace may rest upon us, upon these gifts present before us, and upon all your people."

The "Anaphora" is the portion of the Byzantine liturgy which par-
allels the Eucharistic Prayers of the Roman rite. In the Anaphora of
the liturgy of John Chrysostom, the priest recounts Christ's words of
institution at the Last Supper and then says, "We offer to you, yours
of your own, on behalf of all and for all."[22] The Mass is the return to
God of the fruits of the earth, bread and wine, the natural gifts which
he gives to his children. But in his abounding mercy, God enhances
even these gifts, as shown in the "Epiclesis":

> We offer to you this rational and unbloody worship: and we ask,
> we pray and we entreat you: send down your Holy Spirit upon
> us and upon these gifts here present, and make this bread the

20 For this and the following two quotations, see LJC, 9.
21 For this and the following quotation, see LJC, 11.
22 For this and the following block quotation, see LJC, 14.

precious body of your Christ, and that which is in this chalice the precious blood of your Christ, changing them by your Holy Spirit, so that they may be for the communicants: sobriety of soul, forgiveness of sins, fellowship of your Holy Spirit, fulfilment of the kingdom of heaven, confidence before you and not for judgment or condemnation.

Through the power of the Holy Spirit at work in the words of Institution, God transforms the natural gifts of bread and wine into the body and blood of Christ. Then, those who consume Christ's flesh and blood in sacramental Communion are transformed: they are further divinized by the Holy Spirit, forgiven and empowered, so that they may live in the kingdom and pass the judgment of God. With the Eucharist now upon the altar, the priest prays: "we offer you this rational and unbloody worship for those who have gone to their rest in faith" and "for the whole world."[23] This indicates that the Eucharist is beneficial not only to those who receive holy communion, but also to those who cannot consume the sacrament. It is a true sacrifice which is offered for the dead and for every person. Hence, the priest exhorts the people to pray regarding the consecrated gifts: "That our loving God, who has received them as a spiritual fragrance upon his holy, heavenly and mystical altar, may send down on us in return his divine grace and the gift of the Holy spirit."[24] The Eucharistic Christ is a sacrificial gift given to God upon his altar in heaven, and in response to this sweet smelling offering God sends down the gift of the Holy Spirit upon those who participate in this offering and upon those for whom they pray.

The prayers which precede reception of the Eucharist emphasize the need to receive the Sacrament worthily as well as the divinizing effects of sacramental Communion. The priest prays for a worthy and life-giving reception of the Eucharist: "make us worthy to partake with a pure conscience of your awesome and heavenly mysteries at this sacred and spiritual table: for the forgiveness of sins, for the pardon of offenses, for the fellowship of the Holy Spirit, for the

23 LJC, 14 and 15, respectively.
24 For this and the following quotation, see LJC, 16.

inheritance of the kingdom of heaven, for confidence before you, and not for judgment or condemnation." The entire assembly then prays audibly *to* the Eucharist:

> I believe, O Lord, and confess that you are truly Christ, the son of the living God, who came into the world to save sinners, of whom I am first. Accept me this day, O Son of God, as a partaker of your mystical supper. I will not tell your mystery to your enemies, nor will I give you a kiss as did Judas, but like the thief, I confess to you: Remember me, O Lord, when you come into your kingdom. Remember me, O master, when you come into your kingdom. Remember me, O Holy One, when you come into your kingdom. May the partaking of your Holy Mysteries, O Lord, be unto me not for judgment or condemnation, but for the healing of soul and body. God, be merciful to me, a sinner. God, cleanse me of my sins and have mercy on me. I have sinned without number, forgive me, O Lord.[25]

This prayer emphasizes the true presence of Christ in the Eucharist, the need to receive the Eucharistic Lord with faith and repentance, and the divinizing power of the Eucharist: it heals the sinner in soul and body. Following reception of the sacrament, the choir prays: "you made us worthy to partake of your holy, divine, immortal and life-giving Mysteries. Preserve us in your holiness that we may meditate all the day upon your justice." The deacon then prays, "Having received the divine, holy, immaculate, immortal, heavenly, and life-giving, awesome mysteries of Christ, let us rightly give thanks to the Lord." The people respond: "Lord, have mercy. Help and save, have mercy and protect us, O God, by your grace." The Eucharist is a divine and divinizing mystery. We receive the Eucharist with thanksgiving and we beg to receive God's saving grace by doing so.

The Liturgy of Basil the Great

The Anaphora of the liturgy of Basil the Great begins with a prayer that highlights the divinizing work of the Holy Spirit. Before recounting

---

25 For this and all ensuing quotations in this paragraph, see LJC, 19–20.

Christ's words of institution from the Last Supper, the priest affirms how through Christ "the Holy Spirit was made manifest, the Spirit of truth, the grace of sonship, the pledge of the inheritance to come, the first fruit of the eternal good things, the life-giving power, the source of sanctification."[26] These descriptions of the Holy Spirit show how he is given to sinners to bring about a real change within them, and not merely to impute a new legal status to them. The priest continues, "Through him every rational and intelligent creature is empowered, worshipping you."[27] The Holy Spirit which Christ gives transforms sinners: he sanctifies them, gives them life, and empowers them to worship the true God.

The Anaphora includes an extended "Remembrance" prayer which recounts the saving work of the eternal Word and highlights central elements of Catholic soteriology. This prayer is worth quoting at length:

> For You fashioned a man by taking dust from the earth, and honoured him, O God, with your own image. You placed him in the Paradise of delight and promised him immortal life and the enjoyment of eternal good things if he kept your commandments. But when he disobeyed you, the true God, who had created him, and when he had been led astray by the deception of the serpent, and been slain by his own transgressions, you banished him from Paradise into this world by your just judgment, O God, and returned him to the earth, from which he had been taken.[28]

Humans are God's image and, if they had kept God's commandments, would have remained in a state of paradise and lived forever with God. But through disobedience they incurred physical death and were banished from God's intimate presence in Eden. Yet God did not abandon them:

26 "The Divine Liturgy of St Basil the Great," page 12. All references are to the English version available online: www.ukrcatholic.org/fileadmin/user_upload/PDFs/Our_Faith/The_Divine_Liturgy_of_St_Basil.pdf. I henceforth cite this as "LBG" ("Liturgy of Basil the Great") along with the page number.

27 LBG, 12.   28 LBG, 12–13.

In your Christ, you established for him the salvation which comes through rebirth. For you did not utterly turn away from your creature, O Good One, nor did you forget the work of your hands, but you visited us in diverse ways through your compassionate mercy.... And when the fullness of time had come, you spoke to us through your Son, through whom you had also made the ages. He is the brightness of your glory and the express imprint of your substance. He bears all things by the word of his power.[29]

In mercy, God revealed himself to sinners through the law, the prophets, miracles and angels. Finally, he spoke to us through his divine, eternal Word, the Creator of all things who came to give us new birth precisely by becoming one with us:

He did not consider equality with you, God and Father, as something to be grasped; and though he is God before the ages, he appeared on earth and lived among mortals. Taking flesh of a holy Virgin, he emptied himself, taking the form of a servant, being made in the likeness of our lowly body, *so that he might make us in the likeness of the image of his glory*. For as sin had entered the world through a man, and through sin death, your only-begotten Son—who is in your bosom, God and Father, being born of a woman, the holy Mother of God and Ever-Virgin Mary, being born under the law—*was well-pleased to condemn sin in his flesh*, so that all who had died in Adam might be given life in your Christ himself.[30]

The sin of Adam causes all of humanity to be enslaved to sin and death. God becomes human in order to transform us into the image of the Incarnate Son. The Son, as man, conquers sin by living as a servant of God. In doing so he becomes the new Adam and the source of victory over sin and death for all of humanity. Consequently:

Having lived in this world, giving us saving commandments, and turning us from the error of idols, he brought us to the

---

29 LBG, 13.   30 LBG, 13, emphasis added.

knowledge of you, the true God and Father, and acquired us for himself as a people all his own, a royal priesthood, a holy nation.

Christ saves us from intellectual error and idolatry by teaching us his commandments and the truth about God. He brings us to knowledge and faith in the true God and so makes us God's people. The "Remembrance" concludes:

> When he had cleansed us by water and sanctified us by the Holy Spirit, he gave himself as an exchange to death, by which we had been held captive, sold under sin. And when he had descended through the Cross into Hades, so that he might fill all things with himself, he loosed the pangs of death. And rising on the third day and making a way for all flesh to the resurrection of the dead—for it was not possible for the Prince of life to be mastered by corruption—*he became the first fruit* of those that sleep, the first-born of the dead, so that he might have pre-eminence in all things. And he ascended into heaven and took his seat at the right hand of your majesty on high; and he will come again to reward each according to their works.[31]

By his death, descent to the dead, and resurrection from the dead Christ conquered death itself and opened up the possibility of the resurrection for all. He became the "first fruit," the first sacrificial gift which humanity offers to God from the fruit of the land which God himself provides. As all followed in Adam's sin and death, so now through the gift of the Holy Spirit and through the practice of good works we all can follow in Christ's victory over sin and death: we can be offered with him and in him to the Father as a sacrificial gift.

The ensuing prayers in the Anaphora of Basil testify to the sacrificial nature and divinizing power of the Eucharist. In the "Anamnesis," the priest presents the bread and wine to the Father as gifts on behalf of the people: "We offer to you, yours of your own, on behalf of all and for all."[32] After calling upon the Holy Spirit to transform the bread and wine into the body and blood of Christ, the priest prays: "unite all of us, who share in this one bread and cup,

---

31 LBG, 13–14, emphasis added.   32 LBG, 14.

with one another into the communion of the one Holy Spirit, and let none of us partake of the holy body and blood of your Christ unto judgment or condemnation." The Eucharist unites those who receive it worthily in the power of the Holy Spirit. The priest then prays for God's divinizing grace to be poured out in response to the Eucharistic sacrifice:

> Remember, O Lord, those who have brought these gifts, and those for whom, through whom, and on behalf of whom they have brought them. Remember, O Lord, those who bring offerings and do good work in your holy Churches, and who remember the poor. Reward them with your riches and heavenly gifts of grace; for earthly things grant them heavenly ones; for temporal ones, eternal, for corruptible, incorruptible.[33]

The Eucharist is not beneficial only to those who receive it. As a sacrificial gift which is offered to the Father, it is also beneficial to all those who have participated in its offering and for whom it is offered. Both the offering and the consumption of the sacrificial victim contributes to our salvation:

> O God who has received these gifts, cleanse us of every pollution both of flesh and spirit, and teach us to attain perfect holiness through reverence for You: that with the pure witness of our conscience, receiving a portion of your blessed gift, we may be united to the holy Body and Blood of your Christ; and that, receiving them worthily, we may have Christ dwelling in our hearts and may become a temple of your Holy Spirit. Yes, O God! And make none of us guilty of these tremendous and heavenly mysteries, nor let us be wounded in spirit or body from an unworthy participation in them, but grant that until our last breath we may receive worthily our share of your blessed gifts for a viaticum of eternal life, for an acceptable defense at the dread judgment-seat of your Christ; that together with all your saints who have pleased You since time began, we

---

33 LBG, 16.

may become partakers of the eternal blessing you have promised to those who love You, O Lord![34]

The Eucharist is a gift which God enables us to offer to him and
to share in. We join God in the sacrificial feast at his altar. When we
unite ourselves to the sacrificial offering and worthily partake in it,
Christ strengthens our union with him and abides in us with the Holy
Spirit. He empowers us to become like him and live like him, and so
to pass our judgment and receive eternal life: "Bless those who have
bowed their heads to You; sanctify them, strengthen them, confirm
them, keep them from every evil work, incline them towards every
good work, and make them worthy to partake without condemnation
of these your spotless and life-giving mysteries, for the forgiveness of
sins and the fellowship of the Holy Spirit."[35] Christ is at work "sanctifying those who partake" of him in the Sacrament.[36] As the faithful
open their mouths to receive the Eucharist from the priest, the priest
prays audibly in their place: "The precious and most holy Body and
Blood of our Lord and God and Savior Jesus Christ is given to me,
for the remission of my sins, and unto life everlasting."[37]

CONCLUSION AND SYNTHESIS

What does Jesus save us from and *how does he do so?* In this chapter
we have explored the way in which Catholic Eucharistic liturgies
provide answers to these questions. We have focused upon the Roman rite liturgies of the Traditional Latin Mass and the contemporary Mass of Pope Paul VI as well as the Byzantine divine liturgies of
John Chrysostom and Basil the Great. We can now synthesize the
soteriological concepts that are expressed in the numerous prayers
and actions of those liturgies. First, humans are fallen and in need
of salvation. Adam's sin led to his own death and banishment from
God's presence in Eden as well as to the sin and death of his descendants. All are sinners who are destined to die. Second, God does not
abandon us to sin and death but rather seeks our salvation through

34 LBG, 19.   35 LBG, 20.
36 LBG, 21.   37 LBG, 22.

the giving of the law and prophets and, ultimately, through the Incarnation of the eternal Word.

Third, the Incarnate Lord saves us in a variety of ways. Through his example, teaching and miracles he leads us out of idolatry and to the worship of the true God. By his obedience unto death he offers God the supreme sacrifice of love and so conquers the power of sin and the devil. His resurrection from the dead conquers death and hell and his Ascension into heaven opens access to eternal life. The incarnate Lord's work culminates in the gift of the Holy Spirit, who grants us a share in Christ's life and thus the capacity to participate in his victory over sin, death and hell and his entrance into eternal life. In all of these ways, the Son of God became man in order to bring about our rebirth in grace as sons of God. Fourth, each and every human person will be judged on their works by Christ and therefore they must freely choose to receive the gift of the Holy Spirit and cooperate with his gifts of grace. We receive the Spirit, are forgiven of our sins, and conform our lives to Christ through repentance and faith in what Christ has revealed; by obedience to Christ's commands and the practice of good works; and especially through prayer and participation in the liturgy of the Eucharist.

Fifth and finally, the liturgy of the Eucharist itself is a means of saving and divinizing contact with the Incarnate being and work of Christ. The liturgy is a Christocentric, sacrificial and eschatological act of worship. Through and with the ordained priest, the baptized faithful look to God in his sanctuary and pray to the holy Trinity in the name of Christ. They also repeatedly worship Christ himself as eternal Word, Creator, and giver of grace, forgiveness and eternal life. Through the ministry of the ordained priest, the assembly approaches God's altar and offers him the oblations of bread and wine, products of their human work. Yet their very capacity to offer these oblations is itself a result of God's prior gift of life and land to humanity. The presentation of bread and wine upon God's altar, therefore, is an acknowledgment of God's good gift of creation. Yet the ritual oblation does not end there, for the assembly prays that God will accept the gifts and send his Holy Spirit upon them in order to transform them into the supernatural and divine gift of Christ's flesh and blood, soul and divinity. This miraculous conversion occurs in the consecration in the Eucharistic Prayers (Roman rite) and Anaphora (Byzantine), both of which testify to the true presence and sacrificial nature of the Eucharist.

Once the body and blood of Christ are on the altar, the priest and people "offer" the Eucharist to God for the salvation of themselves and for all sinners, living and dead. They pray that, as a result of the offering of the Eucharist, God will hear their prayers and pour forth his saving and life-giving grace upon them in this life, save them from eternal damnation, and bring them to eternal life. Yet the priest and people's "offering" of the Eucharist does not suggest that Christ needs to be offered by them or that there is anything lacking in his self-sacrifice which he offered to the Father in his Paschal Mystery. Rather, the "offering" of the liturgical assembly is itself a merciful gift from Christ: he has enabled them, through the sacramental hands of the priest, to associate themselves with his own historical and eternal gift of self in love and worship to the Father on their behalf. Christ offers himself to the Father on the cross and continues to do so in heaven, regardless of what we do; but he allows us to unite ourselves to and cooperate with his offering through our gifts of bread and wine, our prayers, our sacramental consecration, and above all through our reception of holy Communion.

We are offered to the Father through, with and in Christ above all by worthily receiving the Eucharist in sacramental Communion. When we receive Christ in this way, so long as we do not receive him with the intent to betray him as Judas did, then we are healed, nourished, and strengthened with Christ's very being and with the Holy Spirit: we are divinized, saved from our sinful inclinations, and empowered to obey Christ's commandments. We are given the grace needed to abide in Christ, to pass our eschatological judgment before him, and consequently to live with Christ forever. The Incarnate and life-giving presence of Christ to us in the Eucharist is summarized in the reading of John 1:1–14 (the "Last Gospel") at the conclusion of the Traditional Latin Mass: the eternal Word has been made flesh in our presence and we have seen his glory, the glory of the only-begotten Son of the Father; and the sacrificial offering and sacramental reception of this Son, the life and light of the world, has given us new birth as sons of God. We are now living sacrifices which are offered as gifts to the Father upon his altar in his sanctuary of heaven: through, with, and in Christ, we now enjoy the sanctifying presence of the divine glory.

~

COMPREHENSION QUESTIONS

1. Why is the liturgy an important source of soteriology?
2. What is *ad orientem* worship and what does it symbolize?
3. How does the direction, movements and structure of the TLM manifest the theocentric and sacrificial nature of the liturgy?
4. How is the penitential rite of the TLM a microcosm of the Christian life?
5. How do the prayers and readings of the Mass of the Catechumens (Preparation and Instruction) testify to the divinity and saving power of Christ?
6. What is the Offertory and what does it indicate about our relationship to Christ's sacrifice?
7. What are the words of Consecration and what is their biblical source?
8. In what sense does the ordained priest and liturgical assembly "offer" the Eucharist to the Father?
9. What blessings does the liturgical assembly pray for in response to their "offering" and its "acceptance" by God?
10. In the Roman Canon, what three Old Testament figures and sacrifices are mentioned in comparison to the sacrifice of Christ?
11. How does the Roman canon depict the Eucharist like a whole burnt offering and a peace offering?
12. How do the prayers of the Communion rite (TLM and Mass of Paul VI) testify to the nature and saving effects of holy Communion?
13. What does the "Last Gospel" (Jn. 1:1–14) indicate about the being and saving power of Christ?

14. What is symbolized by the presentation and preparation of the gifts in the Mass of Paul VI?
15. What do the priest and assembly pray for in the presentation and preparation of the gifts?
16. What is the "Mystery of Faith" which follows the consecration?
17. What are the three soteriological points in Eucharistic Prayer II?
18. How does Eucharistic Prayer III interpret Malachi 1:11?
19. According to Eucharistic Prayer III, what is "pleasing" (*placari*) to God and how do we become "one body, one spirit" in Christ and "an eternal gift" to God?
20. What are the central events of salvation history in the Preface of Eucharistic Prayer IV?
21. According to Eucharistic Prayer IV, how do we become a "living victim?"
22. How do the prayers of the Liturgy of John Chrysostom (LJC) testify to the need for cooperation between God's grace and human freedom?
23. How do the prayers preceding the Anaphora of LJC indicate the priestly and sacrificial nature of the liturgy of the Eucharist?
24. How does the Anaphora of LJC show that the Eucharist is a salvific sacrifice both as offered and as consumed?
25. What are the major features of the prayer which the entire assembly prays audibly prior to the reception of the Eucharist in the LJC?
26. What does the beginning of the Anaphora of the liturgy of Basil the Great (LBG) indicate about the impact of the Holy Spirit upon sinners?
27. What are the major features of salvation history as recounted in the "Remembrance" within the Anaphora of LBG?
28. What are the major features of the "Anamnesis" within the Anaphora of LBG?

CONCLUSION

A SYNTHESIS OF CATHOLIC SOTERIOLOGY

THIS book has explicated and analyzed the content of Catholic soteriology. We have done so through a close and analytic reading of the actual texts of Scripture and Tradition: the Old and New Testaments, the doctrinal statements of the Council of Trent and popes, and the texts of Roman and Byzantine Eucharistic liturgies. In this conclusion, we will synthesize the major speculative and practical soteriological fruits of our preceding textual analysis. We do so by offering a response to the two fundamental questions which we identified at the outset of this book and which we have consistently returned to: first, *what* does God save us from? Second, *how* does God save us?

WHAT DOES GOD SAVE US FROM?

In this section we examine the nature of, and relationship between, the enemies of the human race: sin, hell, the devil, and death. We also consider, in response to influential soteriological works such as Gustaf Aulén's *Christus Victor*, to what degree if any we can say that Christ saves us from God's "law" and "wrath."[1]

Sin and Hell

Sin is the *fundamental enemy* which plagues humanity. But what exactly is sin? Catholic soteriology makes a distinction between "actual sin" and "Original Sin." Actual sin refers to a deliberate human choice to do that which the agent knows, or ought to know, is evil. An "evil" is that which is contrary to God's will and to the objective goods to which we are ordered by our God-given nature. Through

---

1 Gustaf Aulén, *Christus Victor: An Historical Study of the Three Main Types of the Idea of the Atonement*, trans. A.G. Herbert (Wipf and Stock, 2003), 67–69 (on the law), 111, 114–16, and 118 (on wrath).

actual sin we set our will against God's will: it is like when a passenger jumps off of a moving train. They may do so because they reject the ultimate destination of the train or merely the route which is being used to get there. But either way, the passenger's will is no longer in harmony with the will of the train: they have gone their separate ways. The first ever actual sins were committed by the father and mother of the human race in Eden. Tempted by the devil, they disobeyed God's command to abstain from the tree of the knowledge of good and evil. The essence of their sin, and the root cause of all subsequent actual sin, is a lack of trust in the goodness of God. We reject God's commandment in a particular instance because we do not think that following that commandment in that instance will make us happier. And this means that God does not want what is best for us, or he would not have given us that commandment at all. Therefore, God is not to be trusted. This line of thinking leads to rebellion which may be total (we reject everything God commands) or selective (we pick and choose which commandments to obey), predetermined (we *plan* on disobeying God) or impulsive (we disobey God in a moment of passion or weakness). But even a selective and impulsive rebellion is still a refusal to obey God which stems from a lack of trust in God's goodness.

The actual sins of the first human couple resulted in the fallen *condition* known as "Original Sin." This condition was first experienced by Adam and Eve and subsequently passed on by them to all of their descendants (excluding Mary and Jesus). These descendants possess this condition from the moment of their conception. The condition consists principally in the absence of sanctifying grace and the loss of the grace of original justice. The absence of sanctifying grace means that our souls lack the supernatural life of God and so are incapable of entering into the Beatific Vision. And whereas Adam and Eve began to exist in a state of supernatural intimacy with God, we begin to exist in a merely natural state. And the loss of original justice renders us vulnerable to harm, pain, and bodily death. Whereas Adam and Eve were impassible and immortal because they had access to the tree of life. Human beings remain in God's image and likeness, and their nature remains inherently good, even following the fall.

But we now develop and must live with a nature that is wounded in its physical, intellectual, and moral capacities: we experience bodily diseases and deformities; mental illness and intellectual difficulty in pursuit of the truth; and an inclination of the heart and will to do what is evil (concupiscence). By our natural powers alone, we cannot easily come to know God's existence or will; nor can we completely and consistently abstain from grave sin. The human person in the state of original sin is like a space shuttle that is leaking fuel and which has suffered damage to two of its three engines: the shuttle may be able to takeoff and it may fly relatively farther than most planes, but it will not breach the atmosphere or reach the moon as it was designed to do.

Original sin and actual sin result in *vice*. Concupiscence inclines us to commit actual sin, and repeated actual sins generate vice. A vice is the opposite of a virtue: it is a bad moral habit, a stable disposition of the will which inclines the person to consistently desire and choose even grave evils with delight and without hesitation or remorse. Vice enslaves a person to sin by instilling in them deeply entrenched, disordered passions and attractions. Timeless and universal examples of vice include bad habits like pride, cowardice, anger, lust, sloth, gluttony, and lying. In contemporary American culture, many people seem bound by vice to sins such as pornography, fornication, contraceptives and abortifacients; gluttonous consumption and prideful production of social media and digital entertainment; and even violent means of acquiring wealth such as in the abortion, human trafficking, euthanasia, and transgender industries. Such vices result in the habitual commission of grave actual sins which destroy friendships, families, communities, and human life itself.

Such sins lead to hell, and hell is best understood as the state of eternal vice. It is first and foremost the spiritual state of perpetual refusal to repent of one's sins. The souls in hell delight in their sins more than anything, and the idea of letting go of sin is horrific to them. They committed mortal sin on earth and they refused to repent and receive God's forgiveness prior to their death. Hence, they get to cling to their mortal sin and delight in it forever. Hell is like a person who insists upon entering an airport and boarding a flight to Hawaii with their unleashed, feral Rottweiler. They will not be allowed through security or onto the plane if they insist upon bringing the untethered, mad dog. And so too you cannot enter the eternal presence of God and the saints in heaven if you insist upon bringing your mortal sins with you. There is no place for an unrestrained and violent dog in an airport or on a plane, and there is no place for sin before the direct and unmediated presence of God's glory. Airline security may walk you and the dog outside and delay the flight for hours as they attempt to persuade the dog lover to send the beast away where it cannot harm anyone. So too, God offers sinners countless opportunities in this life to repent and receive his forgiveness. But eventually the plane has to take off, and so eventually the person has to decide whether they want to be in Hawaii or continue to enjoy the company of the roaming, feral Rottweiler. Hell is choosing to miss the flight and remain locked outside of the airport with the nasty dog.

Understanding sin and hell as the foundational and ultimate enemies of the human race enables us to consider the issue of "the law." The modern notion of *sola fide*, popularized by Martin Luther, views the law as an enemy which Christ saved us from by eliminating any connection between moral duties and eternal life. On this view, the only duty which we *must* fulfill in order to be justified and to receive eternal life is to confess Jesus as "Lord." But such a view is philosophically problematic and difficult to reconcile with Scripture. Christ came to save us from sin. Sin is the refusal to obey God's will and fulfill our moral duties as specified by God's law. If God wants to save us from sin, then he must not save us from law; rather, he must give us his laws and help us to follow them. For to observe the law out of love is to *ipso facto* be saved from sin. It thus seems counterproductive to say that the God who seeks to save us from sin also saves us from his own laws. And even merely saying that we do not *need* to follow the law in this life in order to receive eternal life is problematic. For the very essence of eternal life necessitates that we be free of all sin, and this means that eternal life requires us to completely and perpetually will what God wills as specified in his laws. But how can we definitively embrace God's will in eternity if we have not embraced it in this life, even if only through an act of sincere repentance made just before death? Even if we bracket these philosophical difficulties, the idea that law is an enemy and that *sola fide* is the only duty necessary for salvation still faces formidable opposition from the texts of Scripture. For both the Old and New Testaments clearly and repeatedly depict God instituting laws and connecting their observance, or lack thereof, to our eternal reward or punishment. Christ gave numerous ritual and moral commandments and said that we must observe those commandments if we wish to receive eternal life. And he insisted that our response to his commandments, including his demanding moral laws, would be the criteria by which he judged our eternal destination. Hence, we should think of God's law exclusively as a gift, and never as an enemy.

The Devil

The devil and his demons are fallen angels who can harm the human body and tempt the soul to sin. The devil successfully tempted Adam and Eve to sin and his conflict with Christ and his disciples is depicted regularly in the New Testament: Christ was tempted by the devil in the wilderness; Judas was inspired by the devil to betray Christ; Christ drove demons out of possessed people; and Christ came to destroy the works of the devil.[2] Only God knows how many temptations to sin (thoughts, feelings, sights, sounds, movements, etc.) occur as a result of the devil's activity. And only God knows how many people's bodies are oppressed or possessed by the devil. But that these things can and do occur is a given of divine revelation. Hence, the performance of the rite of exorcism remains a real, albeit typically private, ministry within the Catholic Church. And prayer for strength against the presence and power of the devil, such as the prayer to Michael the Archangel, remains central to Catholic spirituality. And while the devil can harm our bodies, he is a greater threat to our souls. For by tempting us to sin he tempts us to sever ourselves from the life of grace and so to approach the brink of eternal damnation. Yet the demons cannot compel our wills; the freedom to choose good or evil, and the culpability which results, remains our own. So while

---

2 Mt. 4, Lk. 22, and 1 Jn. 3:8, respectively.

we must be on guard against the devil's temptations, we do this first and foremost by being on guard against any and all temptations to sin; the question of where the temptations come from—the demons, the world, our own inclinations, or some combination of the above— is secondary. We conquer the devil when we conquer sin.

Death and Punishment

Death is a punishment of sin. If Adam and Eve had not sinned then they would not have died and neither would their descendants so long as they remained sinless. But following their sin, God informed Adam and Eve that they would one day return to the dust from whence they came: he banished them from Eden and hence from access to the tree of life, the source of their impassibility and immortality. Death is thus a punishment which God gives to the human race. A "punishment" (or, the "wrath of God") refers to some kind of burden or loss which God wills upon a sinner in response to their sin. God may *actively* or *permissively* will to punish us. He actively willed that *if* Adam and Eve sinned, *then* they would become passible and mortal and pass on such a fallen nature to their descendants.[3] God then permits or actively wills any particular instance of suffering or death which follows in human history. Why does God punish sinners? The answer is out of love, as a means to save us from sin. When a parent punishes their misbehaving child, they do so not to vent their anger or take revenge, but rather to prevent the child from causing further harm and to correct their errant behavior. The punishment serves these ends by curbing the child's freedom, making them hesitant to sin again, and reminding them of their dependence upon their parents for the things which they enjoy. The punishment of passibility and mortality God imposes upon humanity, as well as specific instances of pain or death, can serve similar purposes: mortality reminds us

---

3 The Church leaves open the question of whether death is merely the result of God's withdrawal of the grace of original justice (i.e., mortality is integral to human nature and immortality is merely the result of a supernatural gift from God) or whether it is actively imposed upon sinners by God (i.e., human nature is naturally immortal even apart from the grace of original justice, but God afflicts the fallen human person with mortality).

of our dependence upon God and of the fragility of this life; pain and death prevents heinous sinners from carrying out as much evil as they may desire; and suffering provides occasions for people to serve those in need and to practice heroic virtue.

Does God punish the damned in hell? God merely permits hell insofar as it is the definitive spiritual state of impenitence and sin. He actively wills that we repent during our life on earth, receive his forgiveness, and cling to him eternally in heaven. But if we refuse to do so, then certain limits need to be imposed upon the freedom of the damned, even if only for the sake of the blessed in heaven. This is especially the case once the bodies of the damned rise. Surely the damned want, for instance, to be in the presence of the risen saints and to curse them, tempt them, and attack them; and surely God will not allow such a thing, as it would seem incompatible with the joy which constitutes the experience of the saint in heaven. No saint wants to listen to blasphemies all day anymore than a loving husband wants to hear insults hurled at his beloved wife. And the unrepentant priests of Molech cannot be allowed near the child saints in heaven whom they sent through fire in this life.[4] So the peace and order of the eternal city of God requires that God impose at least some form of penal restraint upon the damned. This punishment does not lead to their conversion, it merely limits their capacity to do evil, both for their own sake and for the sake of the blessed in heaven.

Freedom from punishment follows from freedom from sin. Hence, we need to be saved primarily from sin, and only secondarily and consequently from punishment. To reverse this order is akin to a patient who wants to be saved from the cure rather than from the disease. Catholic soteriology maintains that we will not be definitively free of the punishments of pain and death until we are definitely free of sin. Pain ceases when our purification and satisfaction for sin is completed in Purgatory. And death is conquered only after we enter the Beatific Vision, when our bodies rise from the grave on the last day. As the Hebrews in Egypt first had to offer right worship to the true God, and only then could be freed from physical slavery, so

4 See Lev. 20:1–5 and 2 Kgs 21:6, etc.

too God saves each person from their spiritual slavery (sin) before he saves them from their physical slavery (bodily corruption and death). And similarly, Christ had to first conquer sin through obedience unto death before he conquered death by his resurrection. And so the person who seeks to conquer death must first seek, with God's help, to conquer sin. And if the example and teaching of Christ are any indication, then the conquest of sin will necessarily involve the pain of the cross.

HOW DOES GOD SAVE US?

In the previous section we considered the nature of and relationship between sin, hell, the devil, death and punishment. We identified sin and hell as the foundational and ultimate enemies of the human race. In this section we consider *how* God saves us from these enemies. We begin with a fuller account of the distinction between the ends and means of salvation.

Salvation: Ends and Means

Salvation consists above all in eternal life, and therefore eternal life is the ultimate *end* of all of God's salvific activity on our behalf. Eternal life consists primarily of the Beatific Vision and secondarily of the communion of saints and the resurrection of the body. The Beatific Vision is the direct knowledge and love of God as he is in his divine essence, and this participation in the life of the Trinitarian communion of persons satisfies every longing of the human mind, heart and will. Eternal life is completely beyond the mere natural capacity of the human person and therefore can only be received as a gift of supernatural grace from God. Eternal life is given to all souls who die in the state of grace, meaning, they possess sanctifying grace and its theological virtues of faith, hope, and charity. Reception of sanctifying grace requires repentance from all sin and continual abiding in the state of grace requires avoidance of mortal sin. And even all venial sins must be repented of, and satisfied for, prior to entrance into the Beatific Vision and the communion of saints. For all sin is excluded from the eternal presence of God. Hence, deification or theosis is central to the concept of salvation: through reception and cooperation with the gift of grace, we enter into supernatural communion with God, participate in the life of the holy Trinity, and become like God. Deification begins in this world and culminates in eternal life.

How does God deliver us from sin and bring us into divinizing communion with himself? This is a question about the *means* which God employs to save us from sin and its consequences. First and foremost, God must *offer* us the gifts of deification and eternal life. For these gifts, by their very nature as supernatural grace, are not owed to us. And so we can ask about the particular ways in which God makes this offer to us. Second, we must *accept* God's offer and *cooperate* with its requirements. And so we can ask about what such acceptance and cooperation looks like. And third, acceptance and cooperation necessitates that we *trust* in the goodness of the offer and the offerer. For recall that at the root of every actual sin is a lack of trust in the goodness of God. And trust in the goodness of God is innate to deification and eternal life, since these supernatural gifts are none other than loving communion with God and participation in his own divine nature. We do not want to be a temple of God and become like God if we do not trust in his goodness. And we have not been freed from sin if we continue to doubt God's goodness. And so we can ask about what God does to persuade us of his goodness and of the goodness of eternal communion with him. In the ensuing sections we consider the various means by which God offers us communion with himself; how we accept and cooperate with that offer; and how God helps us to do so by fostering our trust in his goodness.

Moral and Ritual Sacrifices in the Old Testament

In the opening chapters of Genesis God blessed Adam and Eve with life in paradise and gave them one command, namely, to abstain from the fruit of the tree of the knowledge of good and evil. He warned them that disobedience to his command would result in death. This story shows that what God wills from human beings, first and foremost, is the *moral sacrifice* of *obedience*. This obedience would have involved a true death to self for Adam and Eve insofar as it necessitated resistance to the pleasures of mind, taste, and sight which the forbidden fruit offered. Obedience may have also resulted in the experience of physical harm and death, if we grant that the serpent was a violent figure. Adam and Eve failed to offer the sacrifice of obedience. Following their sin, God asked them if they ate the forbidden fruit. By doing so, God was giving them another opportunity to offer a moral sacrifice, namely, a sacrifice of *repentance:* they could admit their sin, ask for forgiveness, resolve to sin no more, and even offer to make some form of reparation for their sin. But rather than repent, Adam blames his disobedience on God and Eve; Eve blames her disobedience on the serpent. And so the man, the woman, and the serpent are cursed.

Despite the fall, sacrifice remains central to the relationship between God and humanity. In the *protoevangelium* of Genesis 3:15, God promises that the offspring of Eve will crush the head of the serpent's offspring, yet the serpent's offspring will strike the heel of Eve's offspring. This indicates that Eve will be victorious, but only through sacrifice. She will be wounded in battle, yet will conquer her enemy nonetheless. The implication is that the descendants of Eve can conquer the power of sin, but they must do so through the moral sacrifices of repentance and obedience. And in the fallen world, these moral sacrifices must be offered amidst the pains and toils of history and in the shadow of bodily death. The first ever animal sacrifice is depicted in Genesis 3:21, when God clothes Adam and Eve with animal skins. He does so in order to partially repair and limit the damage of sin: in their fallen state, the nakedness of Adam and Eve increases their shame, temptation, and vulnerability. The provision of clothes is an expression of God's mercy towards them, but this gift comes at a cost: the life of the animal.

The primordial sacrifices in Eden anticipate the numerous ritual and moral sacrifices which follow in Genesis. Abel offers the first fruits of his flock as a pleasing sacrifice to God, while Cain's sacrifice is found wanting; Cain's murderous jealousy follows, and Abel becomes the first victim of religious persecution. This story indicates that those who offer right worship to God will often be hated by those who do not. Noah alone among fallen humanity offers the moral sacrifice of obedience, and as a result he and his family are saved from the flood. Afterwards, Noah's animal sacrifices please God and result in God's covenant blessing upon Noah, his family, and the entire world. Melchiz'edek is the first priest in Scripture, and he is also the king of [Jeru-] Salem. He offers bread and wine to God in gratitude for Abraham's military victory and in petition for blessing upon Abraham. God later commands Abraham to offer his son Isaac in sacrifice upon the mountain of Moriah. God had previously given Isaac to Abraham and Sarah in a miraculous conception. God also promised to bless Abraham with numerous descendants through Isaac and to bless the entire world through Isaac's line. And so now God was testing Abraham's trust in the goodness and veracity of God. Abraham attempted to carryout the command, all the while trusting that God could raise Isaac from the dead and that God himself would provide the sacrifice. God rewards Abraham for his trust by halting the sacrifice, providing a ram in Isaac's place, and confirming his covenant blessing upon Abraham, Isaac, and the whole world through Isaac's line.

The salvific value of sacrifice is central to the narrative of Exodus. God comes to the aid of his enslaved Hebrew people in Egypt by asking Pharoah to give them three days to offer sacrifices to God in the wilderness. When Pharaoh refuses, God promises to punish the Egyptians and liberate his people from Egypt. Physical liberation is ultimately in the service of right worship. And in order to receive this physical liberation, the Hebrews must conduct the Passover ritual in obedience to God's command. This ritual was a public symbol of their rejection of Egyptian idols and of their commitment to the one God. In response to the Passover sacrifice, God spares the Hebrews from the plague of death and sets them free from Egypt. Their freedom is secured when they cross the red sea in obedience to God. At Sinai, God enters into a new covenant with his people, a familial relationship which involves both moral and ritual duties on man's part and blessings and promises bestowed by God. This covenant is symbolically sealed through animal sacrifices: the blood of bulls is sprinkled upon the people and upon God (the altar), and the people then dine with God upon the sacrificial meat atop God's holy mountain and in the presence of God's glory.

The establishment of enduring laws of ritual worship at Sinai perpetuates the presence of God and the salvific functions of sacrifice
to the Chosen People. In obedience to God's commands, the Isra-
elites build the ark of the covenant, the tabernacle, and its various
altars and liturgical items. This tabernacle is later replaced by the
temple of Solomon in Jerusalem. The Ark is the throne or footstool
of God, and the tabernacle/temple is his home. There God dwells
in glory and is present to his people as king and savior. He guides
them through the wilderness, gives them victory in Canaan, and establishes the kingdom of David in Jerusalem. All the while, the Levites are the divinely appointed priests who serve God in his temple
and mediate between God and the people. The fundamental task of
the Levites, and specifically the descendants of Aaron, is to offer oblations and sacrifices to God on behalf of the people. Sacrifices are
oblations in which the thing which is offered is killed; it is made a
victim. Bread is burnt upon an altar; wine is poured out; an animal
is killed, its blood is poured out, and its body burnt. These rituals are
fundamentally symbolic: they represent a gift of food to God upon
his table, and the burning of the victim represents God's consumption of the meal and/or the rising of the pleasing aroma to God in
heaven. Through observance of the laws regarding ritual sacrifices,
and through observance of God's moral laws summarized in the Ten
Commandments, the people remain pleasing to God and God remains present in glory to his people from the temple.

The manner, ends and symbolism of ritual sacrifice varied. In
terms of animal sacrifices, a holocaust was burnt entirely for God;
a peace offering was burnt only partially, with the priest and the offerer eating the remainder; a sin or guilt offering was burnt partially
and only the priest ate the remainder. Hence, the *manner* of sacrifice
or *what was done* to the victim always included killing and burning,
but it could also include consumption. The location of these sacrifices in the temple of Jerusalem, upon Mt Moriah, was a reminder of
Abraham's sacrifice of obedience. It was also a reminder of Eden, the
primordial temple of God's glory, where death entered the world due
to the failure of man to offer right sacrifice, and yet where God sacrificed the first animal for sinners and promised ultimate victory to

humanity through sacrifice. The ends for which these sacrifices were offered were thanksgiving, petition, communion, and atonement: we surrender our animals to God in grateful recognition that all of our blessings come from him; we offer our prized possessions as a sign of trust that God will answer our prayers and continue to provide for our needs; we share a meal with God as a member of his family; and we pour out blood upon the altar to symbolize the gift of our lives to God and the recognition that all life belongs to him. The value of these ritual sacrifices is bound up with the interior moral sacrifices from which they proceed and which they further cultivate. This is seen especially in atonement sacrifices: the sinner placed their hand upon the head of the animal and audibly confessed to the priest the sin or impurity for which they were offering the sacrifice; and for those who sought to atone for sins committed against their neighbors, they first had to pay recompense to their neighbor. And so the ritual sacrifices of atonement which were offered to God had to be accompanied by the moral sacrifices of confession and satisfaction. Hence, ritual sacrifices of atonement fostered and enacted essential elements of the moral sacrifice of repentance.

The saving function and close relationship between moral and ritual sacrifices is displayed throughout the history of the Chosen People. The priority of moral sacrifice over ritual sacrifice is emphasized in the stories of king Saul's disobedience (1 Sm. 13 and 15), in Isaiah's critique of ritual sacrifice and accompanying moral exhortation (Isa. 1:11–20), and in Psalm 51's call for contrition, confession and interior cleansing prior to the offering of animals. Various figures exemplify this proper relation between ritual and moral sacrifice. Job is obedient to God even amidst terrible social, physical, and material loss. He remains certain that one day he will rise from the dead and see God in the flesh with his own eyes. And he prays for the friends who errantly accused him of sin throughout his sufferings. Consequently, God rewards Job with two times the goods which he had lost. In Daniel 3 and 6, respectively, Shad'rach, Me'shach, Abed'nego and Daniel refuse to worship false gods even when threatened with death. They are cast into a raging furnace of fire and into a lions' den, and yet God saves each one of them as a reward for their obedience. God subsequently grants them positions of power in the kingdom of Babylon and punishes their enemies. Yet unconditional obedience does not always result in salvation from bodily death, and even the heroes from the book of Daniel eventually died. Moral sacrifice must ultimately be offered, as it was by Job, with the hope of bodily resurrection and eternal life. We see this on dramatic display in 2 Macc. 7 in the story of the seven martyred brothers and their martyred mother. They offer their obedience unto death as sacrifices in atonement for the sins of the nation. These themes converge and reach their zenith in Isaiah's Suffering Servant (Isa. 52:13–53:12), who is led like a lamb to the slaughter and who is misunderstood and rejected as a sinner who is being punished by God. In reality, the Servant suffers and goes to death freely as a sacrifice in atonement for the sins of the people. As a result, he is rewarded with life and offspring, and the people are cleansed and made righteous.

To summarize: in the Old Testament, God begins to lead his people away from sin and into communion with himself through the establishment and enactment of ritual and moral sacrifices. Through observance of God's ritual and moral commands, we *ipso facto* abstain from sin, at least on a material level. And these material actions in turn further foster the interior dispositions which they are meant to express. Those who observed God's commands and offered him pleasing moral and ritual sacrifices enjoyed the presence of his glory in the temple and had confidence to go before him on the day of judgment. Insofar as they truly received God's revelations with faith, sincerely repented of their sins, and responded to his commandments with trusting obedience, then they may have dwelled in the supernatural state of grace and really exercised the theological virtues of faith, hope, and charity.[5] Even so, their salvation was not complete, for when they died they did not receive eternal life. Despite the holiness of figures like the Maccabean martyrs, the ultimate end of salvation was not yet realized. That gift was not yet offered, and the holiness necessary to achieve it was not yet established.

5 See Aquinas, ST III, Q. 62, art. 6, ad 1–3.

The Incarnation and Public Ministry of Christ

Who is Jesus? The meaning of the name "Jesus" reflects Jesus' mission as our savior and also points towards his identity as God himself (Emmanuel—God with us). The titles "Christ/Messiah," "Son of God" and "Son of Man" identify Jesus as the royal descendant of David through whom God promised to deliver his chosen people from their pagan oppressors, bring the exiled tribes home, and establish a universal and permanent kingdom of God in the world. As "only-begotten Son of God," Jesus is the eternal Word and Son of the Father through whom all things were created and who, with the Father and the Holy Spirit, is God. The divine Son assumed a complete human nature, body and soul, in the womb of his biological mother Mary. Jesus is therefore one person who is both fully divine and fully human, capable of acting with both divine power and human power.

Why did God become human? How does Jesus' divine and human natures contribute to his saving work? As God, Jesus is the divine shepherd who will lead his wayward and oppressed sheep back to good pastures; he is the eschatological temple through which God dwells in glory with his people; he is the source from which the river of life flows; the giver of bread from heaven and the Spirit of God which raises the dead to life; the lawgiver whose commands illuminate the way; and the judge who eternally separates the sheep from the goats. Jesus' divinity makes him the object of our worship, the ultimate source of our life, and the basis of our hope. By assuming a human nature, the eternal Son manifests God's love for humanity, the sanctity of every human life, and the ultimate destiny of each person, namely, eternal communion with God. By assuming a human nature which was subject to growth, pain and death, the Son affirmed the goodness of human life at all stages of development and even amidst suffering and the shadow of death. The Son healed, elevated and perfected human nature in a unique and unparalleled way by uniting it to his own divine personhood and by living a life of perfect virtue. He gave us the supreme example of how to live righteously, including when doing so will lead to persecution, and even when that persecution is actualized. The humanity of the God-man is now the exemplar for all other men, such that all men must now be conformed to him.

How did Jesus establish the kingdom of God in the world? The kingdom consists of God's conquest of the powers of evil and his active reign in human affairs. This kingdom is present above all in Jesus himself: his human will is always perfectly united to his divine will, such that no amount of suffering, threats, human or demonic temptation is able to lead him to sin. Jesus himself, with his human will, conquers every power of sin. And through his example, teaching, and demonstrations of power he begins to share his conquest with us. By his example and teaching Jesus teaches us the truth about God and about life in the kingdom; he thus saves us from ignorance, error, and the idolatry and sin which result from them. Through his miraculous works such as walking on water, calming the wind and sea, and multiplying bread, Jesus provides compelling proof of his divinity and thus of the presence of God in the world and of his absolute power over all things. By miraculously healing the sick and raising the dead, Jesus demonstrates his power over death itself, his capacity to give new life, and the merciful goodness of God. And by driving out demons, Jesus conquers the forces of Satan and grants physical freedom to the oppressed. As God and man, Jesus himself conquers sin, error, death, and the devil; and as God and man, he draws us to share in his victory through faith in his teachings, imitation of his example, and above all through reception of the life-giving grace which he offers as the eternal Word and only-begotten Son. As man, Jesus is the pattern to which we must be conformed; as God, he gives us the grace which enables us to be conformed to that pattern.

The Paschal Mystery

What purpose did Jesus' Passion serve within his saving mission? Jesus knew that his enemies would attempt to put him to death and he insisted that he had the power to escape their hands. Yet he chose to endure the suffering and death which they inflicted upon him. He did so out of obedience to the Father and out of love for sinners. The Passion was a witness to the truth, for Jesus refused to recant his teaching, including his claims regarding his own divinity, even in the face of persecution and death. By doing so, he enables us to have confidence in the truth of his teaching and in his own goodness and trustworthiness. The Passion was also an example of obedience unto death and the supreme moment of Jesus' conquest over the powers of sin: he remained completely sinless, merciful, and loyal to the Father even as he was physically, socially, and interiorly tormented. He thus shows us that we can, with the help of God's grace, conquer temptation and do what is right even amidst the worst possible circumstances. And by sharing in our pain and death, Jesus shows us that God does not command anything which God himself has not done first: he told us to pick up our crosses and follow him, and to lay down our lives for our friends; Jesus does this first. Christ goes before us as our leader, and he gives us the grace to follow him.

The Passion was a sacrifice which fulfills the moral sacrifices of the Old Testament. In contrast to Adam and Eve, Jesus chose obedience to God even in the face of death. In doing so he imitated and surpassed the sacrifices of obedience offered by Noah, Abraham, Shad'rach, Me'shach, and Abed'nego, Daniel, Job and the Maccabean martyrs. Like Abel and the heroes of Daniel, Jesus was persecuted for exemplifying and teaching right worship. While the mother and her seven sons in Second Maccabees died to atone for the sins of the nation, Jesus offered his death in atonement for the sins of the entire world. In this way he fulfilled the prophecy of the Suffering Servant (Isa. 53). Like Abraham, Jesus gave back to God the precious gift of life which God had given to him, and he trusted that God would restore that gift to him. As Noah's obedience resulted in his preservation from death in the flood, so Jesus' obedience unto death resulted in his permanent resurrection from the dead and glorification in heaven. And while Noah's pleasing ritual sacrifices resulted in humanity's protection from all future worldwide floods, Jesus' pleasing self-sacrifice resulted in the opportunity for all of humanity to be protected from the abyss of hell. And as God promised to give Abraham numerous descendants and bless the whole world as a result of his obedience in the face of death, so now Christ's obedience unto death results in God's offer of eternal life and the resurrection of the body for the entire human family.

Why was Jesus' sacrifice pleasing to God, and so much so that it resulted in the offer of eternal life for all sinners? Jesus' Passion was not pleasing to God in itself, but rather was pleasing because Jesus chose to endure it out of obedience. And this obedience has value precisely because it was motivated by Jesus' love for the Father. Jesus did not obey out of fear or some other selfish motivation; rather, he did the Father's will specifically in order to please the Father as an end in itself, for the Father's own sake. Jesus obeyed with certain knowledge of the goodness and trustworthiness of the Father and his command. Jesus also obeyed out of love for sinners, because he knew that his endurance of the Passion was conducive towards their good. As the omniscient, eternal Word made flesh, Jesus' decision to love is absolutely free and undertaken with full knowledge of all that it will entail and result in. And as the divine, only-begotten Son of the Father, Jesus' human acts of love and his gift of self on the cross are so pleasing to the Father that they satisfy for every human sin and merit access to eternal life for the entire world. Christ recapitulates the human story: whereas Adam's sin was so grievous as to result in all of humanity's banishment from the tree of Life, Jesus' love is so pleasing that it results in God's offer of eternal paradise to all. Christ's loving obedience unto death is the supremely pleasing fragrance which rises up to God in heaven.

The Passion also fulfills the ritual sacrifices of the Old Testament. Jesus is like a holocaust insofar as he offered his entire self to God on the cross. As in all animal sacrifices, he handed over his flesh and blood as a gift to God. He poured out his blood, like the blood of atonement sacrifices, as an expression of the return of his life to God and in recognition that God is the Lord of life and the giver of all good things. As the Hebrews' destroyed the Paschal lamb in public rejection of Egyptian idols, so too Jesus publicly chose death over sin. And as the death of the lamb was the ransom payment which resulted in the Hebrews' protection from temporal death and liberation from slavery, so Jesus' death redeems humanity from spiritual slavery and eternal death. As the Hebrews ate the flesh of the paschal lamb and their homes were marked with his blood, so Christians receive Jesus' sacrificial flesh and blood in the Eucharist. Christ's blood, sprinkled upon us from the chalice of the altar, establishes sinners in a new and eternal covenant with God. Like the blood which is sprinkled upon the mercy seat on the Day of Atonement, Christ's sacrificial blood cleanses us from sin and impurity. As Moses and the elders ascended Mt Sinai with the flesh of the peace offerings and there dined with God in his presence, so now we ascend to heaven with the flesh of Christ, through which we have communion with God. As the Letter to the Hebrews makes clear, Christ is the high priest and sacrifice who has entered beyond the veil of the sanctuary of heaven with his own flesh and blood. There he abides eternally as a pleasing gift to God, and those who share in his flesh and blood abide there too and are offered with him.

Christ's Paschal Mystery completes his actualization of the Kingdom of God. Christ conquered the power of sin and error by his loving obedience and witness unto death. Consequently, God exalted him by raising him from the dead and glorifying him at his right hand in heaven. In this way Christ conquered death and hell, and he subjected the demons and all of his creation under his feet. Christ reigns over all things as true God and true man at the right hand of the Father. Sin, death, the devil, and hell have no power over him. Christ is the stone through which God shatters the forces of evil in the world; he is the Son of Man through whom God destroys the beasts of sin and idolatry. But how exactly does Christ's conquest and reign become our conquest and reign? This question highlights the distinction between the objective work of Christ on our behalf and our subjective (i.e., personal) participation in that work. As the next section explains, we participate in Christ's work through the gift of grace and our free cooperation with that grace.

Grace and Free Cooperation

Grace enables sinners to be incorporated into Christ and so to share in his conquest of sin, death, and hell. We enter into life-giving communion with Christ through the grace of justification, which is an absolutely free gift from God which is independent of our merits. Justification forgives our sins and wipes away our guilt by infusing the soul with sanctifying grace, which is a real participation in the divine life of God via the presence and power of the Holy Spirit. Through sanctifying grace we are changed and empowered with the supernatural virtues of faith, hope, and charity, by which the risen Christ lives in us and through us. Alive in Christ, we can imitate his obedient, humble, servile, merciful and sacrificial love for God and neighbor. We receive justification through the sacrament of Baptism or, absent this possibility, through Baptism by desire or blood. Justification is lost through mortal sin and it is restored through the sacrament of Penance or, when Penance is impossible, through the grace of perfect contrition. Those who die in the state of grace will receive eternal life as a merciful gift and reward from God. Having clung to Christ in charity in this life and, if necessary, having been further purified and satisfied for minor faults in Purgatory, their soul will enjoy the Beatific Vision and, at the second coming, receive their risen body in glory. As Christ's conquest of sin through obedience unto death resulted in his conquest of death and hell via resurrection and Ascension, so too we conquer sin in this world with Christ when we live and die in charity, and we subsequently conquer death and hell when we ascend to eternal life and rise from the dead.

The life of grace requires the free cooperation of the human will. Reception of justification in Baptism and Penance requires an act of honest faith and repentance. But this act is itself empowered by God's grace: conversion from unbelief and sin is a process which culminates in justification, and God's grace initiates and sustains every moment of that process. Yet all along the human person must freely choose to cooperate with God's grace, for they can reject it and end the process at any moment. God takes us by the hand and leads us through the blinding darkness towards the light, but we must freely hold on as he does so. This necessity of free cooperation remains even after we are justified. Justification gives the believer the grace which is necessary to observe God's commandments and avoid mortal sin, but we must still make the free choice to do so. The Holy Spirit prompts, directs, and strengthens the believer's mind, heart and will, but these interior aids do not eliminate our moral agency and responsibility. Charity is a supernatural habit which *inclines* us to do God's will, but we must still choose to *act* upon that inclination and act against lingering, disordered inclinations. When we do so then we participate in the merits of Christ and God rewards us by increasing our charity; this increase is supernatural and therefore a gift of grace. Works of charity include prayer, fasting, and almsgiving, through which we participate in Christ's work of satisfaction and so contribute to the reparation of sin in the world.

Catholic soteriology emphasizes the specific, concrete and active manner in which Christ's objective work of salvation must be applied to each believer. Through his Passion, Christ merited our salvation and satisfied for our sins. This means that every person now has the opportunity to receive the grace of justification, to be delivered from sin and hell, and to receive the gift of eternal life. But Christ determines the ways in which we receive these saving fruits of his Passion; we do not. And as the Gospels make clear, Christ does not promise to distribute the fruits of the Passion merely in an *immaterial* manner, nor will he give them in response to purely *intellectual* acts of faith. Rather, Christ instituted *tangible* means through which we receive the grace of forgiveness of our sins and life-giving union with him. Those means are baptism, the words of absolution given to the Apostles, and above all the food and drink of the Eucharist. And reception of these means of justification and spiritual growth presuppose the moral requirement of *repentance*. Following repentance and reception of the sanctifying sacraments, we continue to abide in Christ and grow closer to him through acts of living faith which are both *intellectual and moral*. Such faith recognizes Jesus as "Lord" *and* does the good works which he commands us to do. Obedience to the concrete moral commandments of Jesus, as well as obedience to his sacramental (ritual) commands, is essential to each believer's appropriation of the salvific fruits of the Passion. Those who refuse to obey Christ's commandments are like branches which remove themselves from the vine. They dry up and die, and so will be thrown into the fire. But those who abide in Christ in this world can receive the fulness of the fruits which his Passion merited, namely, to accompany Christ in the Spirit into the eternal house of the Father.

The necessity of obedience to Christ's commands should not surprise us if we consider the biblical narrative as a whole and the logic of the Incarnation. Catholicism insists upon the essential harmony between the Old and New Testaments. And prior to Christ, God led his people to holiness and prepared them to face judgment by giving them specific and concrete commands pertaining to both ritual (the Ark, Temple, Levitical priesthood and sacrifices, etc.) and moral (the Ten Commandments, etc.) behavior. It is fitting that the saving work of Christ would follow, rather than dramatically depart, from this basic approach. Christ was, after all, a Jewish rabbi. But in the early Church figures like Marcion and the gnostics sought to radically divorce Christianity from Judaism and from the concept of moral duties. In the modern and contemporary period, figures like Martin Luther and Gustaf Aulén have attempted to do the same through their concepts of *sola gratia* and *sola fide* and through their rejection of "the law." But such views are inconsistent with the logic of the Incarnation: God became human in order to save us in a tangible and concrete manner which included his own performance of free human acts, including the act of supreme sacrifice, the Passion. God does not want us to relate to him as a mere spirit and in a purely immaterial way. Rather, God willed that we relate to him as our brother in Adam, as the Son of Mary, as a carpenter, rabbi, example, healer, martyr, and as the risen and glorified one. He willed that we not merely know *of* him, but that we be *conformed* to him: that we be united with him and actively share in his mind, his heart, and his will. What pleases God is that we become like Christ, and this conformity is actualized through our obedience to Christ's sacramental and moral commandments. Above all, this conformity is accomplished in the sacrifice and sacrament of the Eucharist.

The Eucharist: Sacrifice and Sacrament of Salvation

The Eucharist is a saving sacrifice. In a ritual sacrifice, an animal is slain, its blood is poured out against the altar, at least a portion of the flesh is burnt upon the altar, and sometimes the remainder is eaten by the priest and those for whom he offers. A moral sacrifice is an act of virtue such as repentance, obedience, almsgiving and martyrdom. Christ's Passion fulfills both forms of sacrifice, for he was slain and his blood was poured out upon the cross as a result of his loving obedience and witness; he then rose from the dead and ascended into heaven like the smoke of a sweet smelling offering. And Christ's sacrificial death was once and for all: he need not and will not ever die or be harmed again. What then, is the relation between the sacrifice of the cross and the sacrifice of the Eucharist? The Eucharist is identical to the cross insofar as both feature the same *priest* and the same *object (victim)* which that priest offers. But the *manner of offering* is distinct, for Christ offered himself in a bloody manner on the cross but does so in an unbloody manner in the Eucharist. But how can the Eucharist be a "sacrifice" if it is an unbloody offering? The Church's answer to this question is multi-layered: (1) the separate consecration first of bread and then of wine symbolically *commemorates* the sacrificial immolation of Christ's flesh and blood upon the cross; (2) through the consecration the sacrificial being and self-giving love of Christ, which he offered in his Paschal Mystery, becomes *really present* under the accidents of bread and wine;[6] (3) Christ actively offers himself upon the altar, as he does in heaven, in *prayers* of praise, thanksgiving, satisfaction and supplication on behalf of sinners; (4) we offer our *prayers* and *good works* as spiritual sacrifices in union with Christ; (5) the priest, and the faithful who are worthily prepared, partake of the sacrificial victim through sacramental *holy communion*; (6) and in all of these ways, the sacrificial *power of the cross is applied* to the assembly and to those for whom they offer the sacrifice. And as the Church has insisted at least as early as the Council of Trent, the power of the cross is applied to the participants at Mass above all when they receive the Eucharist.

For the Eucharist is sacrificial, saving food. The sacrifice of the Mass is not reducible to the reception of holy Communion, but nonetheless reception completes the sacrificial nature of the Mass. Jesus is not merely a whole burnt offering; he is also a sacrifice of atonement and a Passover sacrifice. The Levitical priest had to consume a portion of every atonement sacrifice which he offered; the Jewish

---

6 That is, the substance of bread and wine is completely converted into the substance of Christ's body, blood, soul and divinity, while the accidents of bread and wine remain. This conversion can itself be called a "sacrifice" insofar as it involves a real change to the oblation, namely, to the substance of bread and wine.

people had to consume the flesh of the Passover lamb each year. Jesus was slain on the cross, rose and ascended into heaven as a new atonement and paschal sacrifice; and now we must consume his flesh and blood, or the fruits of his sacrifice will not be applied to us. Christ's sacrifice on the cross will be of no consequence to those who refuse to partake of his sacrificial flesh and blood. The Catholic priest must do so every time he consecrates the Eucharist; the faithful must do so at least annually in the paschal season of Easter. But the Church exhorts the faithful, and has done so explicitly since the Council of Trent, to receive the Eucharist every time they attend Mass and to do so even daily. We must do so worthily, lest we profane the body and blood of Christ and eat and drink condemnation upon ourselves. But if we can do so worthily, absolved of all grave sin, then we ought to do so as often as we are able. And we ought to prioritize our time so that we are able to receive the Eucharist daily, so long as doing so is prudent and fitting in light of our life's circumstances. For Christ instituted the Eucharist to be our "daily" and supersubstantial bread, and he compared this divine food to the daily gift of manna which he gave to the Hebrews. The manna nourished them physically each day on their journey through the wilderness to the Promised Land; the Eucharist is meant to nourish our souls with charity each day on our journey to eternal life and to prepare our bodies to rise again on the last day. What pleases God the most is the sacrifice of his only-begotten Son; we are most pleasing to God when we are conformed to the Son; and we are conformed to the Son above all when we worthily receive his sacrificial flesh and then become what we have received.[7] Our salvation is realized above all in our worthy, frequent reception of the Eucharist, by which we are united to the sacrificial victim, washed in his blood, and offered to the Father through him, with him, and in him, as a sweet smelling offering, as a sacrifice of charity.

7 See Augustine, Sermon 227, in *Sermons on the Liturgical Seasons*, trans. Mary Sarah Muldowney (The Catholic University of America Press, 1959), 195–98.

This book has aimed at introducing readers to the essential and primary content of Catholic soteriology. We did so through an analytic exposition of major biblical, magisterial, and liturgical texts. We showed that Catholic soteriology interprets the saving work of Christ in light of, and in essential continuity with, the ritual and moral sacrifices of the Old Testament as well as its prophecies of salvation. Christ works to bring about our salvation from sin and its consequences through both his eternal divinity and the humanity which he assumed in time. And his infancy, childhood, public ministry, teaching, miracles, example, passion, resurrection, Ascension, Church and sacraments all play a role within his saving mission: all are a means through which he draws us away from sin, into divinizing communion with himself, and ultimately to eternal life. As true God and true man, Christ personally conquers the powers of sin, the devil, death and hell. He does so through his perfect sacrifice of love and obedience unto death, and through his glorious resurrection from the dead and wondrous Ascension into heaven. And he offers us a share in his sacrifice, and hence in his conquest, through the divine gift of grace: we become living members of Christ's mystical body. United to Christ, we die with him to sin in this world; we then rise and ascend with him into God's temple in the new heavens and the new earth; there we pass with Christ beyond the veil into the eternal holy of holies and partake of the tree of life and the river of life which proceeds from God's throne; and there we look upon the face of the Father with the immeasurable love and joy of the Holy Spirit; and the Father looks upon us with an infinitely greater love and joy, as his adopted sons and daughters, as those who have been conformed to his only-begotten Son—the Lion who has conquered, the Lamb who stands as though slain.

RECOMMENDATIONS FOR FURTHER STUDY

In chronological order

Justin Martyr. *First Apology, Second Apology,* and *Dialogue with Trypho.* In *The Fathers of the Church,* Volume 6: *The Writings of Justin Martyr.* Translated by Thomas B. Falls. The Catholic University of America Press, 1948.

Irenaeus of Lyons. *Against Heresies.* Translated and edited by Alexander Roberts, James Donaldson, and Cleveland Coxe. Ex Fontibus Co., 2015.

Origen. *An Exhortation to Martyrdom.* In *Origen: An Exhortation to Martyrdom, Prayer and Selected Works.* Translated by Rowan A. Greer. Paulist Press, 1979.

Athanasius. *On the Incarnation.* Translated by John Behr. St Vladimir's Seminary Press, 2022.

Augustine. *City of God,* Book x. In *The City of God: Books 1–10.* Translated by William Babcock. New City Press, 2012.

Augustine. *The Trinity,* especially Books iv and xiii. Translated by Edmund Hill. New City Press, 1991.

Anselm of Canterbury. *Cur Deus Homo* and *Meditation on Human Redemption.* In *The Complete Treatises.* Edited and translated by Thomas Williams. Hackett Publishing, 2022.

Peter Lombard. *The Sentences,* Book 3. Translated by Giulio Silano. Pontifical Institute of Medieval Studies, 2010.

Thomas Aquinas. *Summa Theologiae,* Tertia Pars. Translated by Lawrence Shapcote. Edited by the Aquinas Institute. See especially the treatise on the Passion of Christ, questions 46–49. The works of Aquinas are available online in Latin and English at www.aquinas.cc.

Bonaventure. *Tree of Life*. In *The Works of Bonaventure*. Translated by Jose de Vink. Martino Fine Books, 2016.

Matthias Joseph Scheeben. *Mysteries of Christianity*, especially chapters XII–XVII. Translated by Cyril Vollert. The Crossroad Publishing Company, 1946.

Réginald Garrigou-Lagrange. *The Love of God and the Cross of Jesus*. Two volumes. Translated by Jeanne Marie. B. Herder Book Co., 1948.

John Paul II. *A Catechesis on the Creed*. Volume 2: *Jesus, Son and Savior*, especially pp. 413–536. Pauline Books & Media, 1996.

Joseph Ratzinger. *The Spirit of the Liturgy*. Translated by John Saward. Ignatius Press, 2000.

INDEX OF SCRIPTURE

INDEX OF SUBJECTS

www.ingramcontent.com/pod-product-compliance
Lightning Source LLC
Chambersburg PA
CBHW020445130626
46549CB00001B/302